SCIENCE

12 + 1 SAMPLE PAPERS

SHIVAM TIWARI
EDUCATOR
M.Sc. (Physics), B.Ed. (Science)

KAUSHLESH DWIVEDI
EDUCATOR
M.Sc. (Chemistry), B.Ed. (Science)

STRICTLY IN ACCORDANCE WITH THE SAMPLE PAPER RELEASED BY THE CBSE ON 16TH SEPTEMBER 2022

Title : CBSE Class 10 Science

Author Name : Mr. Kaushlesh Dwivedi, Mr. Shivam Tiwari

Published By : EduGorilla Community Pvt. Ltd.

Publishers Address : Sector-12/651, First Floor Opp. Arvindo Park, Near Jama Masjid, Indira Nagar, Lucknow, Uttar Pradesh-226016, India

Copyright

ISBN: 9789355564900

+91-63932 16806, +91-78000 04200
book@edugorilla.com
www.edugorilla.com

Disclaimer

Created & Compiled by EduGorilla Publication

Printed by EduGorilla Community Pvt. Ltd.

CBSE X SCIENCE

MIND MAP

SOLVED SAMPLE TEST PAPER

UNSOLVED SAMPLE TEST PAPER

PREVIOUS YEAR PAPER

MOST EXPECTED QUESTION PAPER

SCIENCE (Code No. 086) Classes: X (2022-23)

The subject of Science plays an important role in developing well-defined abilities in cognitive, affective and psychomotor domains in children. It augments the spirit of enquiry, creativity, objectivity and aesthetic sensibility.

Upper primary stage demands that a number of opportunities should be provided to the students to engage them with the processes of Science like observing, recording observations, drawing, tabulation, plotting graphs, etc., whereas the secondary stage also expects abstraction and quantitative reasoning to occupy a more central place in the teaching and learning of Science. Thus, the idea of atoms and molecules being the building blocks of matter makes its appearance, as does Newton's law of gravitation.

The present syllabus has been designed around seven broad themes viz. Food; Materials; The World of The Living; How Things Work; Moving Things, People and Ideas; Natural Phenomenon and Natural Resources. Special care has been taken to avoid temptation of adding too many concepts than can be comfortably learnt in the given time frame. No attempt has been made to be comprehensive.

At this stage, while Science is still a common subject, the disciplines of Physics, Chemistry and Biology begin to emerge. The students should be exposed to experiences based on hands on activities as well as modes of reasoning that are typical of the subject.

General Instructions:

1. There will be an Annual Examination based on the entire syllabus.
2. The Annual Examination will be of 80 marks and 20 marks weightage shall be for Internal Assessment.
3. For Internal Assessment:

   (a) There will be Periodic Assessment that would include:

   - For 5 marks- Three periodic tests conducted by the school. Average of the best two tests to be taken that will have a weightage of 05 marks towards the final result.
   - For 5 marks- Diverse methods of assessment as per the need of the class dynamics and curriculum transaction. These may include - short tests, oral test, quiz, concept maps, projects, posters, presentations and enquiry based scientific investigations etc. and use rubrics for arguing them objectively. This will also have a weightage of 05 marks towards the final result.

   (b) Practical / Laboratory work should be done throughout the year and the student should maintain record of the same. Practical Assessment should be continuous. There will be weightage of 5 marks towards the final result. All practicals listed in the syllabus must be completed.

   (c) Portfolio to be prepared by the student- This would include classwork and other sample of student work and will carry a weightage of 5 marks towards the final results.

COURSE STRUCTUR CLASS X
(Annual Examination)
Marks: 80

Unit No.	Unit	Marks
I	Chemical Substances-Nature and Behaviour	25
II	World of Living	25
III	Natural Phenomena	12
IV	Effects of Current	13
V	Natural Resources	05
	Total	**80**
	Internal assessment	**20**
	Grand Total	**100**

Theme: Materials

Unit I: Chemical Substances - Nature and Behaviour

Chemical reactions: Chemical equation, Balanced chemical equation, implications of a balanced chemical equation, types of chemical reactions: combination, decomposition, displacement, double displacement, precipitation, endothermic exothermic reactions, oxidation and reduction.

Acids, bases and salts: Their definitions in terms of furnishing of H+ and OH– ions, General properties, examples and uses, neutralization, concept of pH scale (Definition relating to logarithm not required), importance of pH in everyday life; preparation and uses of Sodium Hydroxide, Bleaching powder, Baking soda, Washing soda and Plaster of Paris.

Metals and nonmetals: Properties of metals and non-metals; Reactivity series; Formation and properties of ionic compounds; Basic metallurgical processes; Corrosion and its prevention.

Carbon compounds: Covalent bonding in carbon compounds. Versatile nature of carbon. Homologous series. Nomenclature of carbon compounds containing functional groups (halogens, alcohol, ketones, aldehydes, alkanes and alkynes), the difference between saturated hydrocarbons and unsaturated hydrocarbons. Chemical properties of carbon compounds (combustion, oxidation, addition and substitution reaction). Ethanol and Ethanoic acid (only properties and uses), soaps and detergents.

Theme: The World of the Living

Unit II: World of Living

Life processes: 'Living Being'. The basic concept of nutrition, respiration, transport and excretion in plants and animals.

Control and coordination in animals and plants: Tropic movements in plants; Introduction of plant hormones; Control and coordination in animals: Nervous system; Voluntary, involuntary and reflex action; Chemical coordination: animal hormones.

Reproduction: Reproduction in animals and plants (asexual and sexual) reproductive health - need and methods of family planning. Safe sex vs HIV/AIDS. Childbearing and women's health. **Heredity and Evolution:** Heredity; Mendel's contribution- Laws for inheritance of traits: Sex determination: brief introduction: (topics excluded - evolution; evolution and classification and evolution should not be equated with progress).

Theme: Natural Phenomena

Unit III: Natural Phenomena

Reflection of light by curved surfaces; Images formed by spherical mirrors, centre of curvature, principal axis, principal focus, focal length, mirror formula (Derivation not required), magnification.

Refraction; Laws of refraction, refractive index.

Refraction of light by spherical lens; Image formed by spherical lenses; Lens formula (Derivation not required); Magnification. Power of a lens.

Functioning of a lens in human eye, defects of vision and their corrections, applications of spherical mirrors and lenses.

Refraction of light through a prism, dispersion of light, scattering of light, applications in daily life (excluding colour of the sun at sunrise and sunset).

Theme: How Things Work

Unit IV: Effects of Current

Electric current, potential difference and electric current. Ohm's law; Resistance, Resistivity, Factors on which the resistance of a conductor depends. Series combination of resistors, parallel combination of resistors and its applications in daily life. Heating effect of electric current and its applications in daily life. Electric power, Interrelation between P, V, I and R. **Magnetic effects of current :** Magnetic field, field lines, field due to a current carrying conductor, field due to current carrying coil or solenoid; Force on current carrying conductor, Fleming's Left Hand Rule, Direct current. Alternating current: frequency of AC. Advantage of AC over DC. Domestic electric circuits.

Theme: Natural Resources

Unit V: Natural Resources

Our environment: Eco-system, Environmental problems, Ozone depletion, waste production and their solutions. Biodegradable and non-biodegradable substances.

Note for the Teachers:

1. The chapter Management of Natural Resources (NCERT Chapter 16) will not be assessed in the year-end examination. However, learners may be assigned to read this chapter and encouraged to prepare a brief write up to any concept of this chapter in their Portfolio. This may be for Internal Assessment and credit may be given Periodic Assessment/Portfolio).
2. The NCERT textbooks present information in boxes across the book. These help students to get conceptual clarity. However, the information in these boxes would not be assessed in the year-end examination.

Mind Map : Chemical reaction and Equations

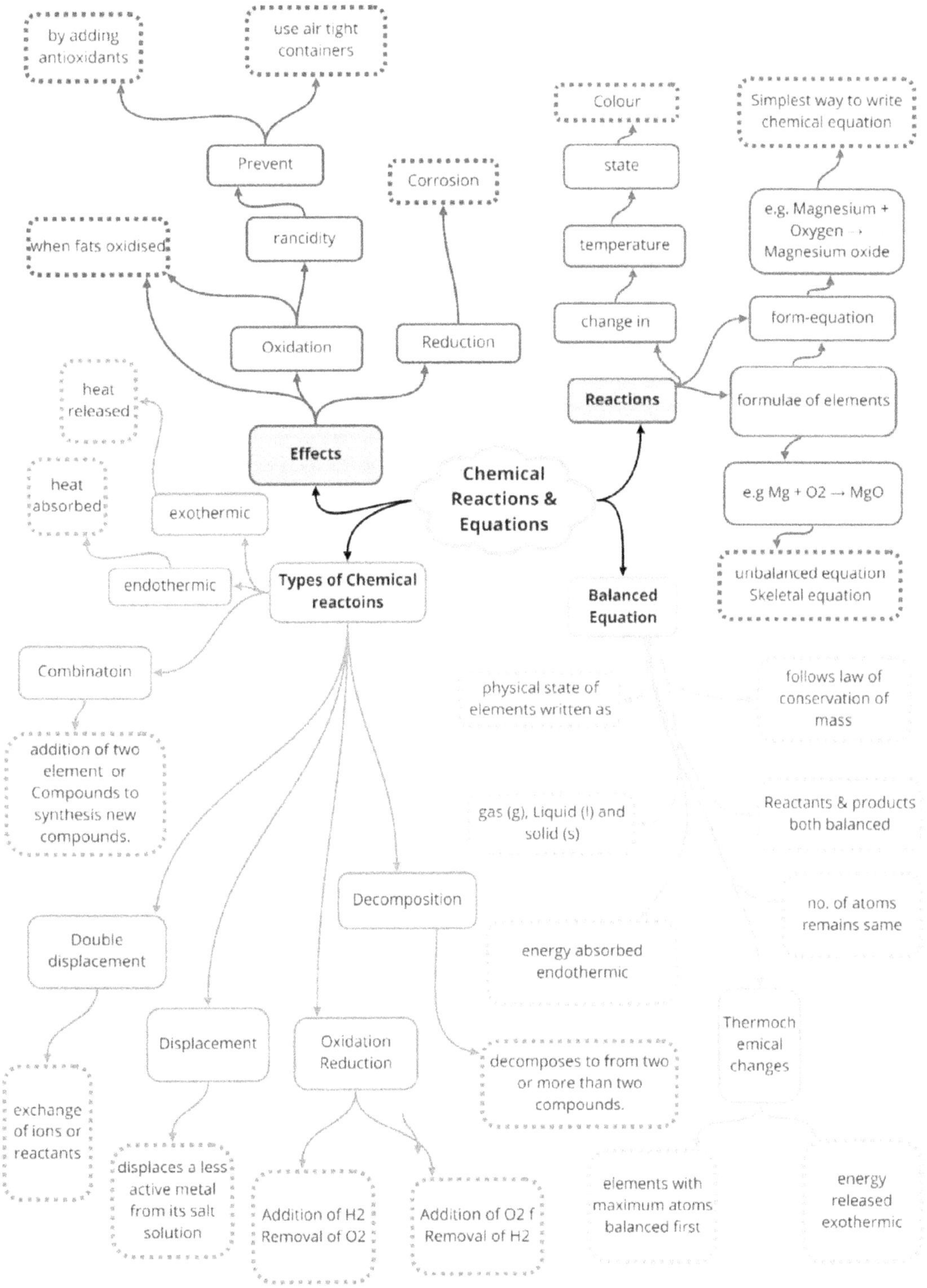

- **Chemical Reactions & Equations**
  - **Effects**
    - Oxidation
      - when fats oxidised
      - rancidity
        - Prevent
          - by adding antioxidants
          - use air tight containers
    - Reduction
      - Corrosion
  - **Reactions**
    - change in
      - temperature
        - state
          - Colour
    - form-equation
      - e.g. Magnesium + Oxygen → Magnesium oxide
        - Simplest way to write chemical equation
    - formulae of elements
      - e.g Mg + O_2 → MgO
        - unbalanced equation Skeletal equation
  - **Types of Chemical reactoins**
    - exothermic
      - heat released
    - endothermic
      - heat absorbed
    - Combinatoin
      - addition of two element or Compounds to synthesis new compounds.
    - Decomposition
      - decomposes to from two or more than two compounds.
    - Double displacement
      - exchange of ions or reactants
    - Displacement
      - displaces a less active metal from its salt solution
    - Oxidation Reduction
      - Addition of H_2 Removal of O_2
      - Addition of O_2 f Removal of H_2
  - **Balanced Equation**
    - physical state of elements written as
      - gas (g), Liquid (l) and solid (s)
    - follows law of conservation of mass
    - Reactants & products both balanced
    - no. of atoms remains same
    - energy absorbed endothermic
    - Thermochemical changes
      - energy released exothermic
    - elements with maximum atoms balanced first

Mind Map : Acid Base and Salt

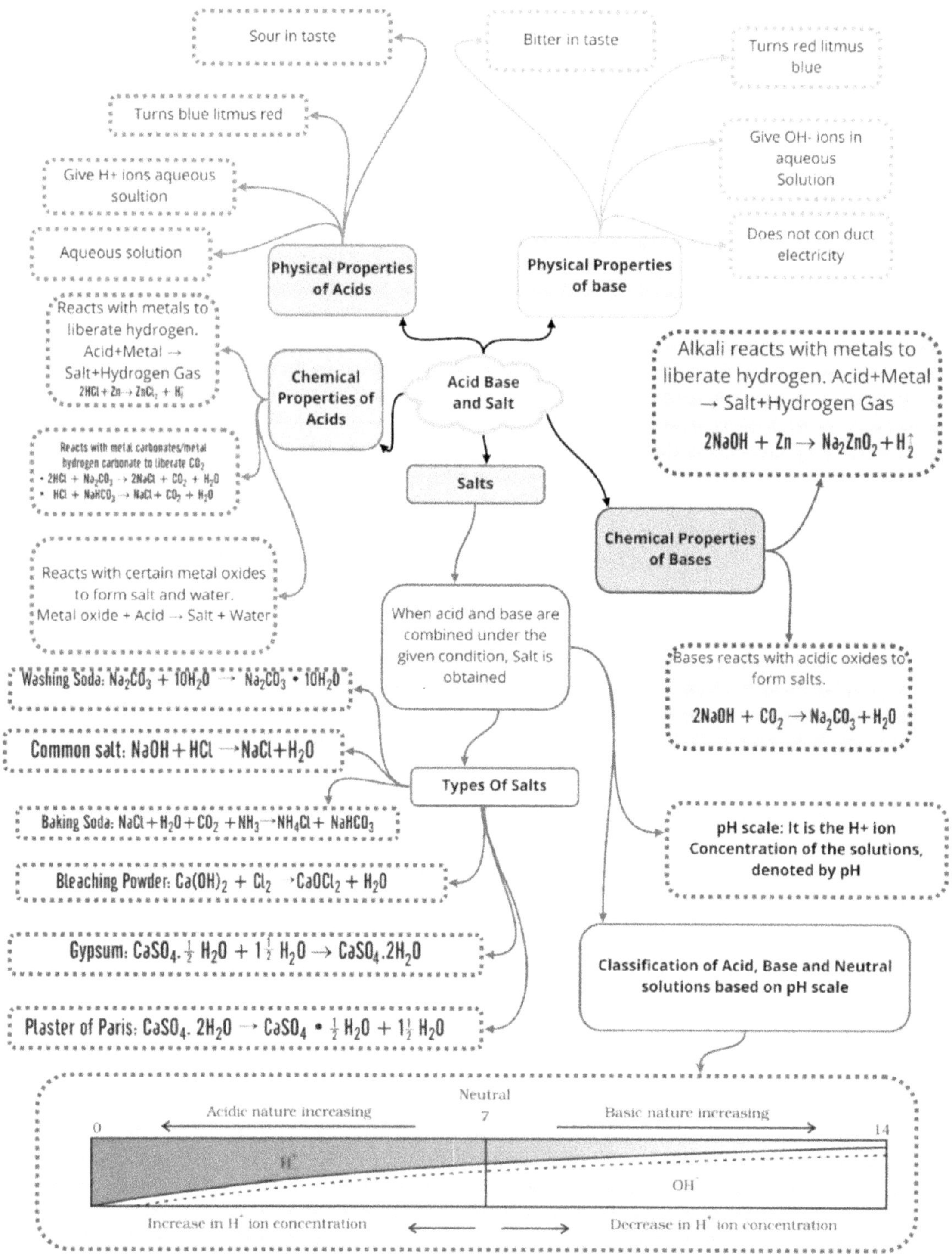

Acid Base and Salt

Physical Properties of Acids
- Sour in taste
- Turns blue litmus red
- Give H+ ions aqueous soultion
- Aqueous solution

Chemical Properties of Acids
- Reacts with metals to liberate hydrogen. Acid+Metal → Salt+Hydrogen Gas
  $2HCl + Zn \rightarrow ZnCl_2 + H_2\uparrow$
- Reacts with metal carbonates/metal hydrogen carbonate to liberate CO_2
  - $2HCl + Na_2CO_3 \rightarrow 2NaCl + CO_2 + H_2O$
  - $HCl + NaHCO_3 \rightarrow NaCl + CO_2 + H_2O$
- Reacts with certain metal oxides to form salt and water. Metal oxide + Acid → Salt + Water

Physical Properties of base
- Bitter in taste
- Turns red litmus blue
- Give OH- ions in aqueous Solution
- Does not con duct electricity

Chemical Properties of Bases
- Alkali reacts with metals to liberate hydrogen. Acid+Metal → Salt+Hydrogen Gas
  $2NaOH + Zn \rightarrow Na_2ZnO_2 + H_2\uparrow$
- Bases reacts with acidic oxides to form salts.
  $2NaOH + CO_2 \rightarrow Na_2CO_3 + H_2O$

Salts
- When acid and base are combined under the given condition, Salt is obtained

Types Of Salts
- Washing Soda: $Na_2CO_3 + 10H_2O \rightarrow Na_2CO_3 \cdot 10H_2O$
- Common salt: $NaOH + HCl \rightarrow NaCl + H_2O$
- Baking Soda: $NaCl + H_2O + CO_2 + NH_3 \rightarrow NH_4Cl + NaHCO_3$
- Bleaching Powder: $Ca(OH)_2 + Cl_2 \rightarrow CaOCl_2 + H_2O$
- Gypsum: $CaSO_4 . \frac{1}{2} H_2O + 1\frac{1}{2} H_2O \rightarrow CaSO_4 . 2H_2O$
- Plaster of Paris: $CaSO_4 . 2H_2O \rightarrow CaSO_4 \cdot \frac{1}{2} H_2O + 1\frac{1}{2} H_2O$

pH scale: It is the H+ ion Concentration of the solutions, denoted by pH

Classification of Acid, Base and Neutral solutions based on pH scale

Neutral 7

0 ← Acidic nature increasing | Basic nature increasing → 14

H^+ | OH^-

Increase in H^+ ion concentration ⟵ ⟶ Decrease in H^+ ion concentration

Mind Map : Metals and Non-Metals

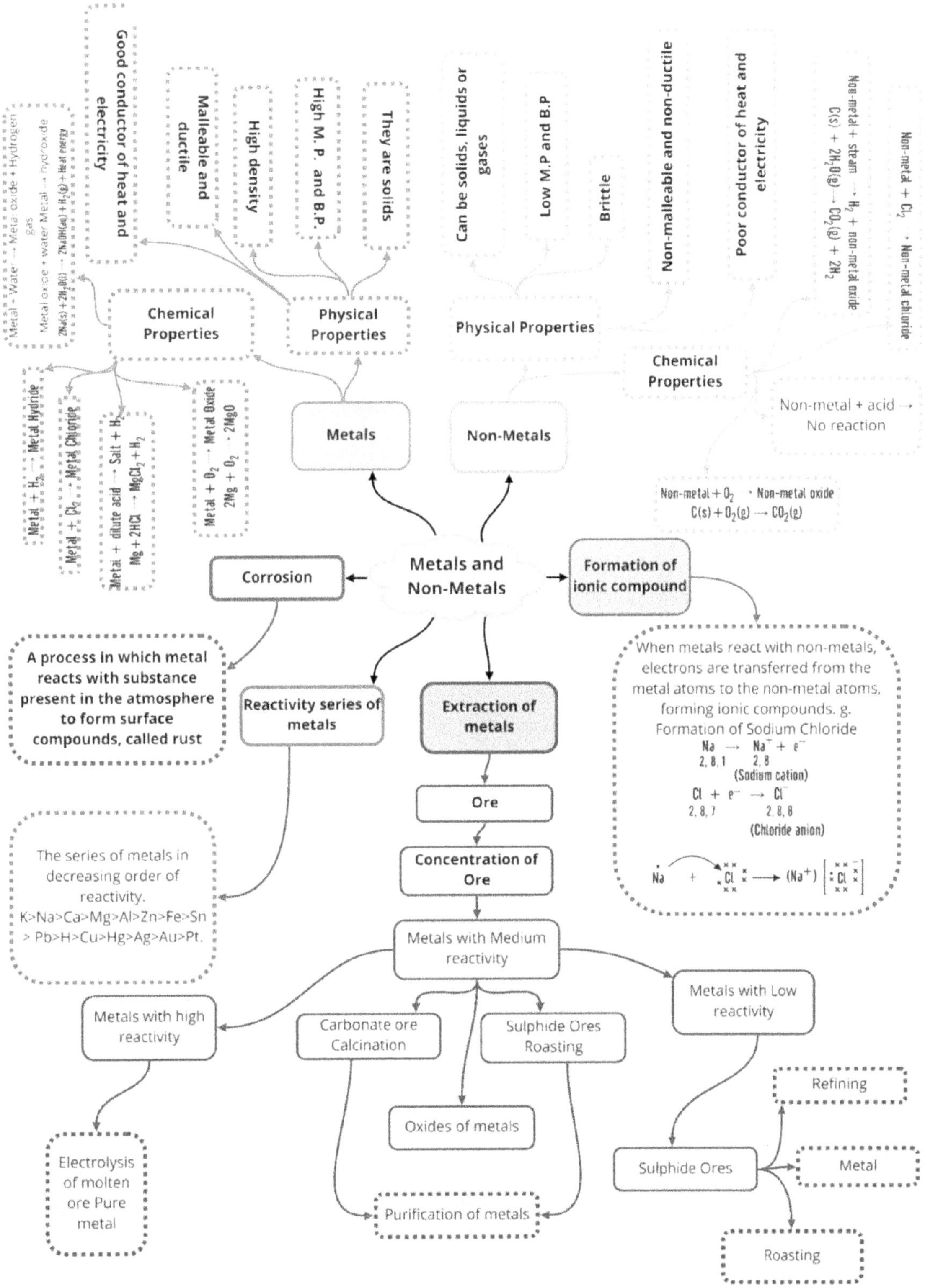

Metals and Non-Metals

- **Metals**
  - **Physical Properties**
    - They are solids
    - High M. P. and B.P.
    - High density
    - Malleable and ductile
    - Good conductor of heat and electricity
  - **Chemical Properties**
    - Metal + Water → Metal oxide + Hydrogen gas
    - Metal oxide + water Metal → hydroxide
    - $2Na(s) + 2H_2O(l) \rightarrow 2NaOH(aq) + H_2(g)$ + Heat energy
    - Metal + H_2 → Metal Hydride
    - Metal + Cl_2 → Metal Chloride
    - Metal + dilute acid → Salt + H_2; $Mg + 2HCl \rightarrow MgCl_2 + H_2$
    - Metal + O_2 → Metal Oxide; $2Mg + O_2 \rightarrow 2MgO$
- **Non-Metals**
  - **Physical Properties**
    - Can be solids, liquids or gases
    - Low M.P and B.P
    - Brittle
    - Non-malleable and non-ductile
    - Poor conductor of heat and electricity
  - **Chemical Properties**
    - Non-metal + steam → H_2 + non-metal oxide; $C(s) + 2H_2O(g) \rightarrow CO_2(g) + 2H_2$
    - Non-metal + Cl_2 → Non-metal chloride
    - Non-metal + acid → No reaction
    - Non-metal + O_2 → Non-metal oxide; $C(s) + O_2(g) \rightarrow CO_2(g)$
- **Corrosion**
  - A process in which metal reacts with substance present in the atmosphere to form surface compounds, called rust
- **Formation of ionic compound**
  - When metals react with non-metals, electrons are transferred from the metal atoms to the non-metal atoms, forming ionic compounds. g. Formation of Sodium Chloride
  - $Na \rightarrow Na^+ + e^-$ (2, 8, 1 → 2, 8) (Sodium cation)
  - $Cl + e^- \rightarrow Cl^-$ (2, 8, 7 → 2, 8, 8) (Chloride anion)
  - $Na + Cl \rightarrow (Na^+)[Cl]^-$
- **Reactivity series of metals**
  - The series of metals in decreasing order of reactivity. K>Na>Ca>Mg>Al>Zn>Fe>Sn > Pb>H>Cu>Hg>Ag>Au>Pt.
- **Extraction of metals**
  - Ore
    - Concentration of Ore
      - Metals with Medium reactivity
        - Carbonate ore Calcination → Purification of metals
        - Oxides of metals
        - Sulphide Ores Roasting → Purification of metals
      - Metals with high reactivity
        - Electrolysis of molten ore Pure metal
      - Metals with Low reactivity
        - Sulphide Ores
          - Refining
          - Metal
          - Roasting

Mind Map : Carbon and its Compound

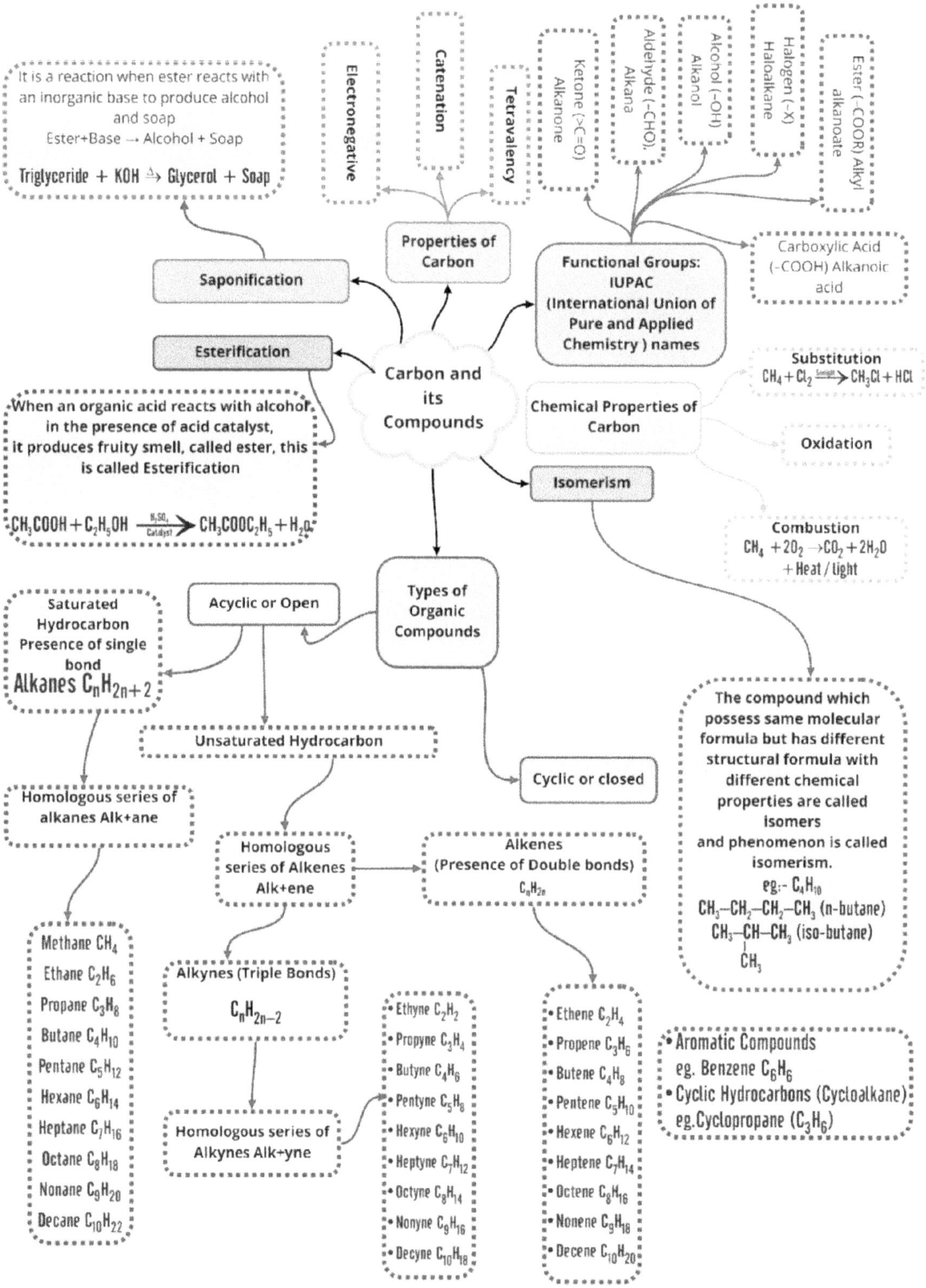

Carbon and its Compounds

Saponification

It is a reaction when ester reacts with an inorganic base to produce alcohol and soap

Ester+Base → Alcohol + Soap

Triglyceride + KOH $\xrightarrow{\Delta}$ Glycerol + Soap

Properties of Carbon

- Electronegative
- Catenation
- Tetravalency

Functional Groups: IUPAC (International Union of Pure and Applied Chemistry) names

- Ketone (>C=O) Alkanone
- Aldehyde (–CHO). Alkana
- Alcohol (–OH) Alkanol
- Halogen (–X) Haloalkane
- Ester (–COOR) Alkyl alkanoate
- Carboxylic Acid (-COOH) Alkanoic acid

Esterification

When an organic acid reacts with alcohol in the presence of acid catalyst, it produces fruity smell, called ester, this is called Esterification

$CH_3COOH + C_2H_5OH \xrightarrow[Catalyst]{H_2SO_4} CH_3COOC_2H_5 + H_2O$

Chemical Properties of Carbon

- Substitution: $CH_4 + Cl_2 \xrightarrow{Sunlight} CH_3Cl + HCl$
- Oxidation
- Combustion: $CH_4 + 2O_2 \rightarrow CO_2 + 2H_2O$ + Heat / light

Isomerism

The compound which possess same molecular formula but has different structural formula with different chemical properties are called isomers and phenomenon is called isomerism.

eg:- C_4H_{10}

$CH_3-CH_2-CH_2-CH_3$ (n-butane)

$CH_3-CH(CH_3)-CH_3$ (iso-butane)

Types of Organic Compounds

Acyclic or Open

Saturated Hydrocarbon Presence of single bond

Alkanes C_nH_{2n+2}

Homologous series of alkanes Alk+ane

- Methane CH_4
- Ethane C_2H_6
- Propane C_3H_8
- Butane C_4H_{10}
- Pentane C_5H_{12}
- Hexane C_6H_{14}
- Heptane C_7H_{16}
- Octane C_8H_{18}
- Nonane C_9H_{20}
- Decane $C_{10}H_{22}$

Unsaturated Hydrocarbon

Homologous series of Alkenes Alk+ene

Alkenes (Presence of Double bonds) C_nH_{2n}

- Ethene C_2H_4
- Propene C_3H_6
- Butene C_4H_8
- Pentene C_5H_{10}
- Hexene C_6H_{12}
- Heptene C_7H_{14}
- Octene C_8H_{16}
- Nonene C_9H_{18}
- Decene $C_{10}H_{20}$

Alkynes (Triple Bonds) C_nH_{2n-2}

Homologous series of Alkynes Alk+yne

- Ethyne C_2H_2
- Propyne C_3H_4
- Butyne C_4H_6
- Pentyne C_5H_8
- Hexyne C_6H_{10}
- Heptyne C_7H_{12}
- Octyne C_8H_{14}
- Nonyne C_9H_{16}
- Decyne $C_{10}H_{18}$

Cyclic or closed

- Aromatic Compounds eg. Benzene C_6H_6
- Cyclic Hydrocarbons (Cycloalkane) eg.Cyclopropane (C_3H_6)

Mind Map : Classification of elements

Classification of Elements

Old theories

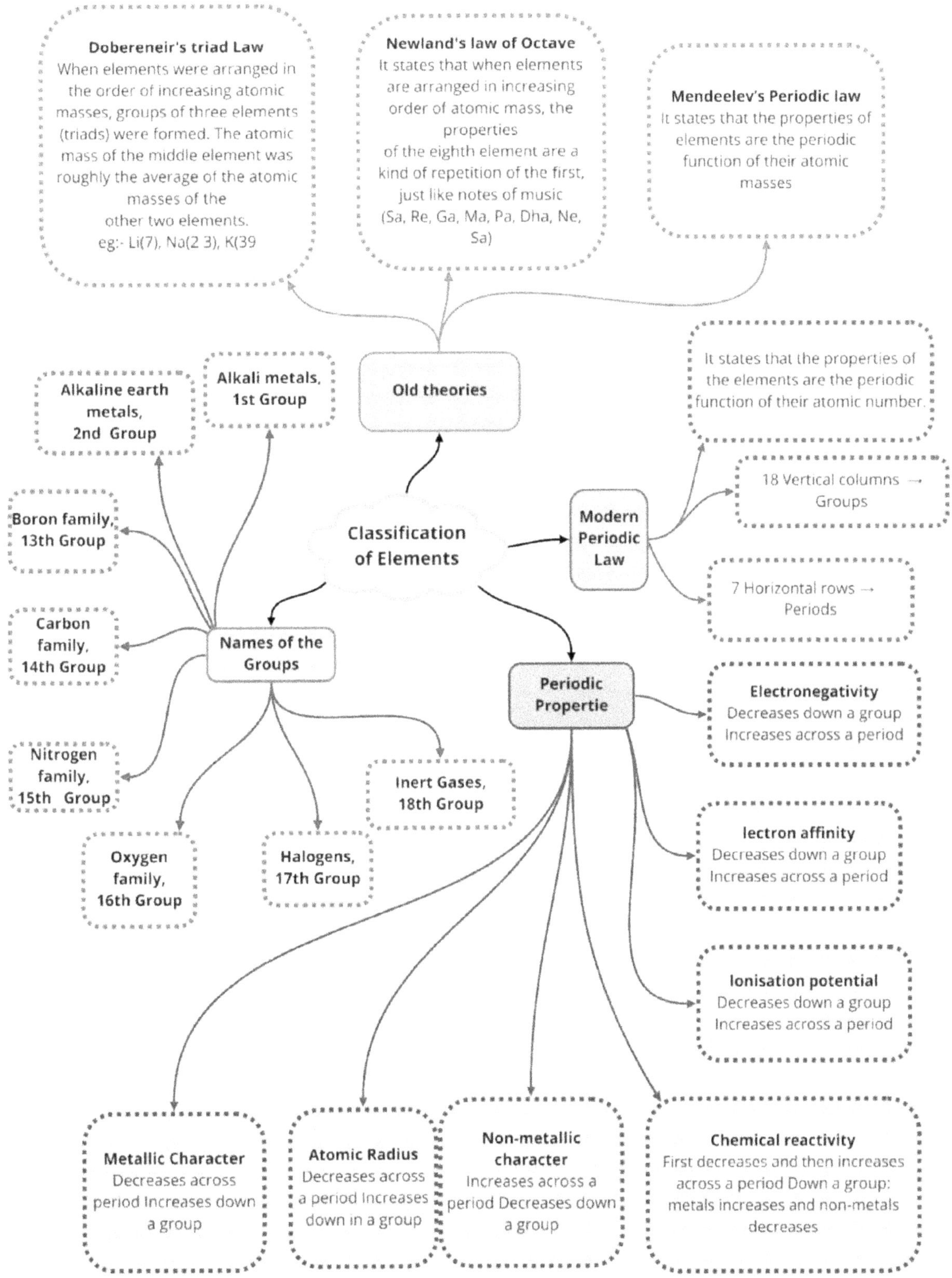

Dobereneir's triad Law
When elements were arranged in the order of increasing atomic masses, groups of three elements (triads) were formed. The atomic mass of the middle element was roughly the average of the atomic masses of the other two elements.
eg:- Li(7), Na(2 3), K(39

Newland's law of Octave
It states that when elements are arranged in increasing order of atomic mass, the properties of the eighth element are a kind of repetition of the first, just like notes of music (Sa, Re, Ga, Ma, Pa, Dha, Ne, Sa)

Mendeelev's Periodic law
It states that the properties of elements are the periodic function of their atomic masses

Modern Periodic Law

- It states that the properties of the elements are the periodic function of their atomic number.
- 18 Vertical columns → Groups
- 7 Horizontal rows → Periods

Names of the Groups

- Alkali metals, 1st Group
- Alkaline earth metals, 2nd Group
- Boron family, 13th Group
- Carbon family, 14th Group
- Nitrogen family, 15th Group
- Oxygen family, 16th Group
- Halogens, 17th Group
- Inert Gases, 18th Group

Periodic Propertie

Electronegativity
Decreases down a group Increases across a period

lectron affinity
Decreases down a group Increases across a period

Ionisation potential
Decreases down a group Increases across a period

Metallic Character
Decreases across period Increases down a group

Atomic Radius
Decreases across a period Increases down in a group

Non-metallic character
Increases across a period Decreases down a group

Chemical reactivity
First decreases and then increases across a period Down a group: metals increases and non-metals decreases

Mind Map : Life Processes

Life Processes

Respiration in Animal (Human Beings)

Parts of Human Respiratory System
- Alveoli
- Bronchioles
- Trachea
- Lungs
- Bronchi
- Nostrils

Mechenism of Breathing
- Expiration
- Gaseous exchange
- Inspiration

Nutrition

- Autotrophic nutrition in plants.
- Process Invilved is Photosynthesis

Various steps included in Heterotrophic nutrition in animals
- Ingestion
- Digestion
- Absorption
- Assimilation
- Egestion

Alimentary canal and their secretions
- Mouth (saliva)
- Pharynx
- Oesophagus
- Stomach (HCl, Gastric Juice)
- Small Intestine
- Large Intestin
- Anus

Double Circulation in Human

Circulatory system in Human
- Blood
- Heart
- Vlood Vessels

Transportation in Plants
- Phleom (Transport of water)
- Xylem (Transport of food)

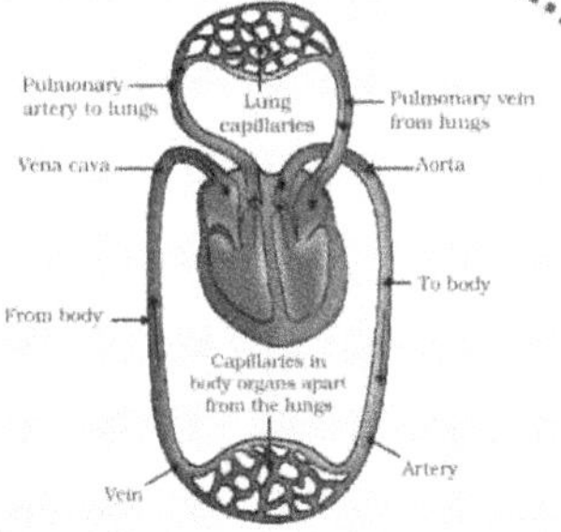

Pulmonary artery to lungs
Lung capillaries
Pulmonary vein from lungs
Vena cava
Aorta
To body
From body
Capillaries in body organs apart from the lungs
Vein
Artery

Figure 6.11
Schematic representation of transport and exchange of oxygen and carbon dioxide

Excretion

In Plants: Process involved is Transpiration

In Human: Kidney helps in formation of urine

In Human, basic unit of kidney-Nephron
Parts of Nephron
- Bowman's Capsule
- Glomerulus
- Proximal Convoluted Tubule
- Loop of Henle
- Distal Comvoluted Tubule

Mind Map : Control and Co-ordination

control and co-ordination

Types by Glands
- **Hormones Secreted by Glands**
  - **Plants Hormones (Growth Hormones)**
    - Auxin
    - Gibberellin
    - Cytokinin
    - Abscisic acid
    - Ethylene
- **Exocrine Glands (With Duct)**
- **Endocrine Glands (Ductless)**
- **Thyroid Gland** Thyroxine Hormone
- **Pituitary Gland** Growth Hormone, Tropic Hormone, Prolactin, Vasopressin, Oxytocin
- **Parathyroid** Parathyroid Hormon
- **Thymus** Thymosin
- **Adrenal Gland** Adrenalin, cortisol
- **Pancreas** Insulin, Glucagon

Plant Movements (Tropic movements)
- **Hydrotropism** (Response to water)
- **Phototropism (Response to light)** Shoots show positive phototropism
- **Geotropism (Response to gravity)** Roots show positive geotropism
- **Chemotropism (Response to chemicals)** Growth of Pollen tube towards a chemical produced by Ovule

Nervous system in Humans
- **Neuron: Unit of Nervous system**
  - **Parts of Neuron**
    - Cell body
    - Dendrites
    - Axon
- **Autonomic Nervous System**
  - • Sympathetic • Parasympathetic
    - Spinal cord
- **Central Nervous system**
  - **Brain**
    - **Fore brain (Thinking part of brain)**
      - Cerebrum
      - Thalamus
      - Hypothalamus
    - **Mid brain** (Controls involuntary actions, Change in pupil size, Reflex actions)
    - **Hind brain**
      - Cerebellum: Controls posture and balance
      - Pons: Controls involuntary actions
      - Medulla Oblongata: Control involuntary actions
- **Peripheral Nervous System**
  - Cranial Nerves(arises from brain) 12 pairs
  - **Autonomic Nervous System**
    - •Sympathetic
    - •Parasympathetic
  - **Reflex action**
    - •Involuntary
    - •Sudden actions
  - Spinal Nerves (arises from spinal cord) 31 pairs
  - Reflex arc Receptors→Sensory Neuron→Spinal Cord→Motor Neuron→Effectors

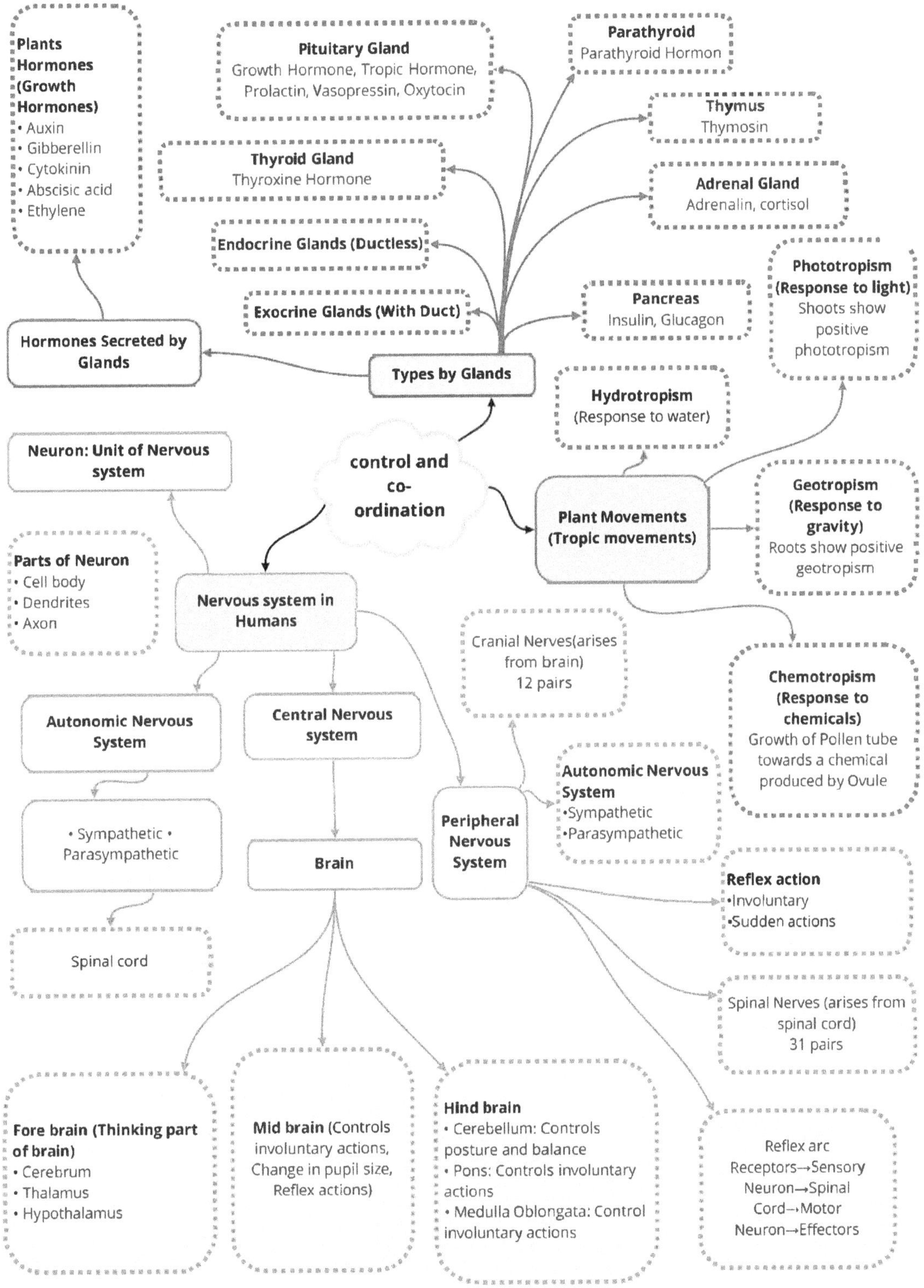

Mind Map :How do organisms reproduce

How do organisms reproduce

Sexual reproduction

Budding
- Bulb like projection comes out of the cells
- Reproduction through buds
- eg. Yeast, Hydra

Reproduction through vegetative parts of Plants
- ThroughLeaves- Bryophyllum
- Through Eyes P-aotato
- Through stem-Rose
- Through Roots

Fragmentation
- Breaking into two or more fragments
- Eg. Spirogyra

Spore formation
- Convered by hard protective coat to withstand condition
- Fungus
- Spore germinates

Sexual reproduction in animals (Human Beings)

Male Reproductive System
- Sperm duct
- Testis (Release Sperm)
- Penis

Part of Sperm
- Head
- Middle piece
- Tail

Female Reproductive System
- Ovaries
- Oviduct
- Ova (egg)
- Uterus

- Fertilization: Ova (from ovaries) fuses with sperm (from testis) to from zygote
- Implantation of embryo in uterus
- develops into baby

Sexual reproduction in Plants

Through Seeds
- contains Embryo
- Ovary forms fruit and Ovules from seeds

Seed dispersal
- By Wind
- By Water
- By Animal

Through Flowers

Fertilization

Fusion of male and female gametes develops into embryo

Pollination

Self Pollination
Pollen grains on stigma of same flower

Cross Pollination
Pollen grains on stigma of another flower

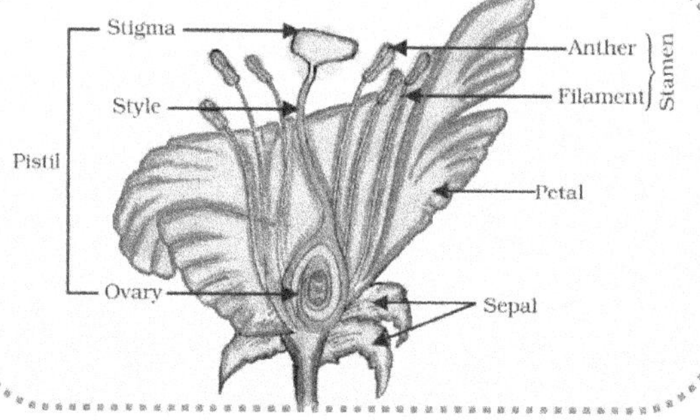

- Stigma
- Style
- Pistil
- Ovary
- Anther
- Filament
- Stamen
- Petal
- Sepal

Mind Map :Heredity and evolution

Heredity and Evolution

Determination human beings
Speciation
Geographical isolation
Reproductive isolation
Natural Selection
Genetic drift

variations
Somatic Variation
Gamete Variation
Asexual Variation
Sexual Variation

Law of Segregation
Monony hybrid Cross
All red
Self Pollination Phenotype
F1 generation Genotype
Genotype
Hybrid
F2 Generation Cross Pollination
Phenotype
Genotype
1RR:2Rr:1rr
3 red:1 White

Gregor John Mendel Heredity
Low of Independents Assortnent
Dihybrid Cross
F1 generation Genotype
Hybrid RRYY
F2 generation
Phenotype
Round yellow
Wrinkled Yellow
Round Green
Wrinkled Green
Genotype
1:2:2:4:2:2:
1:1:1:1

Self Pollination Phenotype
All round Yellow
Cross Pollination

Six in
Male
22 + XY
22 autosomes XY sex chromosome
Female
22 + xx
22 autosomes XX sex chromosome
(XX) Daughter
(XY) Son
(XY) Son
(XX) Daughter

Darwin's theory of Evidence
Vestigial
Organs present but no function
Paleontologica
Study of Fossils
Micro-evolution
Auatomical
Analogous Organs
Morphological
Homologous Organs

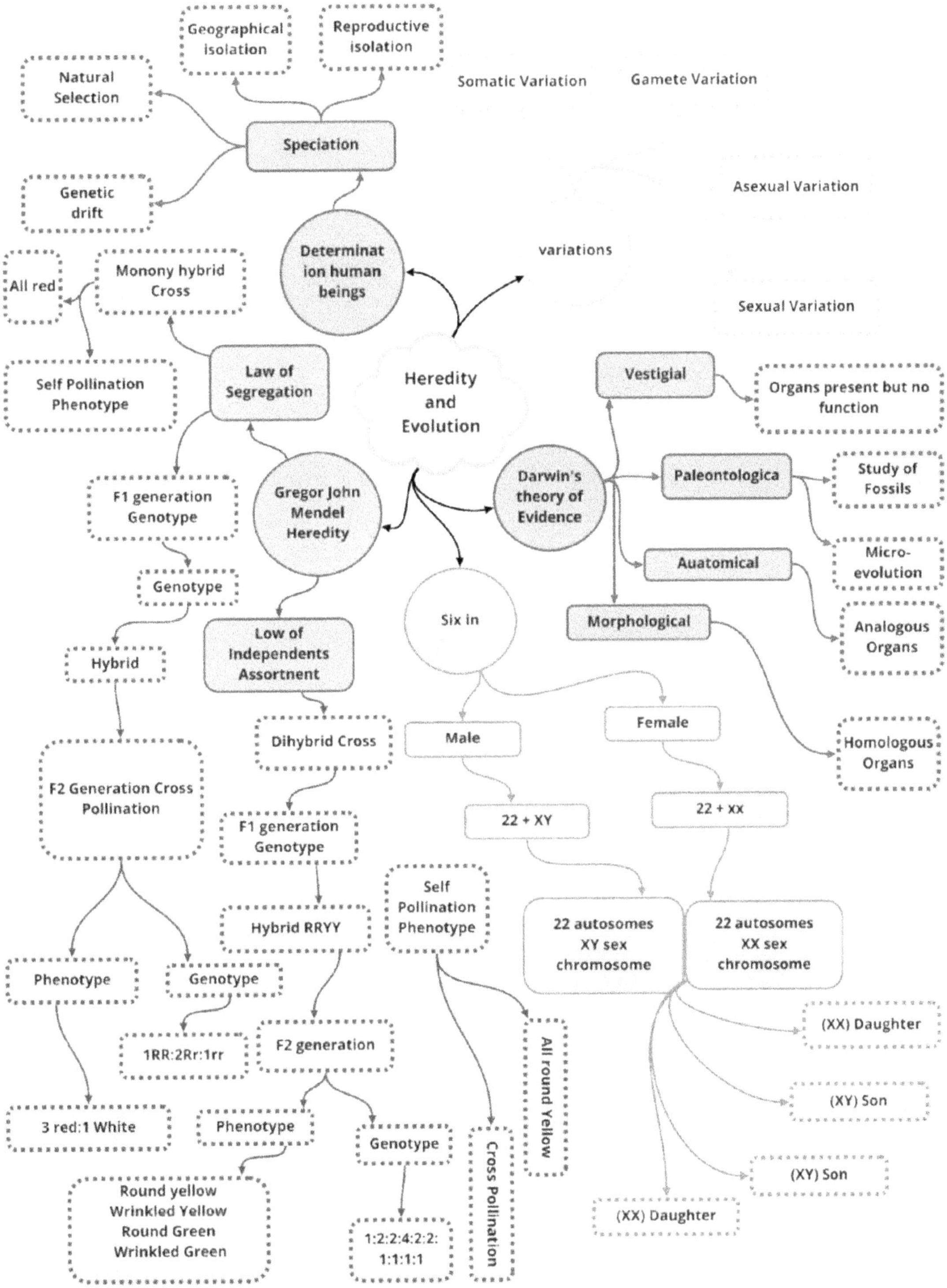

Mind Map : Light reflection and Refraction

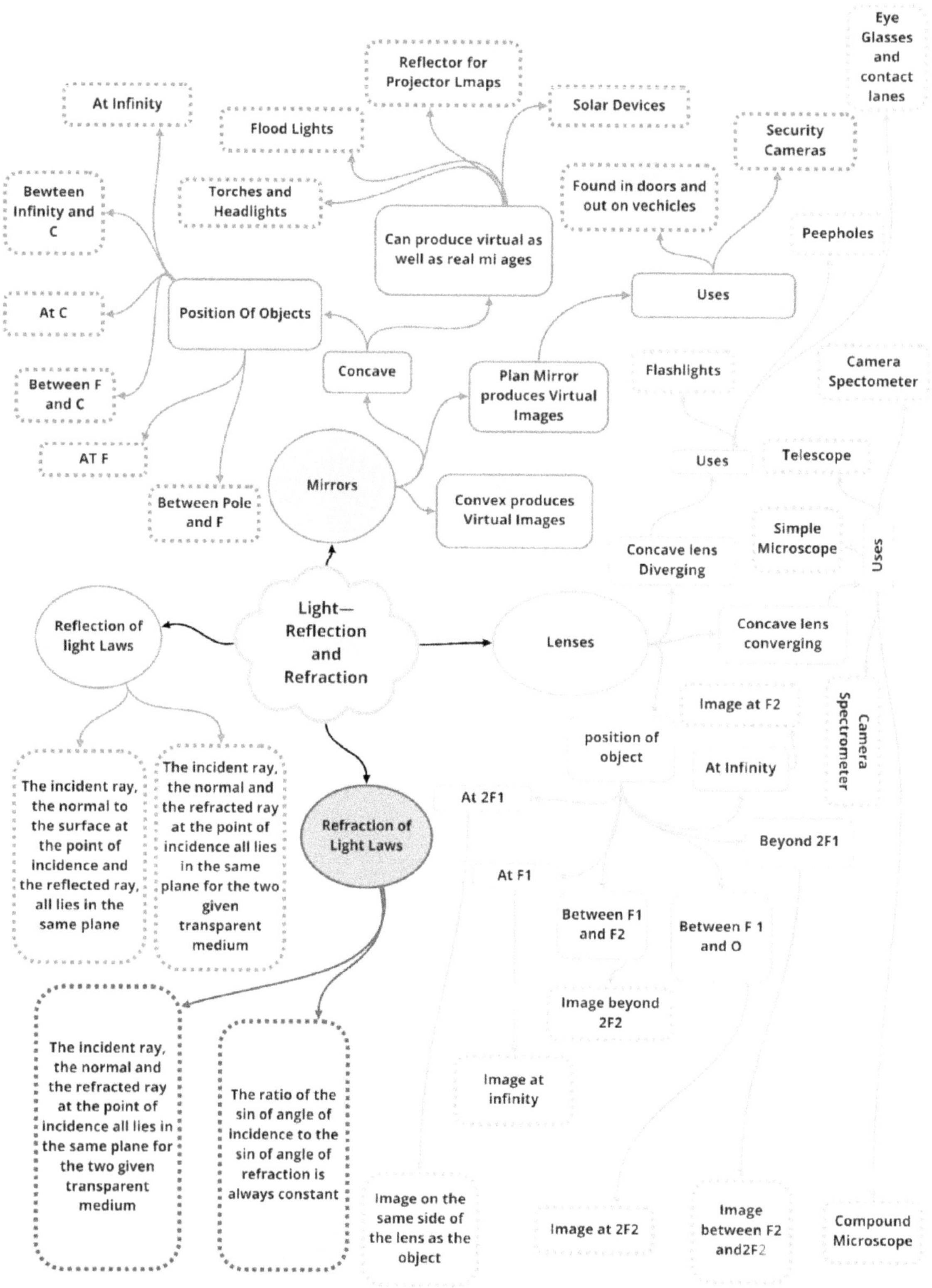

Light— Reflection and Refraction

Mirrors

Concave

Position Of Objects

At Infinity

Bewteen Infinity and C

At C

Between F and C

AT F

Between Pole and F

Can produce virtual as well as real mi ages

Reflector for Projector Lmaps

Flood Lights

Torches and Headlights

Solar Devices

Plan Mirror produces Virtual Images

Uses

Found in doors and out on vechicles

Security Cameras

Convex produces Virtual Images

Reflection of light Laws

The incident ray, the normal to the surface at the point of incidence and the reflected ray, all lies in the same plane

The incident ray, the normal and the refracted ray at the point of incidence all lies in the same plane for the two given transparent medium

Refraction of Light Laws

The incident ray, the normal and the refracted ray at the point of incidence all lies in the same plane for the two given transparent medium

The ratio of the sin of angle of incidence to the sin of angle of refraction is always constant

Lenses

Concave lens Diverging

Uses

Flashlights

Peepholes

Eye Glasses and contact lanes

Camera Spectometer

Concave lens converging

Uses

Telescope

Simple Microscope

Camera Spectrometer

Compound Microscope

position of object

Image at F2

At Infinity

At 2F1

Beyond 2F1

At F1

Between F1 and F2

Between F 1 and O

Image beyond 2F2

Image at infinity

Image on the same side of the lens as the object

Image at 2F2

Image between F2 and2F2

Mind Map :Human Eye and Colourful World

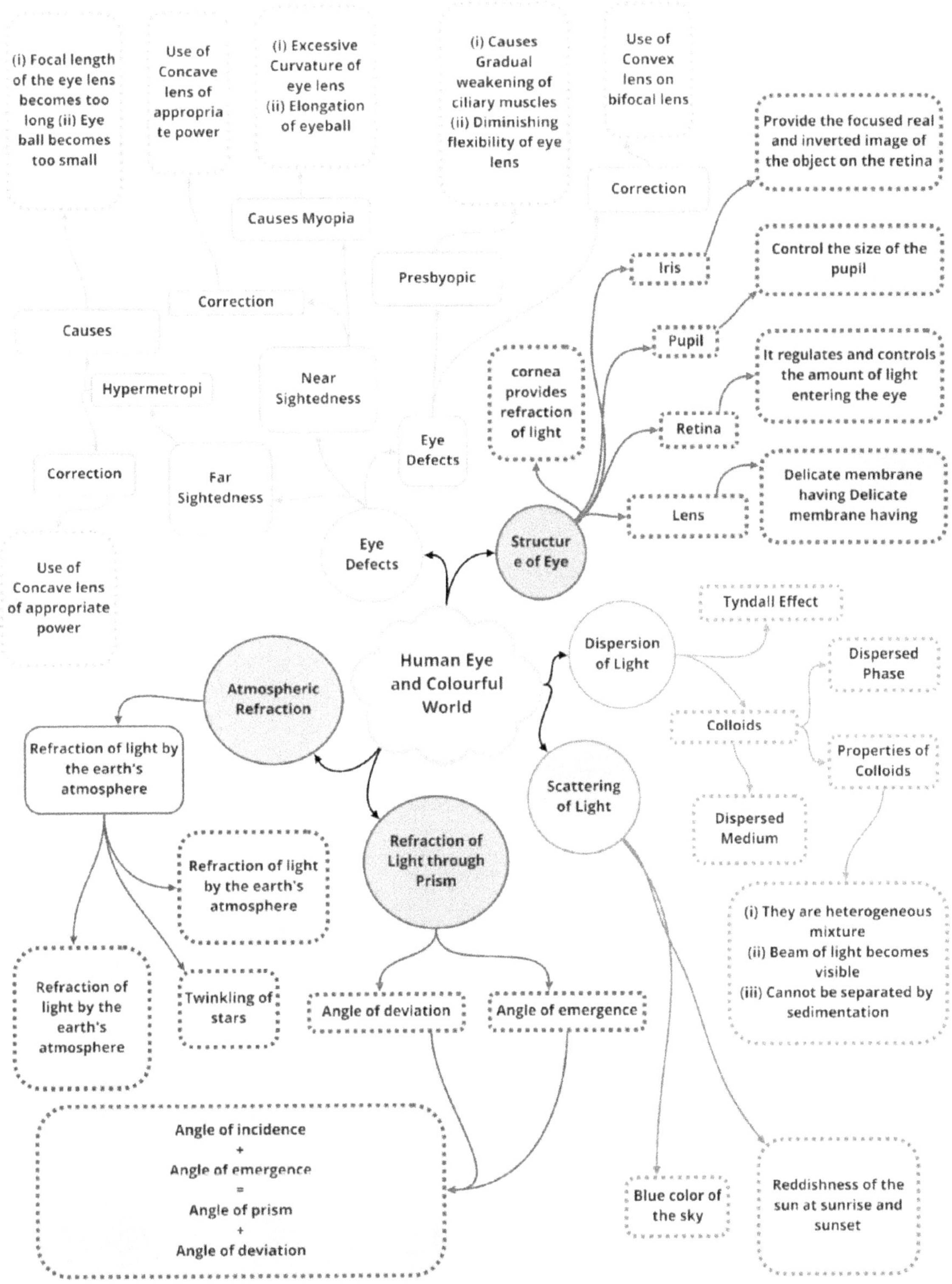

Human Eye and Colourful World

Eye Defects

- Eye Defects
  - Near Sightedness
    - Causes Myopia
      - (i) Excessive Curvature of eye lens (ii) Elongation of eyeball
    - Correction
      - Use of Concave lens of appropriate power
  - Far Sightedness
    - Hypermetropi
      - Causes
        - (i) Focal length of the eye lens becomes too long (ii) Eye ball becomes too small
      - Correction
        - Use of Concave lens of appropriate power
  - Presbyopic
    - (i) Causes Gradual weakening of ciliary muscles (ii) Diminishing flexibility of eye lens
    - Correction
      - Use of Convex lens on bifocal lens

Structure of Eye

- cornea provides refraction of light
- Iris
  - Provide the focused real and inverted image of the object on the retina
- Pupil
  - Control the size of the pupil
- Retina
  - It regulates and controls the amount of light entering the eye
- Lens
  - Delicate membrane having Delicate membrane having

Dispersion of Light

- Tyndall Effect
- Colloids
  - Dispersed Phase
  - Properties of Colloids
    - (i) They are heterogeneous mixture (ii) Beam of light becomes visible (iii) Cannot be separated by sedimentation
  - Dispersed Medium

Scattering of Light

- Blue color of the sky
- Reddishness of the sun at sunrise and sunset

Atmospheric Refraction

- Refraction of light by the earth's atmosphere
  - Refraction of light by the earth's atmosphere
  - Refraction of light by the earth's atmosphere
  - Twinkling of stars

Refraction of Light through Prism

- Angle of deviation
- Angle of emergence

Angle of incidence + Angle of emergence = Angle of prism + Angle of deviation

Mind Map :Electricity

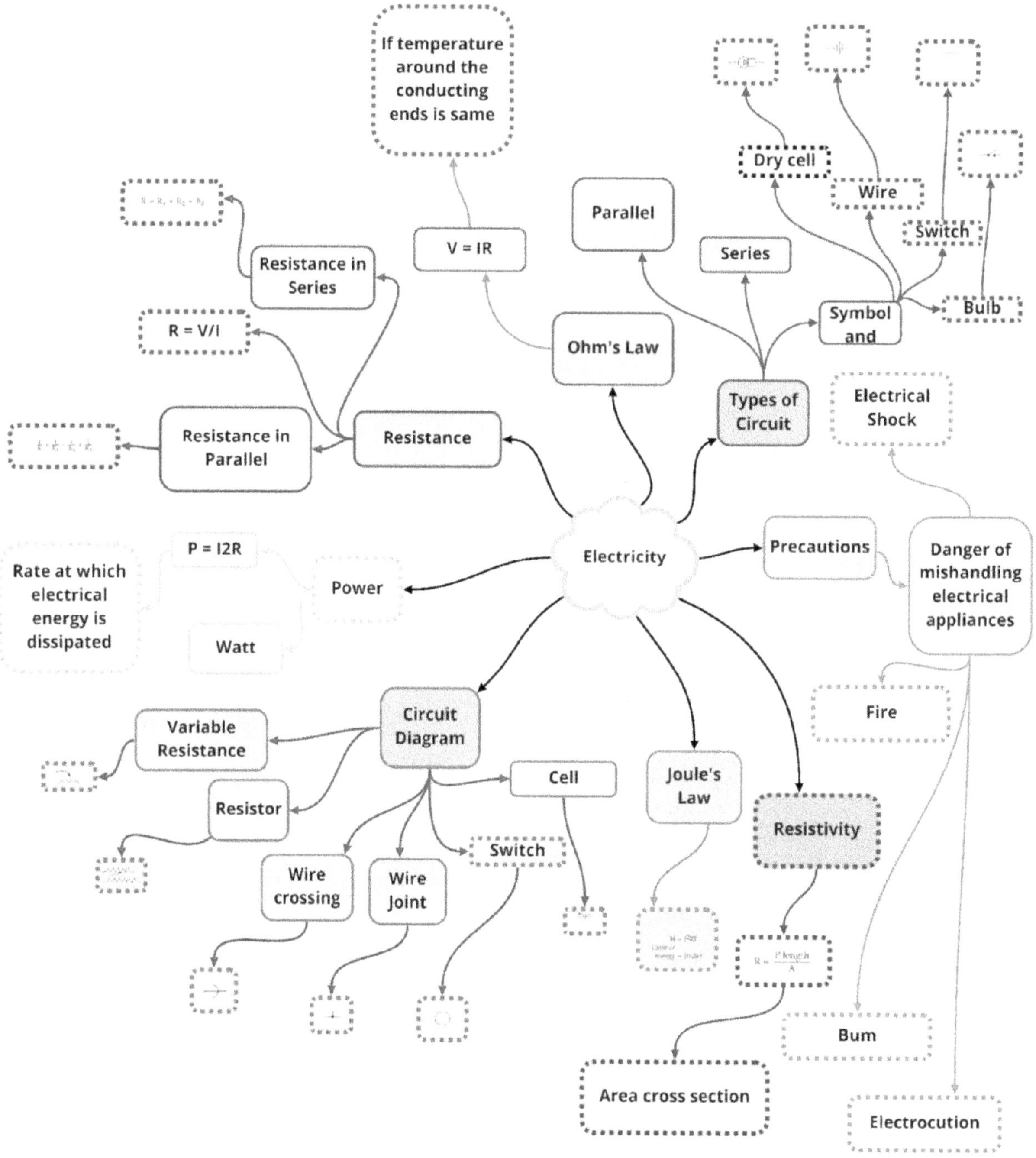

- Electricity
  - Resistance
    - Resistance in Series
    - R = V/I
    - Resistance in Parallel
  - Ohm's Law
    - V = IR
      - If temperature around the conducting ends is same
  - Types of Circuit
    - Parallel
    - Series
    - Symbol and
      - Dry cell
      - Wire
      - Switch
      - Bulb
  - Precautions
    - Danger of mishandling electrical appliances
      - Electrical Shock
      - Fire
      - Bum
      - Electrocution
  - Power
    - P = I2R
    - Rate at which electrical energy is dissipated
    - Watt
  - Circuit Diagram
    - Variable Resistance
    - Resistor
    - Cell
    - Switch
    - Wire crossing
    - Wire Joint
  - Joule's Law
  - Resistivity
    - Area cross section

Mind Map :Magnetic Effect of electric Current

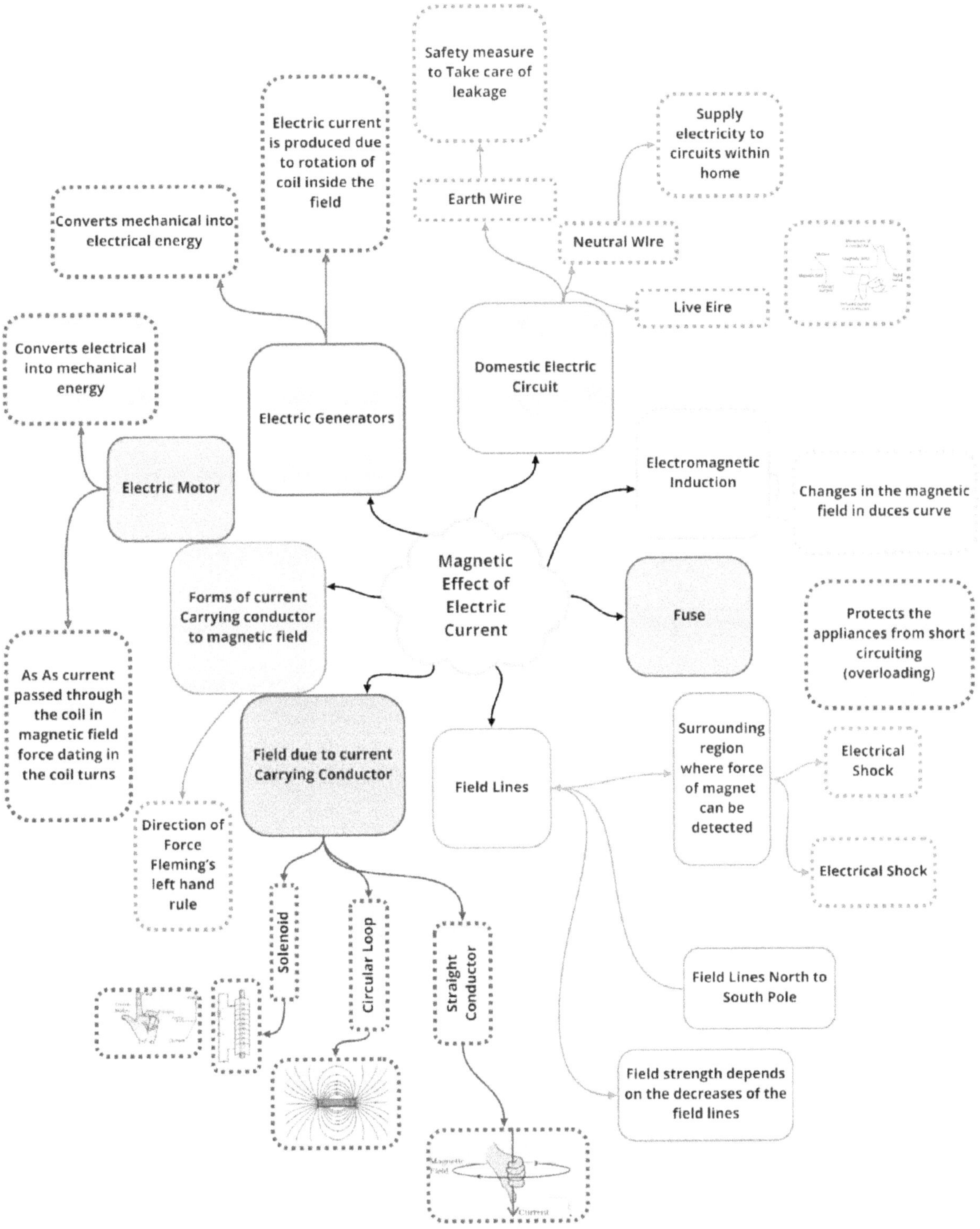

Magnetic Effect of Electric Current

- Electric Motor
  - Converts electrical into mechanical energy
  - As As current passed through the coil in magnetic field force dating in the coil turns
- Electric Generators
  - Converts mechanical into electrical energy
  - Electric current is produced due to rotation of coil inside the field
- Domestic Electric Circuit
  - Earth Wire
    - Safety measure to Take care of leakage
  - Neutral WIre
    - Supply electricity to circuits within home
  - Live Eire
- Electromagnetic Induction
  - Changes in the magnetic field in duces curve
- Fuse
  - Protects the appliances from short circuiting (overloading)
- Forms of current Carrying conductor to magnetic field
  - Direction of Force Fleming's left hand rule
- Field due to current Carrying Conductor
  - Solenoid
  - Circular Loop
  - Straight Conductor
- Field Lines
  - Surrounding region where force of magnet can be detected
    - Electrical Shock
    - Electrical Shock
  - Field Lines North to South Pole
  - Field strength depends on the decreases of the field lines

Mind Map :Sources of Energy

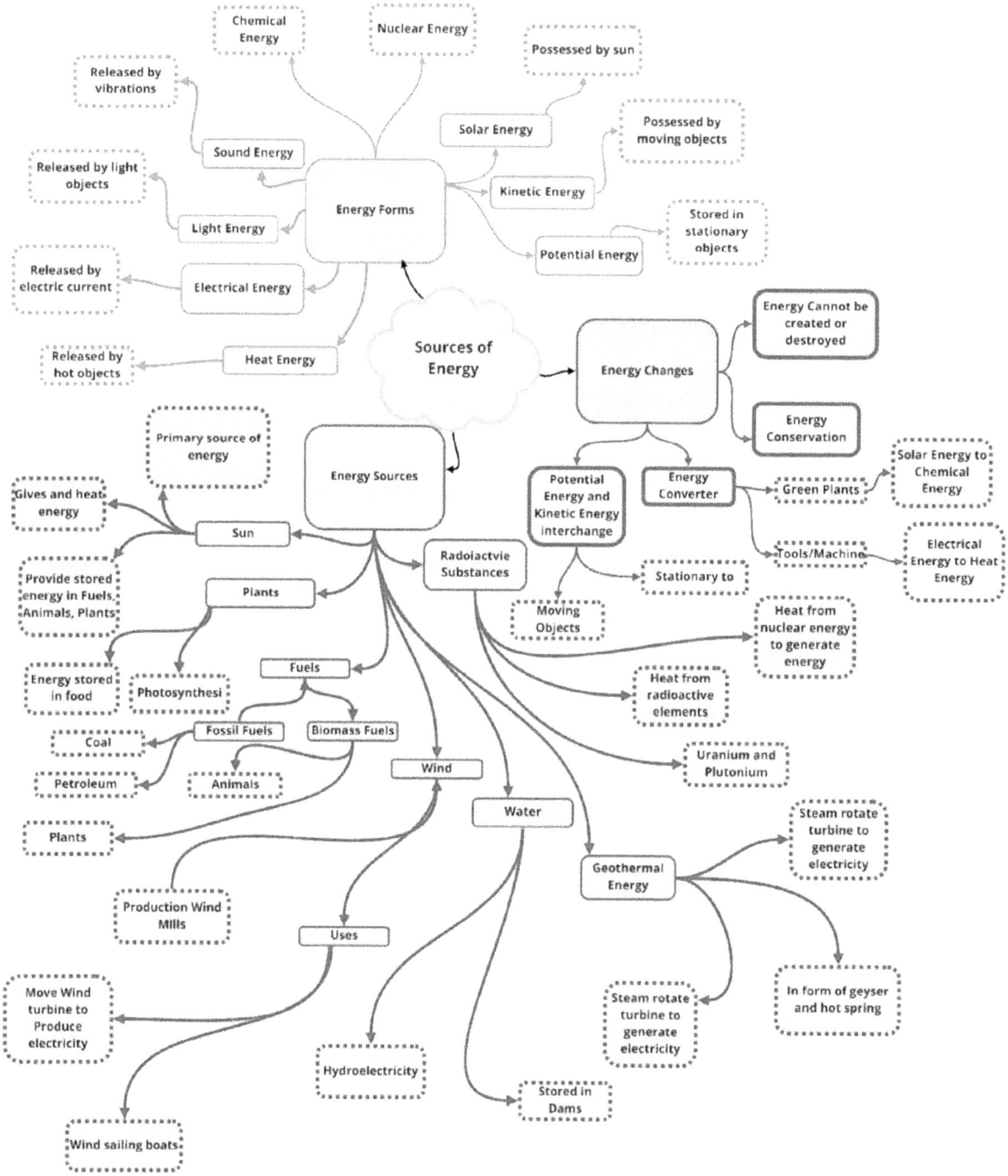

Sources of Energy

- Energy Forms
  - Chemical Energy
  - Nuclear Energy
  - Sound Energy
    - Released by vibrations
  - Light Energy
    - Released by light objects
  - Electrical Energy
    - Released by electric current
  - Heat Energy
    - Released by hot objects
  - Solar Energy
    - Possessed by sun
  - Kinetic Energy
    - Possessed by moving objects
  - Potential Energy
    - Stored in stationary objects
- Energy Changes
  - Energy Cannot be created or destroyed
  - Energy Conservation
  - Potential Energy and Kinetic Energy interchange
    - Stationary to
    - Moving Objects
  - Energy Converter
    - Green Plants
      - Solar Energy to Chemical Energy
    - Tools/Machine
      - Electrical Energy to Heat Energy
- Energy Sources
  - Sun
    - Primary source of energy
    - Gives and heat energy
    - Provide stored energy in Fuels, Animals, Plants
  - Plants
    - Energy stored in food
    - Photosynthesi
  - Fuels
    - Fossil Fuels
      - Coal
      - Petroleum
    - Biomass Fuels
      - Animals
      - Plants
  - Wind
    - Production Wind Mills
    - Uses
      - Move Wind turbine to Produce electricity
      - Wind sailing boats
  - Water
    - Hydroelectricity
    - Stored in Dams
  - Radoiactvie Substances
    - Heat from nuclear energy to generate energy
    - Heat from radioactive elements
    - Uranium and Plutonium
  - Geothermal Energy
    - Steam rotate turbine to generate electricity
    - Steam rotate turbine to generate electricity
    - In form of geyser and hot spring

Mind Map :Our Environment

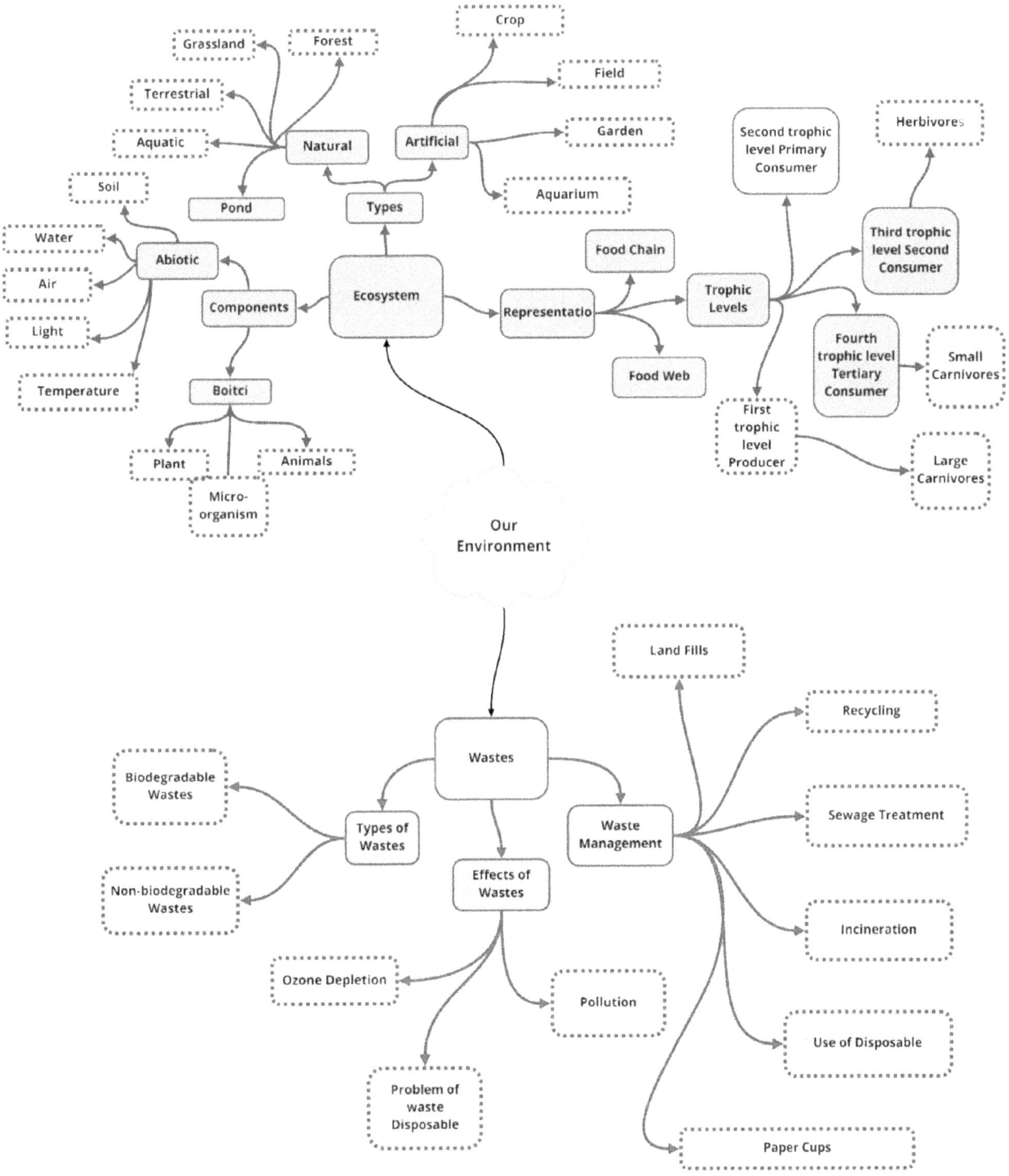

- Our Environment
  - Ecosystem
    - Types
      - Natural
        - Grassland
        - Forest
        - Terrestrial
        - Aquatic
        - Pond
      - Artificial
        - Crop
        - Field
        - Garden
        - Aquarium
    - Components
      - Abiotic
        - Soil
        - Water
        - Air
        - Light
        - Temperature
      - Boitci
        - Plant
        - Micro-organism
        - Animals
    - Representatio
      - Food Chain
      - Food Web
      - Trophic Levels
        - Second trophic level Primary Consumer
        - Third trophic level Second Consumer
          - Herbivores
        - Fourth trophic level Tertiary Consumer
          - Small Carnivores
        - First trophic level Producer
          - Large Carnivores
  - Wastes
    - Types of Wastes
      - Biodegradable Wastes
      - Non-biodegradable Wastes
    - Effects of Wastes
      - Ozone Depletion
      - Pollution
      - Problem of waste Disposable
    - Waste Management
      - Land Fills
      - Recycling
      - Sewage Treatment
      - Incineration
      - Use of Disposable
      - Paper Cups

Mind Map :Management of natural Resources

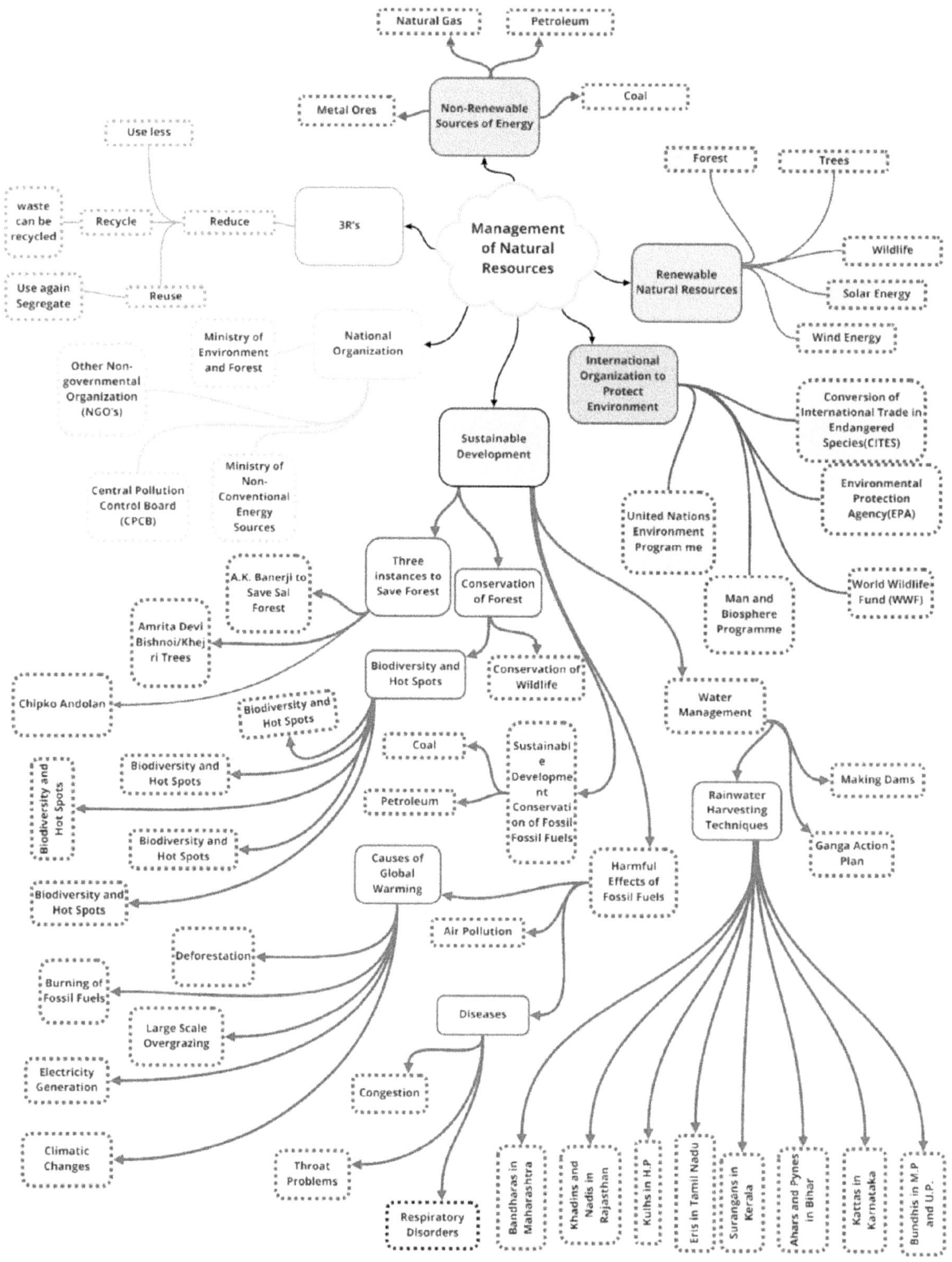

Management of Natural Resources

- Non-Renewable Sources of Energy
  - Natural Gas
  - Petroleum
  - Coal
  - Metal Ores
- 3R's
  - Reduce
    - Use less
    - Recycle
      - waste can be recycled
    - Reuse
      - Use again Segregate
- Renewable Natural Resources
  - Forest
  - Trees
  - Wildlife
  - Solar Energy
  - Wind Energy
- International Organization to Protect Environment
  - Conversion of International Trade in Endangered Species(CITES)
  - Environmental Protection Agency(EPA)
  - World Wildlife Fund (WWF)
  - Man and Biosphere Programme
  - United Nations Environment Program me
- National Organization
  - Ministry of Environment and Forest
  - Other Non-governmental Organization (NGO's)
  - Central Pollution Control Board (CPCB)
  - Ministry of Non-Conventional Energy Sources
- Sustainable Development
  - Three instances to Save Forest
    - A.K. Banerji to Save Sal Forest
    - Amrita Devi Bishnoi/Khejri Trees
    - Chipko Andolan
  - Conservation of Forest
    - Biodiversity and Hot Spots
      - Biodiversity and Hot Spots
      - Biodiversity and Hot Spots
      - Biodiversity and Hot Spots
      - Biodiversity and Hot Spots
      - Biodiversity and Hot Spots
    - Conservation of Wildlife
  - Sustainable Development Conservation of Fossil Fossil Fuels
    - Coal
    - Petroleum
  - Harmful Effects of Fossil Fuels
    - Causes of Global Warming
      - Deforestation
      - Burning of Fossil Fuels
      - Large Scale Overgrazing
      - Electricity Generation
      - Climatic Changes
    - Air Pollution
    - Diseases
      - Congestion
      - Throat Problems
      - Respiratory Disorders
  - Water Management
    - Making Dams
    - Ganga Action Plan
    - Rainwater Harvesting Techniques
      - Bandharas in Maharashtra
      - Khadins and Nadis in Rajasthan
      - Kulhs in H.P
      - Eris in Tamil Nadu
      - Surangans in Kerala
      - Ahars and Pynes in Bihar
      - Kattas in Karnataka
      - Bundhis in M.P and U.P.

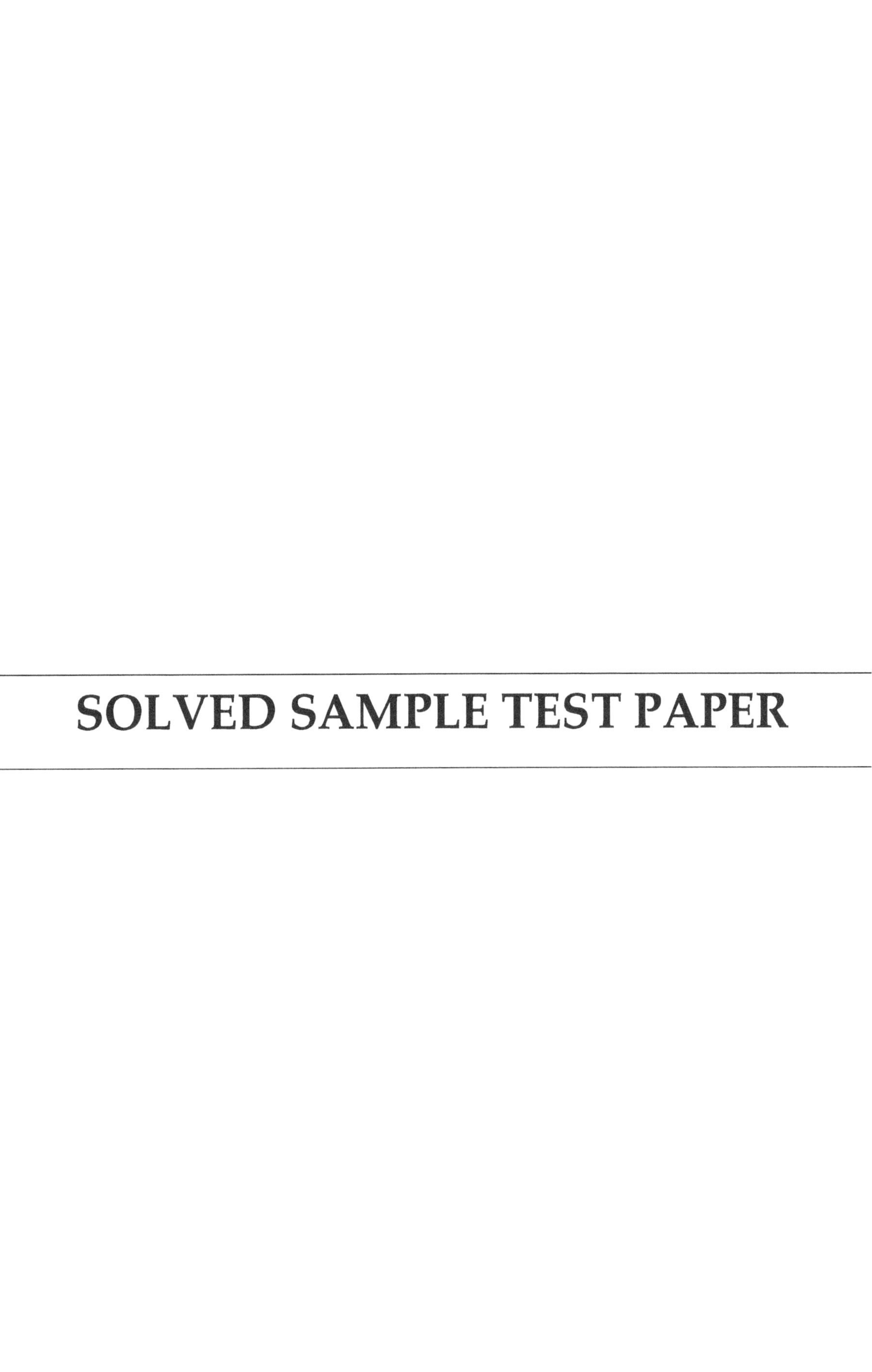

SOLVED SAMPLE TEST PAPER

Class- X Session- 2022-23

SCIENCE

SAMPLE QUESTION PAPER

Time Allowed: 3 Hrs. **Maximum Marks: 80**

General Instructions:

1. This Question Paper has 5 Sections A-E.
2. Section **A** has 20 MCQs carrying 1 mark each
3. Section **B** has 5 questions carrying 02 marks each.
4. Section **C** has 6 questions carrying 03 marks each.
5. Section **D** has 4 questions carrying 05 marks each.
6. Section **E** has 3 case-based integrated units of assessment (04 marks each) with subparts of the values of 1, 1, and 2 marks each respectively.
7. All Questions are compulsory. However, an internal choice in 2 Qs of 5 marks, 2 Qs of 3 marks, and 2 Questions of 2 marks has been provided. An internal choice has been provided in the 2marks questions of Section E
8. Draw neat figures wherever required. Take π =22/7 wherever required if not stated

Section A

Section A consists of 20 questions of 1 mark each

Question 1.

The change in colour of the moist litmus paper in the given set up is due to

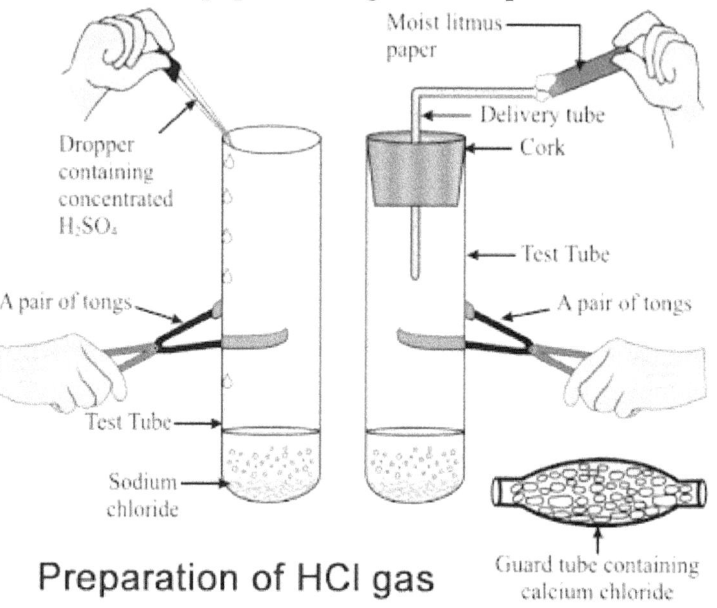

Preparation of HCl gas

(i) Presence of acid
(ii) Presence of base
(iii) Presence of $H^+(aq)$ in the solution
(iv) Presence of Litmus which acts as an indicator

(a) i and ii
(b) Only ii
(c) Only iii

(d) Only iv
Answer. (c) Only iii

Question 2.
In the redox reaction

$$MnO_2 + 4HCl \rightarrow MnCl_2 + 2H_2O + Cl_2$$

(a) MnO_2 is reduced to $MnCl_2$&HCl is oxidized to H_2O
(b) MnO_2 is reduced to $MnCl_2$&HCl is oxidized to Cl_2
(c) MnO_2 is oxidized to $MnCl_2$ & HCl is reduced to Cl_2
(d) MnO_2 is oxidized to $MnCl_2$ & HCl is reduced to H_2O
Answer. (b) MnO_2 is reduced to $MnCl_2$&HCl is oxidized to Cl_2

Question 3.

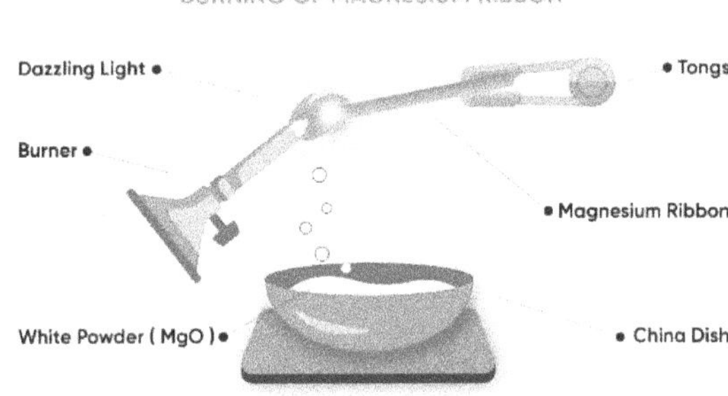

(a) A brown powder of Magnesium oxide is formed.
(b) Colourless gas which tums lime water milky is evolved.
(c) Magnesium ribbon burns with brilliant white light.
(d) Reddish brown gas with a smell of burning Sulphur has evolved.
Answer. (c)Magnesium ribbon burns with brilliant white light.

Question 4.
With the reference to four gases CO_2, CO, Cl_2 and O_2, which one of the options in the table is correct?

Option	Acidic oxide	Used in treatment of water	Product of respiration	Product of incomplete combustion
(a)	CO	Cl_2	O_2	CO
(b)	CO_2	Cl_2	CO_2	CO
(c)	CO_2	O_2	O_2	CO
(d)	CO	O_2	CO_2	CO_2

Answer. (b) CO_2, Cl_2, CO_2, CO

Question 5.

On placing a copper coin in a test tube containing green ferrous sulphate solution, it will be observed that the ferrous sulphate solution

(a) Turns blue, and a grey substance is deposited on the copper coin.

(b) Turns colourless and a grey substance is deposited on the copper coin.

(c) Turns colourless and a reddish-brown substance is deposited on the copper coin.

(d) Remains green with no change in the copper coin.

Answer. (d) Remains green with no change in the copper coin.

Question 6.

Anita added a drop each of diluted acetic acid and diluted hydrochloric acid on pH paper and compared the colors. Which of the following is the correct conclusion?

(a) Ph of acetic acid is more than that of hydrochloric acid.

(b) Ph of acetic acid is less than that of hydrochloric acid.

(c) Acetic acid dissociates completely in an aqueous solution.

(d) Acetic acid is a strong acid

Answer. (a) only i

Question 7.

The formulae of four organic compounds are shown below. Choose the correct option

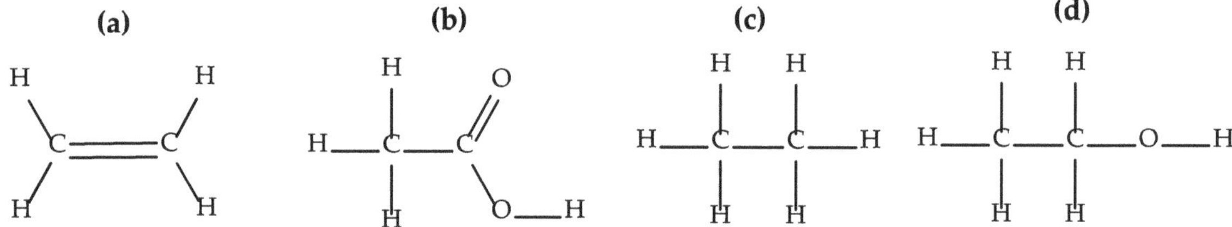

(a) A and B are unsaturated hydrocarbons

(b) C and D are saturated hydrocarbons

(c) The addition of hydrogen in presence of a catalyst changes A to C

(d) The addition of potassium permanganate changes B to D

Answer. (c) The addition of hydrogen in presence of a catalyst changes A to C

Question 8.

In the given transverse Section of the leaf identify the layer of cells where maximum photosynthesis occurs.

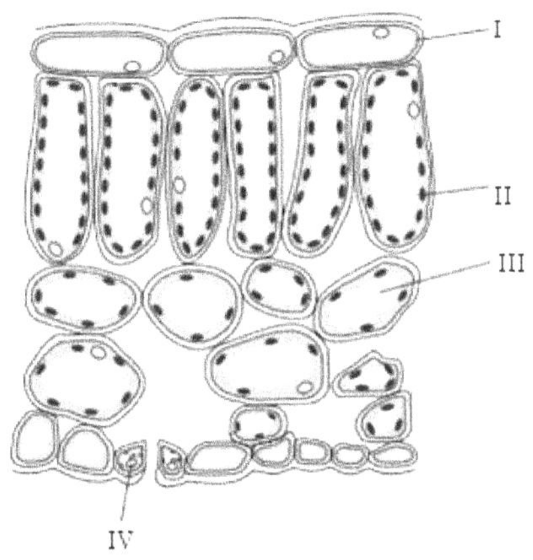

(a) I, II
(b) II, III
(c) III, IV
(d) I, IV
Answer. (b) II, III

Question 9.

Observe the experimental setup shown below. Name the chemical indicated as ' X ' that can absorb the gas which is evolved as a byproduct of respiration.

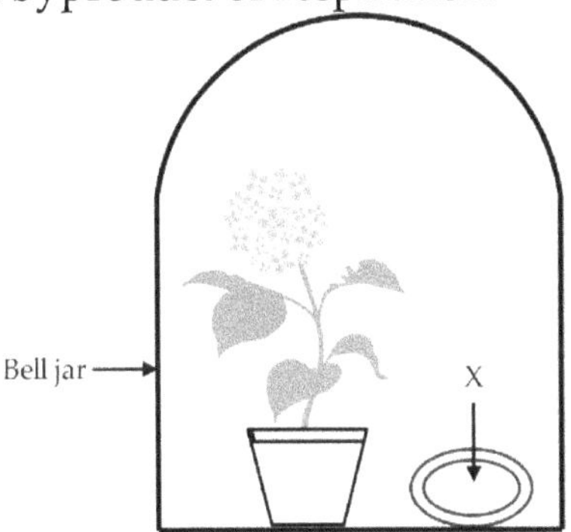

(a) NaOH
(b) KOH
(c)$Ca(OH)_2$
(d) K_2CO_3
Answer. (b) KOH

Question 10.

If a tall pea plant is crossed with a pure dwarf pea plant then, what percentage of F1 and F2 generation respectively will be tall?
(a) 25%, 25%
(b) 50%, 50%
(c) 75%, 100%
(d) 100%, 75%
Answer. (d) 100%, 75%

Question 11.

Observe the three figures given below. Which of the following depicts tropic movements appropriately?

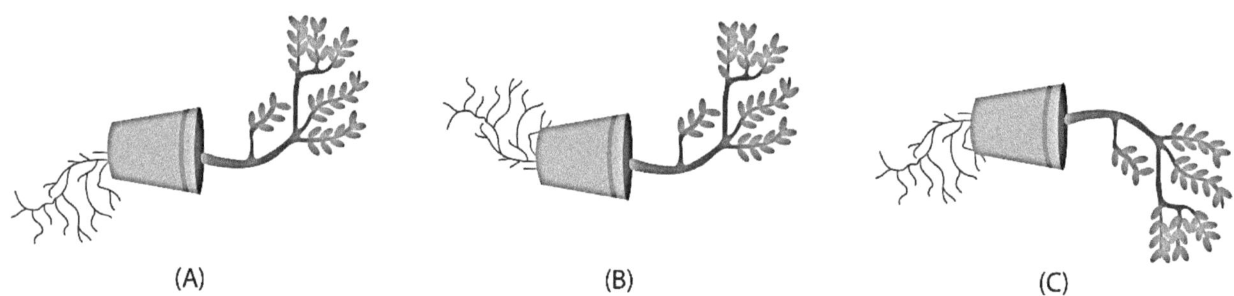

(a) B and C
(b) A and C
(c) B only
(d) C only
Answer. (d) C Only

Question 12.

The diagram shown below depicts pollination. Choose the options that will show a maximum variation in the offspring.

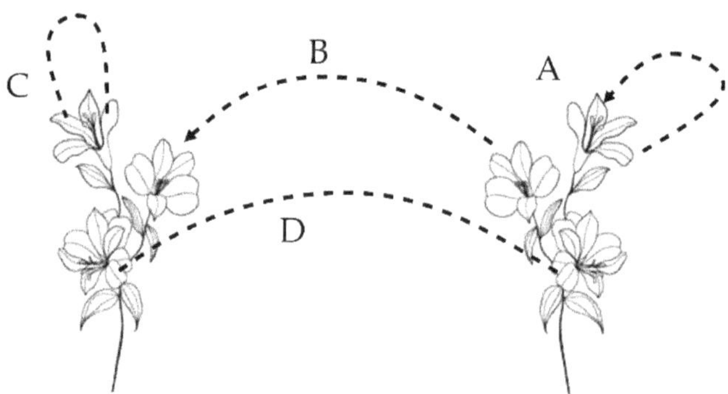

(a) A, B and C
(b) B and D
(c) B, C and D
(d) A and C
Answer. (b) B and D

Question 13.

A complete circuit is left on for several minutes, causing the connecting copper wire to become hot. As the temperature of the wire increases, the electrical resistance of the wire
(a) decreases.
(b) remains the same.

(c) increases.

(d) increases for some time and then decreases.

Answer. (c) increases

Question 14.

A copper wire is held between the poles of a magnet.

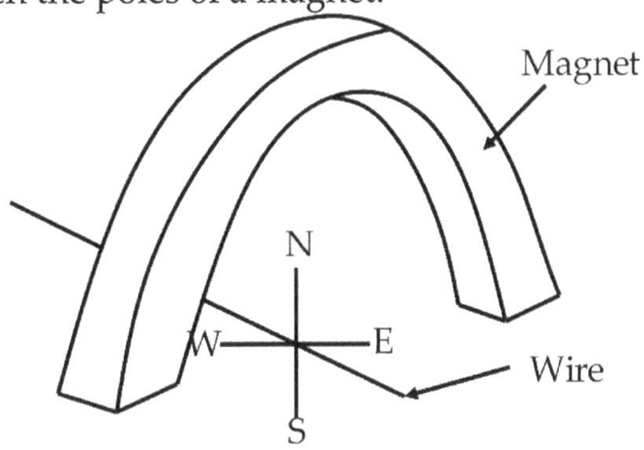

The current in the wire can be reversed. The pole of the magnet can also be changed over. In how many of the four directions shown can the force act on the wire?

(a) 1

(b) 2

(c) 3

(d) 4

Answer. (b) 2 (Either North or South)

Question 15.

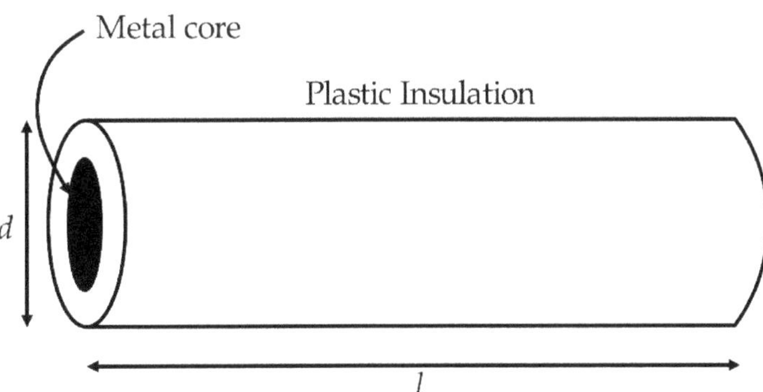

Plastic insulation surrounds a wire having diameter d and length l as shown above. A decrease in the resistance of the wire would be produced by an increase in the

(a) length l of the wire

(b) diameter d of the wire

(c) temperature of the wire

(d) thickness of the plastic insulation

Answer. (b) diameter d of the wire

Question 16.

Which of the following pattern correctly describes the magnetic field around a long straight wire carrying current?

(a) straight lines perpendicular to the wire.

(b) straight lines parallel to the wire.

(c) radial lines originating from the wire.

(d) concentric circles centred around the wire.

Answer. (d) The field consists of concentric circles centred around the wire.

Q. no 17 to 20 are Assertion - Reasoning based questions.

These consist of two statements - Assertion (A) and Reason (R). Answer these questions slecting the appropriate option given below:

(a) Both A and R are true and R is the correct explanation of A

(b) Both A and R are true and R is not the correct explanation of A

(c) A is true but R is false

(d) A is False but R is true

Question 17.

Assertion: Silver bromide decomposition is used in black and white photography.

Reason: Light provides energy for this exothermic reaction.

Answer. (c) A is true but R is false

Question 18.

Assertion: Height in pea plants is controlled by efficiency of enzymes and is thus genetically controlled.

Reason: Cellular DNA is the information source for making proteins in the cell.

Answer. (a) Both A and R are true and R is the correct explanation of A

Question 19.

Assertion: Amphibians can tolerate mixing of oxygenated and deoxygenated blood.

Reason: Amphibians are animals with two chambered heart

Answer. (c) A is true but R is false

Question 20.

Assertion: On freely suspending a current - carrying solenoid, it comes to rest in Geographical N-S direction.

Reason : One end of current carrying straight solenoid behaves as a North pole and the other end as a South pole, just like a bar magnet.

Answer. (a) Both A and R are true and R is the correct explanation of A

Section B

Section B has 5 questions carrying 02 marks each.

Question 21.

A clear solution of slaked lime is made by dissolving $Ca(OH)_2$ in an excess of wate This solution is left exposed to air. The solution slowly goes milky as a faint white precipitate forms. Explain why a faint white precipitate forms, support your response with the help of a chemical equation.

OR

Keerti added dilute Hydrochloric acid to four metals and recorded her observations as shown in the table given below:

Metal	Gas Evolved
Copper	Yes
Iron	Yes
Magnesium	No
Zinc	Yes

Select the correct observation(s) and give chemical equation(s) of the reaction involved.

Answer. Calcium hydroxide reacts with Carbon dioxide present in the atmosphere to form Calcium carbonate which results in milkiness/white ppt / Formation of Calcium carbonate $Ca(OH)_2 + CO_2 \rightarrow CaCO_3 + H_2O$

OR

$Fe + HCl \longrightarrow FeCl_2 / FeCl_3 + H_2$ (No deduction for balancing/ states)

$Zn + HCl \longrightarrow ZnCl_2 + H_2$

Question 22.

How is the mode of action in the beating of the heart different from reflex actions? Give four examples.

Answer.

Beating of heart	**Reflex actions**
Involuntary actions are actions which are not controlled by our will.	Reflex actions are sudden actions in response to something.
They do not need any kind of stimulus to work.	They required stimulus for its action.
These actions are regulated by the brain.	These actions are regulated by the spinal cord.
They do not involve skeletal muscle.	They do involve skeletal muscle.
These actions are performed throughout one's life	These actions are produced in response to an event of an emergency.
This action may be quick or slow.	Reflex actions are always quick.

Question 23.

Patients whose gallbladder are removed are recommended to eat less oily food. Why?

Answer.

Gallbladder stores bile which helps in emulsification of lipids. In the absence of stored bile, emulsification of fats will be negligible/ affected/ less and thus fat digestion will be slow. Hence there are such diet restrictions.

Question 24.

Name the substances other than water, that are reabsorbed during urine formation. What are the two parameters that decide the amount of water that is reabsorbed in the kidney?

Answer.

Glucose, amino acids, salts and a major amount of water are selectively re-absorbed as the urine flows along the tube. The amount of water reabsorbed depends on how much excess water there is in the body and on how much of dissolved waste there is to be excreted.

Question 25.

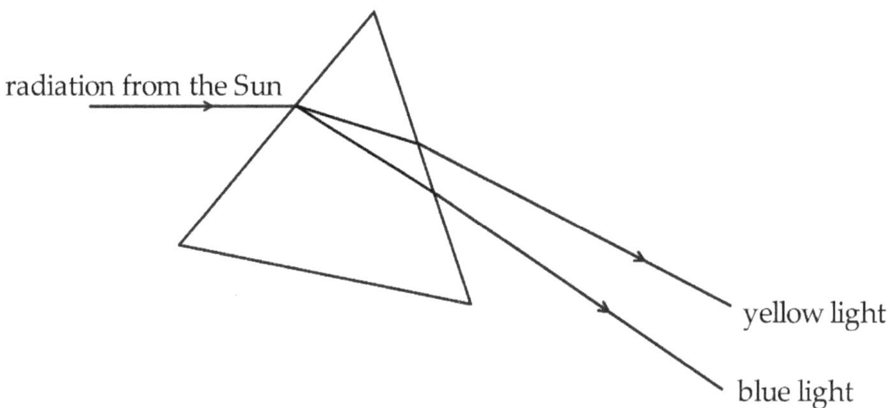

State the phenomena observed in the above diagram. Explain with reference to the diagram, which of the two lights mentioned above will have the higher wavelength?

OR

How will you use two identical prisms so that a narrow beam of white lightincident on one prism emerges out of the second prism as white light? Draw the diagram.

Answer.

Dispersion- The splitting of white light into seven colours on passing through a prism. Velocity is directly proportional to wavelength given constant frequency. So yellow will have greater wavelength than blue as the velocity of yellow light is greater than blue. OR Angle of deflections of the two prisms need to be equal and opposite. While the first prism splits the light in the seven colours due to different angles of deflection, the second prism combines the spectrum along a single ray and the colours again combine to give white light as the emergent light.

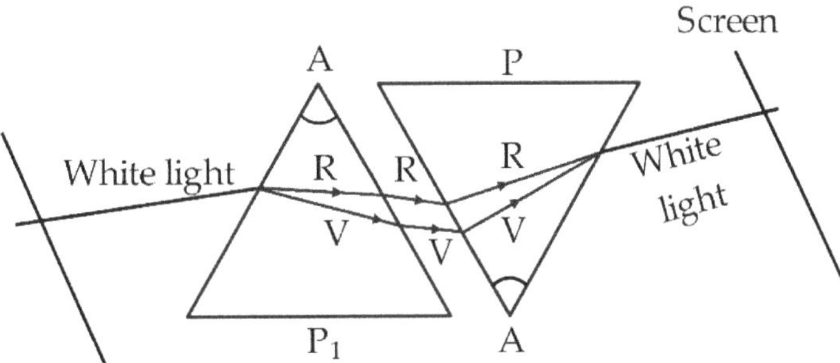

Question 26.

A lot of waste is generated in neighborhood. However, almost all of it is biodegradable. What impact will it have on the environment or human health?

Answer.

Excess generation of biodegradable wastes can be harmful as - Its decomposition is a slow process leading to production of foul smell and gases. It can be the breeding ground for germs that create unhygienic conditions.

Section - C

Q.no. 27 to 33 are short answer questions

Question 27.

(i)

(ii)

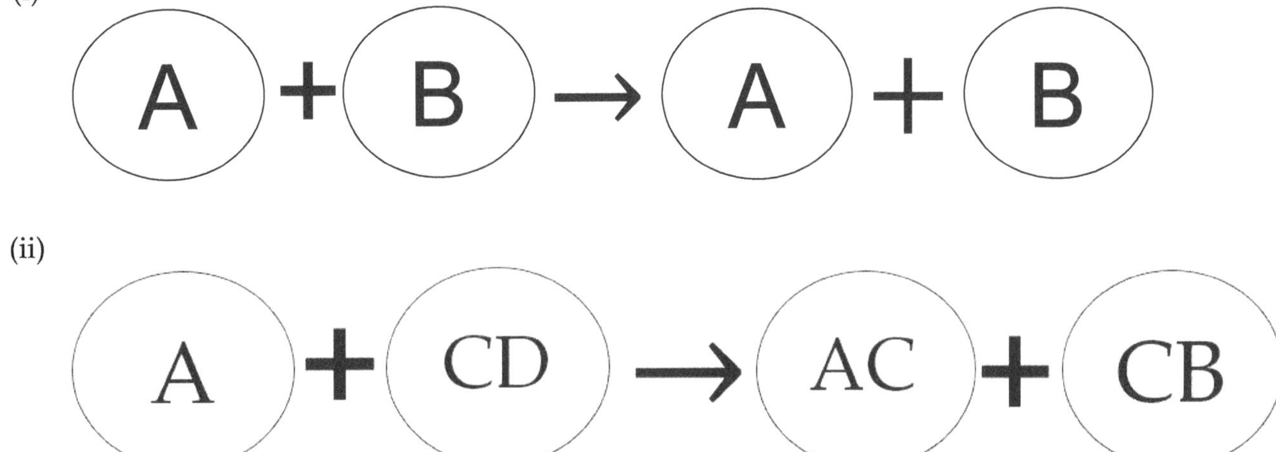

Identify the types of reaction mentioned above in (i) and (ii). Give one example for each type in the form of a balanced chemical equation.

Answer.

(i) Displacement -

Fe(s) + CuSO4(aq) → FeSO4(aq) + Cu(s)

Zn(s) + CuSO4(aq) → ZnSO4(aq) + Cu(s)

Pb(s) + CuCl2(aq) → PbCl2(aq) + Cu(s)

(Any one of the reaction or other displacement reaction.)

(ii) Double displacement

Na2SO4 (aq) + BaCl2(aq) → BaSO4 (s) + 2NaCl(aq).

(Any one of the reaction or other double displacement reaction.)

Question 28.

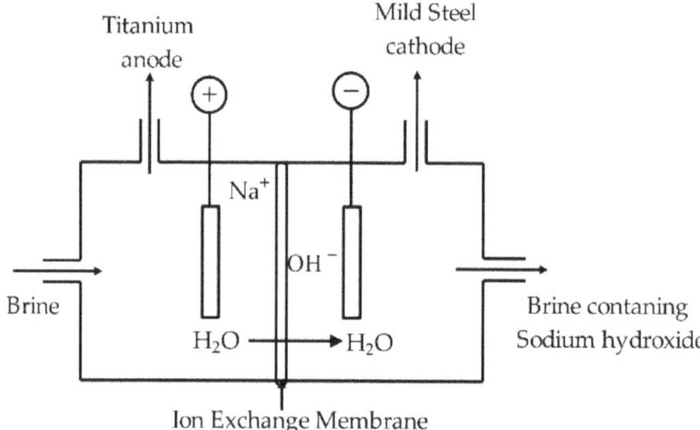

(i) Identify the gasses evolved at the anode and cathode in the above experimental set up.
(ii) Name the process that occurs. Why is it called so?
(iii) Illustrate the reaction of the process with the help of a chemical equation.

Answer.

(i) Anode: Chlorine; Cathode: Hydrogen
(ii) Chlor alkali process as the products obtained are alkali, chlorine gas and hydrogen gas
Electric current
(iii) $2NaCl(aq) + 2H_2O(l) 2NaOH(aq) + Cl_2 (g) + H_2 (g)$

Question 29.

The leaves of a plant were covered with aluminium foil, how would it affect the hhysiology of the plant?

OR

How is lymph an important fluid involved in transportation? If lymphatic vessels get blocked, how would it affect the human body? Elaborate.

Answer.

No photosynthesis will occur so no glucose will be made. Also no respiration will take place as no Oxygen will be taken in.

No transpiration will occur so there would be no upward movement of water or minerals from the soil as there will be no transpirational pull.

Temperature regulation of leaf surface will be affected.

OR

Lymph carries digested and absorbed fat from the intestine (1) and drains excess fluid from extracellular space back into the blood (1). Blockage of lymphatic system will lead to water retention and poor fat absorption in the body

Question 30.

Rohit wants to have an erect image of an object using a converging mirror of focal ength 40 cm.

(i) Specify the range of distance where the object can be placed in front of the mirror. Justify.

(ii) Draw a ray diagram to show image formation in this case.

(iii) State one use of the mirror based on the above kind of image formation.

Answer.

(i) The object has to be placed at a distance between 0 – 40 cm. This is because image **is** virtual, erect and magnified when the object is placed between F and P.

(ii)

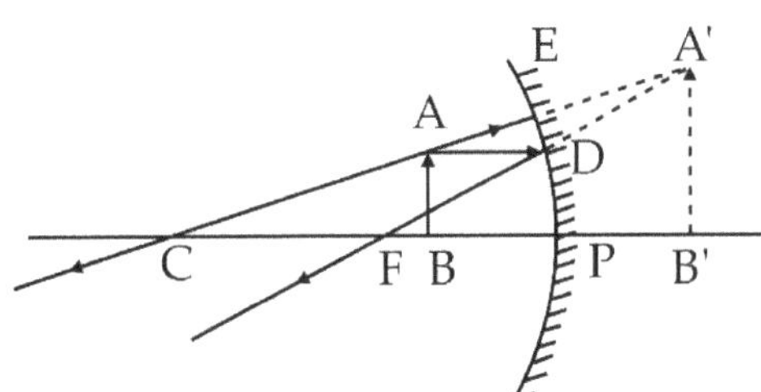

(iii) Used as shaving mirror or used by dentists to get enlarged image of teeth (any one use)

Question 31.

(i) A lens of focal length 5 cm is being used by Debashree in the laboratory as a magnifying glass. Her least distance of distinct vision is 25 cm.

(a) What is the magnification obtained by using the glass?

(b) She keeps a book at a distance 10 cm from her eyes and tries to read. She is. unable to read. What is the reason for this?

(ii) Ravi kept a book at a distance of 10 cm from the cyes of his friend Hari. Hari is not able to read anything written in the book. Give reasons for this?

Answer.

(i) Given, image distance = v = −25 cm, focal length = f = 5 cm, magnification = m =?

From lens formula, $\frac{1}{f} = \frac{1}{v} - \frac{1}{u} = \frac{1}{u} = \frac{1}{v} - \frac{1}{f}\frac{1}{u} = \frac{1}{-25} - \frac{1}{5} = \frac{-1-5}{25} = \frac{-6}{25}$

Object distance = u = $\frac{-25}{6}$ cm. m = $\frac{v}{u} = \frac{-25\times 6}{-25} = 6.$

(ii) This is because the least distance of distinct vision is 25 cm.

Question 32.

A student fixes a white sheet of paper on a drawing board. He places a bar magnet in the centre and sprinkles some iron filings uniformly around the bar magnet. Then he taps gently and observes that iron filings arrange themselves in a certain pattern.

(i) Why do iron filings arrange themselves in a particular pattern?

(ii) Which physical quantity is indicated by the pattern of field lines around the bar magnet?

(iii) State any two properties of magnetic field lines.

OR

A compass needle is placed near a current carrying wire. State your observations for the following cases and give reasons for the same in each case-

(i) Magnitude of electric current in wire is increased.

(ii) The compass needle is displaced away from the wire.

Answer.

(i) When iron filings are placed in a magnetic field around a bar magnet, they behave like tiny magnets. The magnetic force experienced by these tiny magnets make them rotate and align themselves along the direction of field lines mark)

(ii) The physical property indicated by this arrangement is the magnetic field produced by the bar magnet.

(iii) Magnetic field lines never intersect, magnetic field lines are closed curves.

OR

(i) The deflection in the compass needle increases as Magnetic field of the current carrying conductor is directly proportional to current flowing through it.

(ii) The deflection in the needle decreases as the magnetic field is inversely proportional to the perpendicular distance from the wire.

Question 33.

Why is damage to the ozone layer a cause for concern? What are its causes and what steps are being taken to limit this damage?

Answer.

Damage to the ozone layer is a cause for concern because the ozone layer shields the surface of earth from harmful UV radiations from the sun which cause skin cancer in human beings. Synthetic chemicals like chlorofluorocarbons (CFCs) which are used as refrigerants and in the fire - extinguishers are the main reason for the depletion of the ozone layer. Steps taken to limit this damage - Many developing and developed countries have signed and are obeying the directions of UNEP (United Nations Environment Programme) to freeze or limit the production and usage of CFCs at 1986 levels

Section - D

Q.no. 34 to 36 are Long answer questions

Question 34.

Shristi heated Ethanol with a compound A in presence of a few drops of concentrated sulphuric acid and observed a sweet-smelling compound B is formed. When B is treated with sodium hydroxide it gives back Ethanol and a compound C.

(i) Identify A and C

(ii) Give one use each of compound's A and B.

(iii) Write the chemical reactions involved and name the reactions.

OR

(i) What is the role of concentrated Sulphuric acid when it is heated with Ethanol at 443 K. Give the reaction involved.

(ii) Reshu by mistake forgot to label the two test tubes containing Ethanol and Ethanoic acid. Suggest an experiment to identify the substances correctly? Illustrate the reactions with the help of chemical equations

Answer.

(i) A – Ethanoic acid/ Or any other carboxylic acid, C- Sodium salt of ethanoic acid/ any other carboxylic acid/ sodium ethanoate

(ii) Use of A- dil. solution used as vinegar in cooking/ preservative in pickles
Use of B – making perfumes, flavoring agent.

(iii) $CH_3COOH + C_2H_5OH \rightarrow Conc\ H_2SO_4 + CH_3COOC_2H_5 + H_2O$
$CH_3COOC_2H_5 + NaOH \rightarrow CH_3COONa + C_2H_5OH$

OR

(i) Sulphuric acid acts as dehydrating agent

$$H_2SO_4 \xrightarrow[443\ K]{Conc.\ H_2SO_4} C_2H_4 + H_2O$$

(ii) By reaction with sodium carbonate/ bi carbonate, ethanol will not react whereas ethanoic acid gives brisk effervescence

$$2CH_3COOH + 2Na_2CO_3 \rightarrow 2CH_3COONa + H_2O + CO_2$$

OR

$$CH_3COOH + NaHCO_3 \rightarrow CH_3COONa + H_2O + CO_2$$

Question 35.

(i) Why is it not possible to reconstruct the whole organism from a fragment in complex multicellular organisms?

(ii) Sexual maturation of reproductive tissues and organs are necessary link for reproduction. Elucidate.

OR

(i) How are variations useful for species if there is drastic alteration in the niches?

(ii) Explain how the uterus and placenta provide necessary conditions for proper growth and development of the embryo after implantation?

Answer.

(i) The reason is that many multi-cellular organisms are not simply a random collection of cells. Specialised cells are organised as tissues, and tissues are organised into organs, which then have to be placed at definite positions in the body. Therefore, cell-by-cell division would be impractical.

(ii) Sexual maturation of reproductive tissues is a necessary link for reproduction because of the need for specialised cell called germ-cells to participate in sexual reproduction. The body of the individual organism has to grow to its adult size, the rate of general body growth begins to slow down, reproductive tissues begin to mature.
A whole new set of changes in the appearance of the body takes place like change in body proportions, new features appear. This period during adolescence is called puberty. There are also changes taking place that are different between boys and girls. In girls, breast size begins to increase, with darkening of the skin of the nipples at the tips of the breasts. Also, girls begin to menstruate at around this time. Boys begin to have new thick hair growth on the face and their voices begin to crack.

OR

(i) If the niche were drastically altered, the population could be wiped out. However, if some variations were to be present in a few individuals in these populations, there would be some chance for them to survive. Variation is thus useful for the survival of species over time.

(ii)

(a) The lining of the uterus thickens and is richly supplied with blood to nourish the growing embryo.

(b) The embryo gets nutrition from the mother's blood with the help of placenta. It is embedded in the uterine wall.

(c) It contains villi on the embryo's side of the tissue. On the mother's side are blood spaces, which surround the villi.

(d) This provides a large surface area for glucose and oxygen to pass from the mother to the embryo. The developing embryo will also generate waste substances which can be removed by transferring them into the mother's blood through the placenta.

(e) The child is born as a result of rhythmic contractions of the muscles in the uterus.

Question 36.

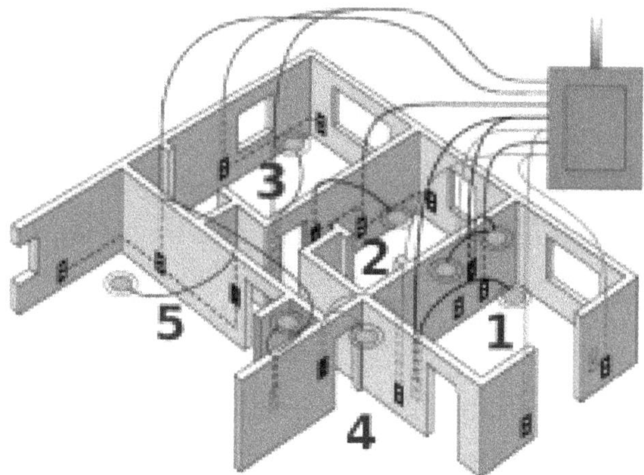

The diagram above is a schematic diagram of a household circuit. The house shown in the above diagram has 5 usable spaces where electrical connections are made. For this house, the mains have a voltage of 220 V and the net current coming from the mains is 22A.

(a) What is the mode of connection to all the spaces in the house from the mains?

(b) The spaces 5 and 4 have the same resistance and spaces 3 and 2 have respective resistances of 20Ω and 30Ω. Space 1 has a resistance double that of space 5 . What is the net resistance for space 5.

(c) What is the current in space 3 ?

(d) What should be placed between the main connection and the rest of the house's electrical appliances to save them from accidental high electric current?

Answer.

(a) All spaces are connected in parallel.

(b) Let Resistance of Space 5 and 4 be R ohms respectively

Resistance of Space 1 = 2 R ohms

Resistance of Space 2 = 30 ohms

Resistance of Space 3 = 20 ohms

(c) Current = 22 A

V = 220 V

$$\text{Total Resistance} = \frac{V}{I} 5\ S$$

Section - E

Q.no. 37 to 39 are case - based/data -based questions with 2 to 3 short sub - parts. Internal choice is provided in one of these sub-parts

Question 37.

(i) Two students decided to investigate the effect of water and air on iron object under identical experimental conditions. They measured the mass of each object before placing it partially immersed in 10ml of water. After a few days, the object were removed, dried and their masses were measured. The table shows their results.

Student	**Object**	**Mass of Object before Rusting in g**	**Mass of the coated object in g**
A	Nail	3.0	3.15
B	Thin plate	6.0	6.33

(a) What might be the reason for the varied observations of the two students?

(b) In another set up the students coated iron nails with zine metal and noted that, iron nails coated with zinc prevents rusting. They also observed that zine initially acts as a physical barrier, but an extra advantage of using zinc is that it continues to prevent rusting even if the layer of zine is damaged. Name this process of rust prevention and give any two other methods to prevent rusting.

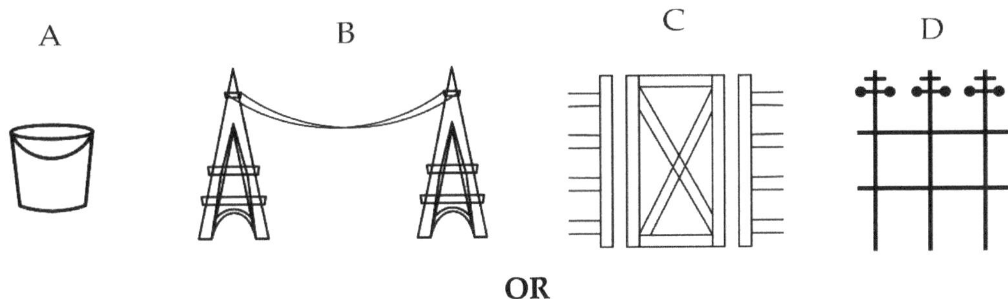

OR

(ii) In which of the following applications of Iron, rusting will occur most? Support your answer with valid reason.

(a) Iron Bucket electroplated with Zinc

(b) Electricity cables having iron wires covered with aluminium

(c) Iron hinges on a gate

(d) Painted iron fence

Answer. (a) Rusting occurs in both A and B so there is an increase in mass.
As the surface area of B is more, extent of rusting is more
(b) Galvanization Oiling/ greasing/ painting/ alloying/ chromium plating or any other

OR

(ii) (c) Iron hinges on a gate -
Iron is in contact with both atmospheric oxygen and moisture/ water vapour.

Question 38.

Pooja has green eyes while her parents and brother have black eyes. Pooja's husband Ravi has black eyes while his mother has green eyes and father has black eyes.

(i) On the basis of the above given information, is the green eye colour a dominant or recessive trait? Justify your answer.

(ii) What is the possible genetic makeup of Pooja's brother's eye colour?

(iii) What is the probability that the offspring of Pooja and Ravi will have green eyes? Also, show the inheritance of eye colour in the offspring with the help of a suitable cross.

OR

(i) 50% of the offspring of Pooja's brother are green eyed. With help of cross show how this is possible.

Answer.

(i) Yes, green eye colour is recessive as it will express only in homozygous condition

(ii) BB, Bb

(iii) bb*Bb

	B	b
B	Bb	bb
B	Bb	bb

Genetic cross -

50% of the offsprings can have green eye colour (0.5)

OR

W. Brother is heterozygous(Bb) and wife is green(bb) - (1)		
Wife bb* Bb brother	B	b
B	Bb	Bb
b	Bb	bb

50% of the offsprings can have green eye colour as per the cross shown.

Question 39.

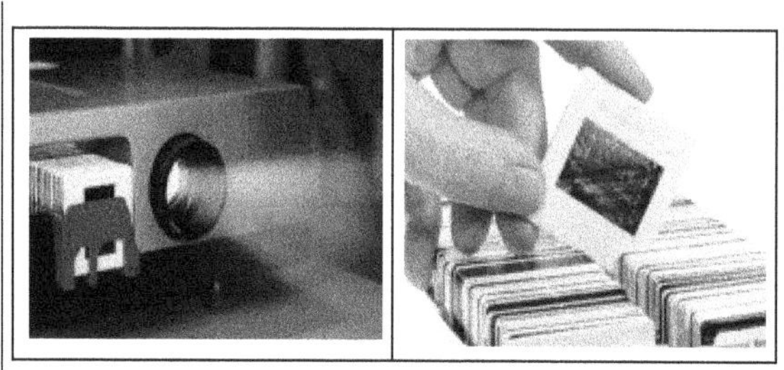

The above images are that of a specialized slide projector. Slides are small ransparencies mounted in sturdy frames ideally suited to magnification and projection, since they have a very high resolution and a high image quality. There is a tray where the slides are to be put into a particular orientation so that the viewers can see the enlarged erect images of the transparent slides. This means that the Gides will have to be inserted upside down in the projector tray.

To show her students the images of insects that she investigated in the lab, Mrs. Iyer orought a slide projector. Her slide projector produced a 500 times enlarged and inverted image of a slide on a screen 10 m away.

(i) Based on the text and data given in the above paragraph, what kind of lens must the slide projector have?

(ii) If v is the symbol used for image distance and u for object distance then with one reason state what will be the sign for $\frac{v}{u}$ in the given case?

(iii) A slide projector has a convex lens with a focal length of 20 cm. The slide is placed upside down 21 cm from the lens. How far away should the screen be placed from the slide projector's lens so that the slide is in focus?

OR

(i) When a slide is placed 15 cm behind the lens in the projector, an image is formed 3 m in front of the lens. If the focal length of the lens is 14 cm, draw a ray diagram to show image formation. (not to scale)

Answer.

(i) Convex Lens

(ii) Negative as the image is real and inverted.

(iii) $\frac{1}{f} = \frac{1}{v} - \frac{1}{u}$

$$\frac{1}{20} = \frac{1}{v} - \frac{1}{-20}$$

$$\frac{1}{v} = \frac{1}{20} - \frac{1}{21}$$

$$= \frac{21 - 20}{420}$$

$$= \frac{1}{420}$$

$$v = 420 \text{ cm}$$

OR

(i)

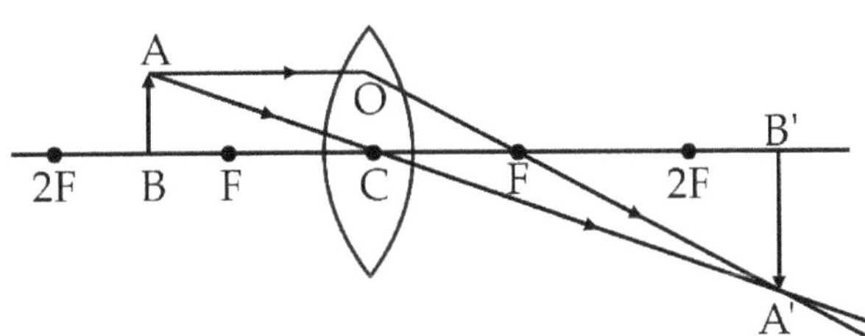

Class- X Session- 2022-23

Science

SAMPLE TEST PAPER-1

Time Allowed: 3 Hrs. **Maximum Marks: 80**

General Instructions:

1. This Question Paper has 5 Sections A-E.
2. Section **A** has 20 MCQs carrying 1 mark each
3. Section **B** has 5 questions carrying 02 marks each.
4. Section **C** has 6 questions carrying 03 marks each.
5. Section **D** has 4 questions carrying 05 marks each.
6. Section **E** has 3 case-based integrated units of assessment (04 marks each) with subparts of the values of 1, 1, and 2 marks each respectively.
7. All Questions are compulsory. However, an internal choice in 2 Qs of 5 marks, 2 Qs of 3 marks, and 2 Questions of 2 marks has been provided. An internal choice has been provided in the 2marks questions of Section E
8. Draw neat figures wherever required. Take π =22/7 wherever required if not stated

Section A

Section A consists of 20 questions of 1 mark each

Question 1

Balanced chemical equation among the following is :

(a) $Fe + H_2O \rightarrow Fe_3O_4 + H_2$

(b) $3Fe + 4H_2O \rightarrow Fe_3O_4 + 4H_2$

(c) $Fe + 4H_2O \rightarrow Fe_3O_4 + H_2$

(d) $Fe + H_2O \rightarrow Fe_3O_4 + 4H_2$

Ans.(b) $3Fe + 4H_2O \rightarrow Fe_3O_4 + 4H_2$

Question 2

$Fe_2O_3 + 2Al \rightarrow Al_2O_3 + 2Fe$ is a:

(i) displacement reaction,

(ii) combination reaction

(iii) double displacement reaction

(iv) redox reaction

(a) (i) and (ii)

(b) (i) and (iii)

(c) (i) and (iv)

(d) (ii) and (iv)

Answer(c) (i) and (iv)

Question 3

The natural indicator is:

(a) Phenolphthalein

(b) Litmus

(c) Methyl orange

(d) All the above

Answer(b) Litmus

Question 4

An ingredient of baking powder is:

(a) Acetic acid

(b) Tartaric acid

(c) Citric acid

(d) Lactic acid

Answer(b) Tartaric acid

Question 5

Which one of the following figures correctly describes the process of electrolytic refining?

(a)

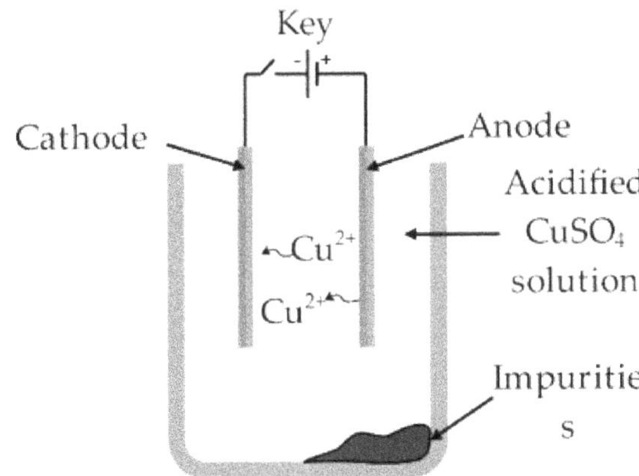

(b)

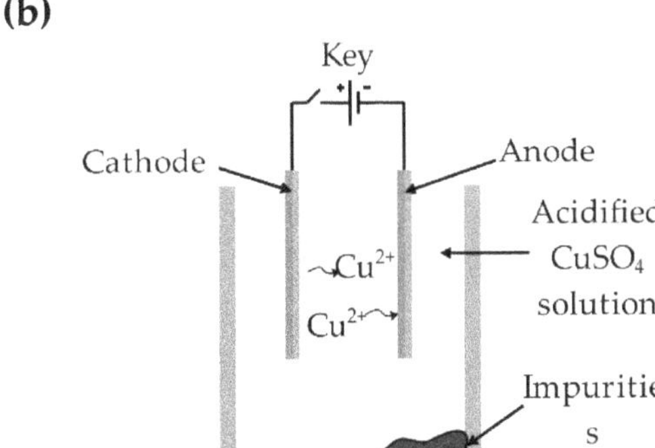

(c)

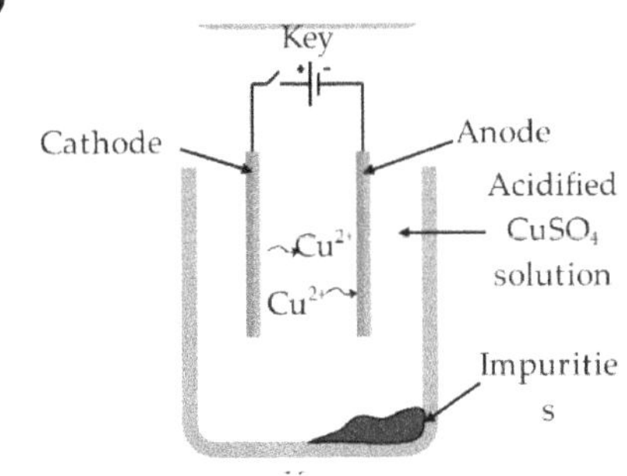

(d)

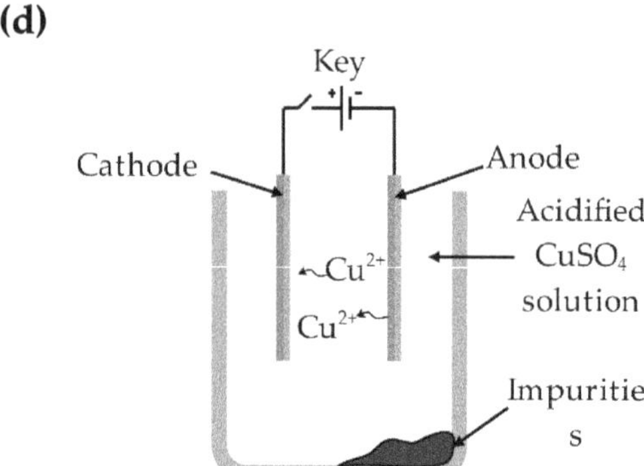

Answer(a)

Question 6

Detergents are effective in:

(a) Soft water

(b) Hard water

(c) River water

(d) All the above

Answer(a) Soft water

Question 7

Soaps are sodium or potassium salts of

(a) Sulphonic acids containing carbon atom 10 to 16

(b) Fatty acids containing carbon atoms 16 to 18

(c) Trihydroxy alcohols

(d) All the above

Answer(d) All the above

Question 8

The chlorophyll in photosynthesis is used for

(a) Absorbing light

(b) Breaking down water molecule

(c) No function

(d) Reduction of CO_2

Answer(a) Absorbing light

Question 9

Proteins after digestion are converted into

(a) Carbohydrates

(b) Small globules

(c) Amino acids

(d) Starch

Ans (c) Amino acids

Question 10

Carbohydrates in the plants are stored in the form of

(a) Glycogen
(b) Starch
(c) Glucose
(d) Maltose

Answer(b) Starch

Question 11

Main site of photosynthesis

(a) Leaf
(b) Stem
(c) Chloroplast
(d) Guard cells

Answer(c) Chloroplast

Question 12

The small pores present of leaf's surface are called

(a) Stomata
(b) Chlorophyll
(c) Guard cells
(d) None of these

Answer(a) Stomata

Question 13

The conductor AB is suddenly moved in the magnetic field when the induced current flows in it as shown in Fig. The conductor AB is moved:

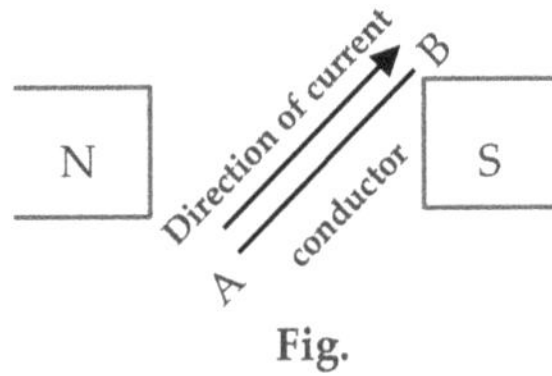

Fig.

(a) Vertically upward
(b) Vertically downward
(c) Towards N-pole
(d) Towards S-pole

Answer(b) Vertically downward

Question 14

Three resistances R_1, R_2, R_3 are connected in series. The total resistance is

(a) $R_s = R_1 + R_2 + R_3$
(b) $R_s = \frac{1}{R_1} + \frac{1}{R_2} + \frac{1}{R_3}$

(c) $R_s = \frac{R_1+R_2}{R_3}$

(d) $R_s = \frac{R_2}{R_1+R_2}$

Answer(a) $R_s = R_1 + R_2 + R_3$

Question 15

The focal length of a lens is 50 cm. Its power would 5 be

(a) 50 dioptre

(b) 2 dioptre

(c) 20 dioptre

(d) None of these

Answer(b) 2 dioptre

Question 16

(i) A real image is always inverted.

(ii) A virtual image is always erect.

(a) Only I is true

(b) Only II is true

(c) Both I and II are true

(d) Neither is true

Answer(c) Both I and II are true

Q. no 17 to 20 are Assertion - Reasoning based questions. These consist of two statements – Assertion (A) and Reason (R). Answer these questions selecting the appropriate option given below: (a) Both A and R are true and R is the correct explanation of A (b) Both A and R are true and R is not the correct explanation of A (c) A is true but R is false (d) A is False but R is true

Question 17

Assertion: The IUPAC nomenclature of

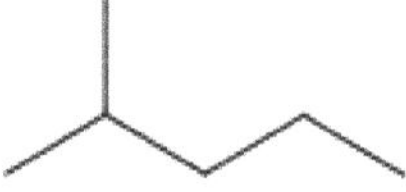

is 2-methyle pentane.

Reason: The substituent (or branch chain) should get lower number.

Answer(a)

Question 18

Assertion(A) : Plants lack excretory org**Answer**

Reason (R) : Plants usually absorb essential nutrients.

Answer(a)

Question 19

Assertion(A): In anaerobic respiration, one of the end product is alcohol.

Reason (R): There is an incomplete breakdown of glucose.
Answer(a)

Question 20
Assertion: If a ray of light is incident on a convex mirror along its principal axis, then the angle of incidence, as well as the angle of reflection for a ray of light, will be zero.
Reason: A ray of light going towards the center of curvature of a convex mirror is reflected back along the same path.
Answer(a)

Section B

Section B has 5 questions carrying 02 marks each

Q. no. 21 to 26 are very short answer questions

Question 21 **[2]**

Write balanced equation for the following reactions:

(a) Magnesium reacts with hydrochloric acid to form magnesium chloride and hydrogen gas.

(b) Copper powder on heating forms black copper (II) oxide.

Answer: (a) $Mg(s) + 2HCl(aq) \longrightarrow MgCl_2(aq) + H_2(g)$

(b) $2Cu(s) + O_2(g) \xrightarrow[\text{Black}]{2CuO(s)}$

OR

Why does dry litmus paper not show colour change with the solution of dry HCl in dry toluene?

Answer:

Dry litmus does not contain any water and dry HCl in dry toluene also does not contain any water. So, HCl gas provides no $H^+(aq)$ ions and dry litmus paper do not show any color change with the solution of dry HCl in toluene.

Question 22 **[2]**

How do plants exchange gases?

Answer:

Plants exchange gases through stomata. Large intercellular spaces ensure that each cell is in contact with air. Carbon dioxide and oxygen are exchanged here.

Question 23

What is the role of acid and mucus in stomach?

Answer:

It kills germs in food and provides acidic meditum for the action of pepsin enzyme to digest the proteins in stomach.

Mucus protccts thc wall of stomach from the action of acid and pepsin

Question 24 **[2]**

What is the role of valves in veins?

Answer:

They prevent the back flow of blood especially when it moves against gravity and under low blood pressure,

Question 25

Find the equivalent resistance of the combination of resistors shown.

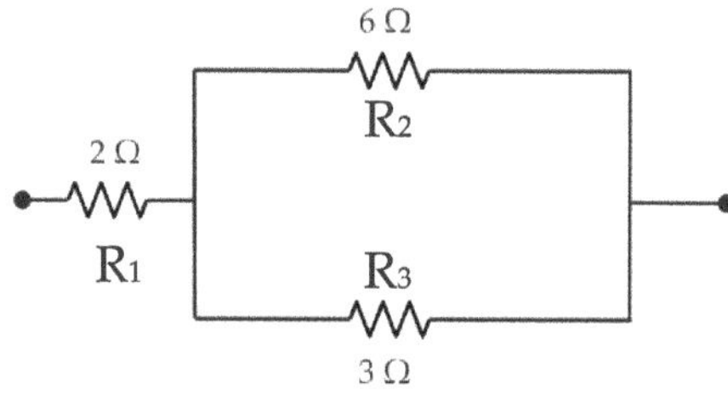

Solution:

$R_2 \& R_3$ are in 11^{al} combination.

$$R' = \frac{R_2 R_3}{R_2 + R_3} = \frac{6 \times 3}{6 + 3}$$

$$R' = 2\Omega$$

$R_1 \& R'$ are in series combination.

$$R_{eq} = R_1 + R'$$

$$= 2 + 2$$

$$\mathbf{R_{eq} = 4\Omega}$$

OR

We can burn a piece of paper by focusing on the sun's rays by using a particular type of lens.

(i) Name the type of lens used for the above purpose

(ii) Draw a ray diagram in support of your answer.

Answer:

(i) Convex lens,

(ii) Fig

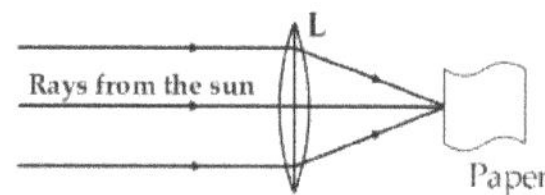

Question 26

Differentiate between Artery and Veins.

Answer:

Arteries carry blood away from the heart (arteriole: small arterial branch). They have thick and flexible walls to cinder higher pressure of blood.

Veins transport blood toward the lieart (venue: small vessel that carries blood from capillaries to veins). They have thimner wall but there are valves in them at regular distance to prevent back flow of blood especially when blood is returning back to heart from lower organs.

Section - C

Q.no. 27 to 33 are short answer questions

Question 27

A carboxylic acid $C_2H_4O_2$ reacts with alcohol in the presence of H_2SO_4 to form a compound X The alcohol on oxidation with alkaline $KmnO_4$ followed by acidification gives the same carboxylic acid, $C_2H_4O_2$. Write the name and structure of

(i) Carboxylic acid

(ii) Alcohol and

(iii) Compound X.

Answer

(i) The carboxylic acid involved in the reaction is acetic acid (CH_3COOH)

```
     H      O
     |    //
 H — C — C
     |    \
     H     OH
```

(ii) The alcohol involved in the reaction is ethanol (CH_3CH_2OH)

```
   H  H
   |  |
 H-C--C-O-H
   |  |
   H  H
```

(iii) X is the ester formed by the condensation of acetic acid and ethanol is ethyl acetate $CH_3COOC_2H_5$.

```
    H   O        H   H
    |   ||       |   |
 H--C---C---O----C---C---H
    |            |   |
    H            H   H
```

Question 28

Write the equations for the following metals which are obtained from their compound's reduction process.

(i) Metal X which is low in reactivity series.

(ii) Metal Y which is middle in reactivity series.by

Answer:

(i) $2HgS(s) + 3O_2(g) \rightarrow 2HgO(s) + 2SO_2(g)$

$$2HgO(s) \xrightarrow{Heat} 2Hg(l) + O_2(g)$$

(ii) $Fe_2O_3(s) + 3C(s) \longrightarrow 2Fe(s) + 3CO(g)$

Question 29

Design an activity to show that CO_2 is produced during breathing.

Answer:

Materials Required:

Two test tubes, a cork with two holes, two ghass tubes bent at right angle, syringe, lime water $Ca(OH)_2$. Procedure:

(i) Take some freshly prepared lime water, Ca(OH)2 in two test tubes,

(ii) Fit cork with two holes in test tubes A and B.

(iii) Fix two glass tubes in this cork of test tube A as shown in the figure.

(iv) Exhale air into the tube and record your observations.

(v) Pass air by the syringe through the lime water contained in test tube B anul record your observations.

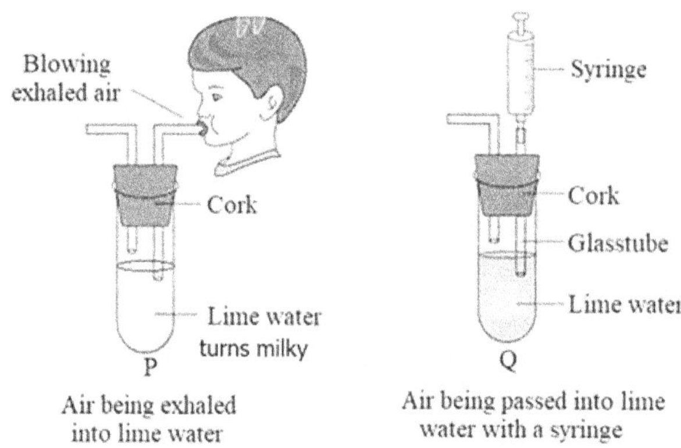

Air being exhaled into lime water

Air being passed into lime water with a syringe

OR

Explain how the air is inhaled during breathing in human,

Question 30

When we watch the sunset on a beach, we can see the sun for several minutes even after it has set. Why?

Answer: This is due to the refraction of sun rays from the earth's atmospheric layers. Sunlight bends towards normal due to the atmosphere. Due to this, the apparent position of the sun gets slightly above the real position. This is why the apparent position of the sun remains above the horizon for some time even after the sun is actually set.

Question 31

What is the cost of heating a tank of water with a 3 kW immersion rod for 80 minutes if electricity costs ₹2 per unit ?

Answer

$$P = 3KW$$
$$t = 80 \text{ min} = \perp .33 \text{ h}$$

$$\text{cost} = \text{F}2$$
$$\varepsilon = P \times t$$
$$\varepsilon = 3 \times 1.33$$
$$\varepsilon = 3.99\text{kWh}$$
$$\text{Cost} = \text{F}2 \times 3.99$$
$$\text{cost} = ₹8$$

(**Answer** ₹ 8.00)

Question 32

Difference between electrical resistance and specific resistance (resistivity) of a conductor.

Answer:

Electrical resistance	**Specific resistance (Resistivity)**
1. The opposition offer by a conductor to the flow of current through it is called electrical resistance. it is equal to the ratio of potential difference to the current flowing through it.	1. Resistivity of a conductor is defined as the resistance of a conductor of unity length and unit area of cross-Section.
2. Resistance of a conductor depends upon the length of area of cross- Section of the conductor.	2. Resistivity of a conductor does not depend on the length of area of cross-Section of a conductor.
3. SI unit of resistance is ohm.	3. SI unit of resistivity is ohm-meter.

OR

Alloys are used in electrical heating devices rather than pure metals. Give reasons.

Answer: This is because the resistivity of an alloy is more than the resistivity of a pure metal and hence more heat is produced in an alloy than in pure metal due to the flow of current. Moreover, alloy does not burn (or oxidize) easily even at higher temperature.

Question 33

What is the composition of urine? Are glucose and proteins normally present in urine? Why? How does volume of urine regulate?

Section - D

Q.no. 34 to 36 are Long answer questions

Question 34

Explain the given reactions with examples.

i. Hydrogenation reaction
ii. Oxidation reaction
iii. Substitution reaction
iv. Saponification reaction
v. Combustion reaction

Answer

(i) The addition of hydrogen to unsaturated hydrocarbons in the presence of Ni catalyst to form saturated hydrocarbons is called a hydrogenation reaction. For example:

$$R_2C{=}CR_2 + H_2 \xrightarrow[\text{Catalyst}]{\text{Ni}} R{-}\underset{H}{\overset{R}{C}}{-}\underset{H}{\overset{R}{C}}{-}R$$

(ii) The addition of oxygen to a substance is called oxidation. Ethanol is oxidized to ethanoic acid warming it with an oxidizing agent alkaline $KmnO_4$ is an example of an oxidation reaction.

$$CH_3CH_2OH \xrightarrow[\text{Heat}]{\text{alk. } KMnO_4} CH_3COOH$$

(iii) The replacement of an atom or a group of atoms with another atom or a group of atoms is called a substitution reaction Hydrogen atom in alkanes are substituted by chlorine atoms on reacting with Cl_2 in the presence of sunlight.

$$CH_4 + Cl_2 \xrightarrow{hv} CH_3Cl + HCl$$

(iv) Esters reacting with a base (or an acid) give sodium salt of carboxylic acid and alcohol. This is called saponification reaction as it is used in the preparation of soap.

$$CH_3COOC_2H_5 + \quad NaOH \longrightarrow CH_3COONa + C_2H_5OH$$

(v) The burning of fuels in the presence of oxygen/ air is called combustion.

$$CH_4 + 2O_2 \longrightarrow CO_2 + 2H_2O + \text{Heat and light}$$

OR

Explain the following:

(i) Reactivity of Al decreases if it is dipped in HNO_3

(ii) Carbon cannot reduce the oxides of Na or Mg

(iii) NaCl is not a conductor of electricity in a solid state whereas it does conduct electricity in an aqueous solution as well as in a molten state

(iv) Iron articles are galvanized.

(v) Metals like Na, K, Ca, and Mg is never found in their free state in nature.

Answer:

(i) Al on dipping in HNO_3 oxidizes to form a coating of aluminum oxide (Al_2O_3) on its surface. This layer is passive. This makes Al less reactive.

(ii) Na and Mg are stronger reducing agents in comparison to carbon. Therefore, carbon cannot reduce the oxides of Na and Mg.

(iii) Sodium chloride is not a conductor of electricity in a solid state because $Na^+$and Cl is not free but is held strongly by electrostatic forces of attraction. An aqueous solution or molten state conducts electricity.

(iv) Iron rusts when kept in the atmosphere for a long time. To prevent rusting a coating of zinc metal is applied to these articles. This protects iron from rusting.

(v) Na, K, Ca, and Mg are highly reactive. These metals react with moisture and other substances present in the atmosphere and therefore are not found in a free state in nature.

Question 35

(i) How is oxygen and carbon dioxide transported in human being? Explain clearly how the air is **inhaled** and exhaled curling breathing in humans

(ii) **(a)** What are two vital functions of the human kidney?

(b) Draw labelled diagram of human urinary system.

Answer:

(i) Exchange of gases in tissues:

(a) Most of oxygen is carried by haemoglobin in blood. On reaching the tissues, it gets diffused into the cells as it is in higher concentration than in the cells.

(b) The carbon dioxide, which is formed in the cells, gets accumulated there in higher concentration as Comparex in the blood, now diffused into the blood.

(c) The CO_2 mostly dissolved in blood plasma reaches the lungs, from where it is expelled out during exhalation.

Mechanism of Inhalation:

The thoracic cavity expands when diaphragm and rib muscles contract. The thorax moves upwards and outwards, increasing the volume inside thoracic cavity. The air pressure in the cavity decreases, hence the air rushes into the lungs through nostrils, trachea, and bronchi.

Mechanism of Exhalation:

Exchange of gases between alveolar nabs and blood occurs anal air having CO_2 enters the alveoli. The thoracic cavity comes back to its original size as diaphragnn muscles relax. Air containing CO_2 is exhaled out through bronchi, trachea, and nostrils.

OR

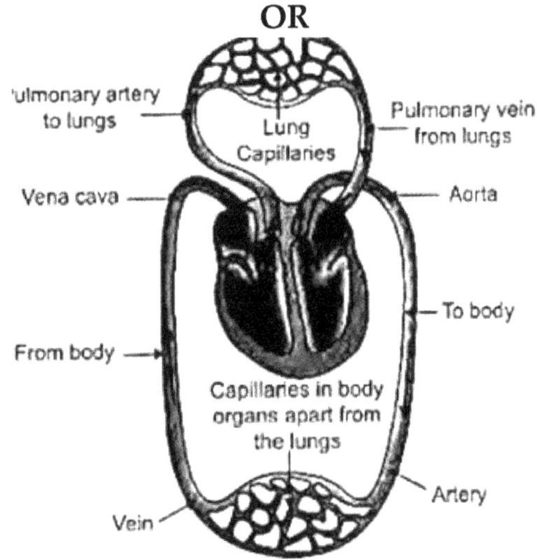

(ii) The two vital functions of kidney are

(a) Excretion of nitrogenous wastes.

(b) Osmoregulation - regulation of water and salt content in blood.

Question 36

A convex mirror used for rear- view on an automobile has a radius of curvature of 4 m. If a bus is located at 4.00m from this mirror, find the position, nature, and magnification?

Answer.

$R = 4\text{ m}$

$u = -4\text{ m}$

$v = ?$

$$f = \frac{R}{2} = \frac{4}{2} = 2\text{m}$$

$$\frac{1}{f} = \frac{1}{v} + \frac{1}{u}$$

$$\frac{1}{2} = \frac{1}{v} + \frac{1}{-4}$$

$$\frac{1}{2} + \frac{1}{4} = \frac{1}{v}$$

$$\frac{3}{4} = \frac{1}{v}$$

$$v = \frac{4}{3}\text{m}$$

$$m = -\frac{v}{u}$$

$$= \frac{-4/3}{-4}$$

$$= \frac{-4}{3} \times \frac{1}{-4}$$

$$m = \frac{1}{3}$$

OR

An object is placed at
(i) 15cm,
(ii) 5cm
In front of a concave mirror of radius of curvature 20cm. Find the position, nature, and magnification of the image in each case.

Answer. The focal length $f = -\frac{20}{2\text{cm}} = -10\text{cm}$

(i) The object distance u=-15cm. then using

$$\frac{1}{f} = \frac{1}{v} + \frac{1}{u}$$

$$\frac{1}{-10} = \frac{1}{v} + \frac{1}{-15}$$

$$\frac{1}{v} = \frac{1}{15} - \frac{1}{10}$$

$$v = \frac{10 \times 15}{-5}$$

$$= -30\text{cm}$$

The image is formed in front of mirror (because v is negative)

Magnification $m = -\frac{v}{u}$

$$m = -\frac{(-30)}{(-15)} = -2$$

Negative implies that the image will be inverted. Therefore, the image is magnified, real and inverted.

(ii) The object distance $u = -5cm$ Then seeing

$$\frac{1}{f} = \frac{1}{u} + \frac{1}{v}$$

$$\frac{1}{-10} = \frac{1}{u} + \frac{1}{v}$$

$$\frac{1}{-10} = \frac{1}{v} + \frac{1}{-5}$$

$$\frac{1}{-10} + \frac{1}{5} = \frac{1}{v}$$

$$\frac{1}{v} = \frac{1}{10}$$

$$v = 10cm$$

virtual, erect &magnified.

Section - E

Q.no. 37 to 39 are case - based/data -based questions with 2 to 3 short sub - parts. Internal choice is provided in one of these sub-parts

Question 37

Aditya was experimenting in the chemistry lab. While heating a test tube, he sensed a smell of burning sulfur and could notice a light brown-colored residue in the test tube. Soon, the students working around him started coughing. When passing by senior watched the scene, he came in and advise them to perform such experiments in the fuming cupboard.

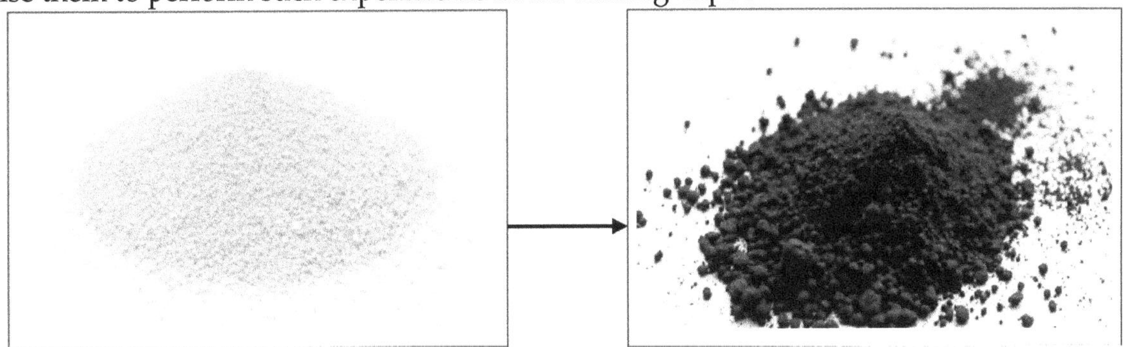

Ferrous Sulphate

(i) Which substance was taken in the test tube?

(ii) Write the equation of the reaction involved.

(iii) Write a precaution to be taken during the experiment.
(iv) What is the name given to such a reaction?

OR

Neeti, Naman's younger sister was very fond of candies and chocolates. She would often throw tantrums if Naman or her parents didn't get her some. Seeing as she ate candies every day before bed, Naman advised his parents to inculcate a habit of brushing her teeth before going to bed otherwise she might develop cavities at a very young age.

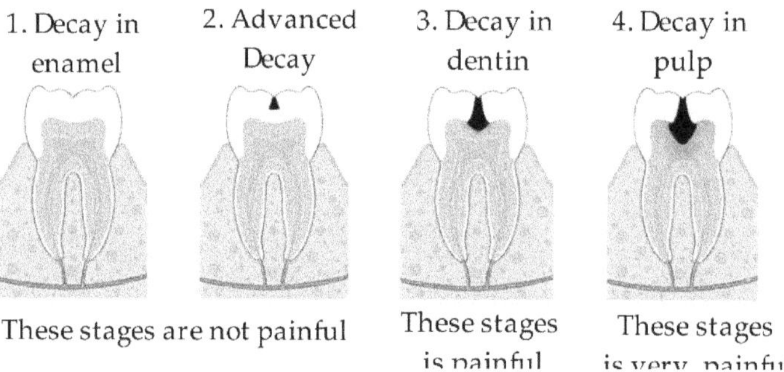

(i) Why did Naman advise so?
(ii) How does brushing help?
(iii) If the pH of a solution is less than 7 then what is the solution called?
(iv) If a solution has a greater $[H^+]$ions in comparison to $[OH^-]$ions, then what is the pH of a solution?

Question 38

Describe double circulation in human beings. Nane the group of aunimal with double circulation? How is it important for them?

Answer:

Such a flow in which blood enters the heart twice is called double circulation. It helps in keeping the oxygenated and deoxygenated blood separate.

The right atrium receives blood from the vena cava and pumps the blood into the right ventricle. Blood is sent to lungs, where it is oxygenated. Then, it is sent through the right and left pulmonary veins to the left atrium where it is pumped to the left ventricle. The blood then travels to the sending north where it leaves the heart and delivers oxygen to different parts of the body.

Birds and mammals have double circulation because they need to maintain a constant body temperature (warm blooded animals or endotherms).

OR

(i) Define excretion.
(ii) Name the brssic filtration unit present in the kidney.
(iii) Draw excretory system in human beings and label the following orgins of excretory system which perform following functions:
(a) Form urine
(b) Is a long tube which collects urine from kidney.
(c) Store urine mintil it is passerl out.

Answer:

(i) Throwing out wastes from the living body.

(ii) Replicon.

(iii) **(a)** Kidney

(b) Ureter

(c) Urinary blacker

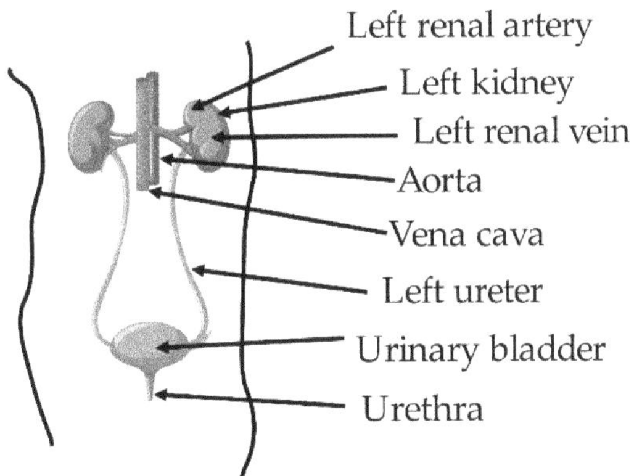

Question 39

The curved surface of a spoon can be considered a spherical mirror. A highly smooth polished surface is called a mirror. The mirror whose reflecting surface is curved inwards or outwards is called a spherical mirror. The inner part works as a concave mirror and the outer bulging part acts as a convex mirror. The center of the reflecting surface of a spherical mirror is called the pole and the radius of the sphere of which the mirror is formed is called the radius of curvature.

(i) When a concave mirror is held towards the sun and its sharp image is formed on a piece of carbon paper for some time, a hole is burnt in the carbon paper. What is the name given to the distance between the mirror and carbon paper?

(a) Radius of curvature

(b) Focal length

(c) Principal focus

(d) Principal axis

Answer(c) Principal focus

(ii) The distance between the pole and focal point of a spherical mirror is equal to the distance between

(a) Pole and center of curvature

(b) Focus point and center of curvature

(c) Pole and object

(d) Object and image.

Answer(b) Focus point and center of curvature

(iii) The focal length of a mirror is 15 cm. The radius of curvature is

(a) 15 cm

(b) 30 cm

(c) 45 cm

(d) 60 cm
Answer(b) 30 cm

(iv) The normal at any point in the mirror passes through
(a) Focus
(b) Pole
(c) Center of curvature
(d) Any point
Answer(c) Center of curvature

(v) In a convex spherical mirror, a reflection of light takes place at
(a) A flat surface
(b) A bent-in surface
(c) A bulging-out surface
(d) An uneven surface
Answer(c) A bulging-out surface

OR

An insulated copper wire wound on a cylindrical cardboard tube such that its length is greater than its diameter is called a solenoid. When an electric current is passed through the solenoid, it produces a magnetic field around it. The magnetic field produced by a current-carrying solenoid is similar to the magnetic field produced by a bar magnet. The field lines inside the solenoid are in the form of parallel straight lines. The strong magnetic field produced inside a current-carrying solenoid can be used to magnetise a piece of magnetic material like soft iron, when placed inside the solenoid. The strength of magnetic field produced by a current carrying solenoid is directly proportional to the number of turns and strength of current in the solenoid.

(i) The strength of magnetic field inside a long current-carrying straight solenoid is
(a) More at the ends than at the centre
(b) Minimum in the middle
(c) Same at all points
(d) Found to increase from one end to the other.
Answer(c) Same at all points

(ii) The north-south polarities of an electromagnet can be found easily by using
(a) Fleming's right-hand rule
(b) Fleming's left-hand rule
(c) Clock face rule
(d) Left-hand thumb rule.
Answer(c) Clock face rule

(iii) For a current in a long straight solenoid N-and S-poles are created at the two ends. Among the following statements, the incorrect statement is

(a) The field lines inside the solenoid are in the form of straight lines which indicates that the magnetic field is the same at all points inside the solenoid.

(b) The strong magnetic field produced inside the solenoid can be used to magnetise a piece of magnetic material like soft iron, when placed inside the coil.

(c) The pattern of the magnetic field associated with the solenoid is different from the pattern of the magnetic field around a bar magnet.

(d) The N - and S-poles exchange position when the direction of current through the solenoid is reversed.

Answer(c) The pattern of the magnetic field associated with the solenoid is different from the pattern of the magnetic field around a bar magnet.

(iv) A long solenoid carrying a current produces a magnetic field B along its axis. If the current is double and the number of turns per cm is halved, then new value of magnetic field is

(a) B

(b) 2B

(c) 4B

(d) B/2

Answer(a) B

Class- X Session- 2022-23

Science

SAMPLE TEST PAPER-2

Time Allowed: 3 Hrs. **Maximum Marks: 80**

General Instructions:

1. This Question Paper has 5 Sections A-E.
2. Section **A** has 20 MCQs carrying 1 mark each
3. Section **B** has 5 questions carrying 02 marks each.
4. Section **C** has 6 questions carrying 03 marks each.
5. Section **D** has 4 questions carrying 05 marks each.
6. Section **E** has 3 case-based integrated units of assessment (04 marks each) with subparts of the values of 1, 1, and 2 marks each respectively.
7. All Questions are compulsory. However, an internal choice in 2 Qs of 5 marks, 2 Qs of 3 marks, and 2 Questions of 2 marks has been provided. An internal choice has been provided in the 2marks questions of Section E
8. Draw neat figures wherever required. Take π =22/7 wherever required if not stated

Section A

Section A consists of 20 questions of 1 mark each

Question 1

A small amount of $CuSO_4$, NaOH and NaCl were added to water present in beakers A, B, and C respectively. The temperature of beaker A and B increases, while that of beaker C decreases. The correct statement(s) is/are:

(i) In beakers A and B, an endothermic process has occurred
(ii) In beakers A and B, an exothermic process has occurred
(iii) In beaker C, an exothermic process has occurred
(iv) In beaker C, an endothermic process has occurred

(a) (i) and (ii)
(b) (i) and (iii)
(c) (i) and (iv)
(d) (ii) and (iv)

Answer. (d)

Question 2

Products obtained as a result of double displacement reaction using $BaCl_2$ and Na_2SO_4 are:

(a) $BaSO_4$ and NaO
(b) $BaCl_2$ and Na_2SO_4
(c) $BaSO_4$ and NaCl
(d) Na_2SO_4 and NaCl

Answer. c

Question 3

Bleaching powder acts as:

(a) Disinfectant

(b) Preservative

(c) Oxidant

(d) Antacid

Answer. (a)

Question 4

Gypsum on heating at 373 K changes to:

(a) Na_2CO_3

(b) $NaHCO_3$

(c) $CaOCl_2$

(d) $CaSO_4 \cdot \frac{1}{2} H_2O$

Answer. (d)

Question 5

Two beakers A and B contain an aqueous solution of $FeSO_4$. In the beaker, zinc granules and in beaker B copper turnings have been placed. A grey coating was observed on zinc but not on copper. From the above observations, we can conclude.

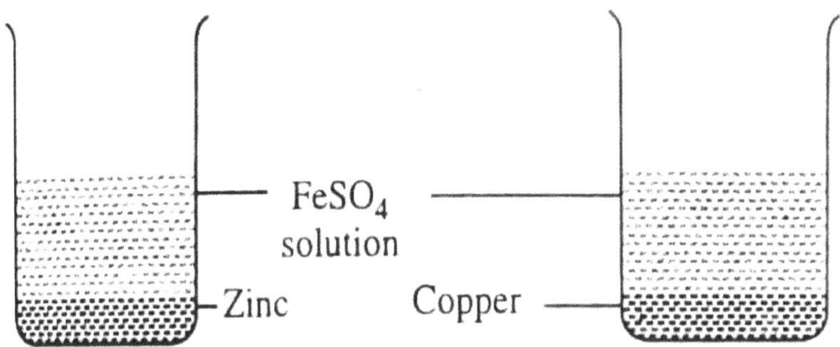

(a) Zinc is more reactive than iron and copper.

(b) Iron is more reactive than zinc and copper.

(c) Iron is more reactive than zinc but less than copper.

(d) Copper is more reactive than iron but less than zinc.

Answer. (a)

Question 6

$$CH_3 - CH_2 - OH \xrightarrow{\text{Alkaline } KMnO_4 + \text{ Heat}}$$

In the above-given reaction, alkaline $KmnO_4$ acts as

(a) Reducing agent

(b) Oxidizing agent

(c) Catalyst

(d) Dehydrating agent

Answer. (b)

Question 7

The structural formula of benzene is

(a)

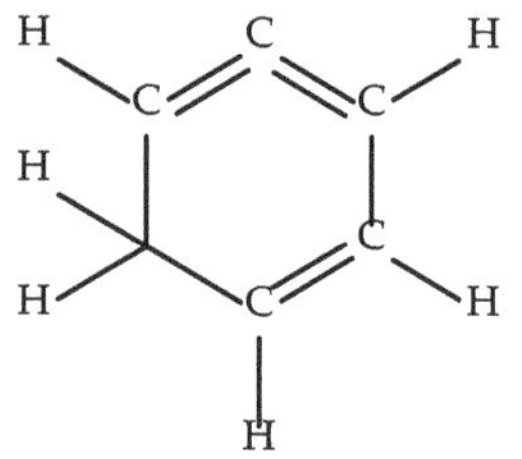

(b)

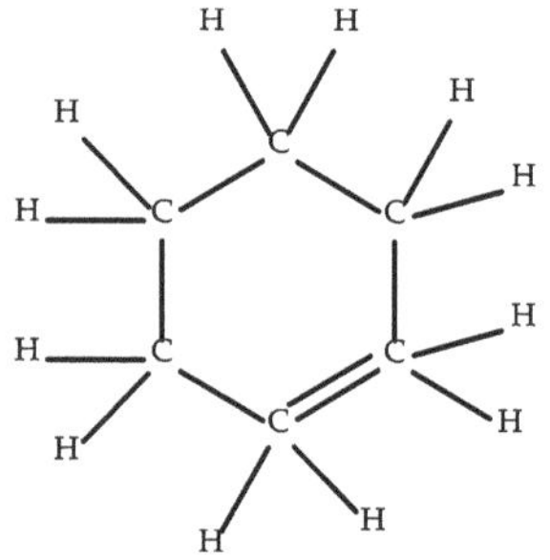

(c)

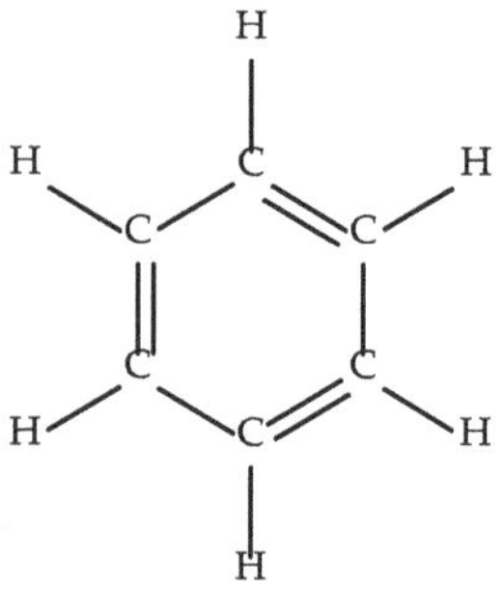

(d)

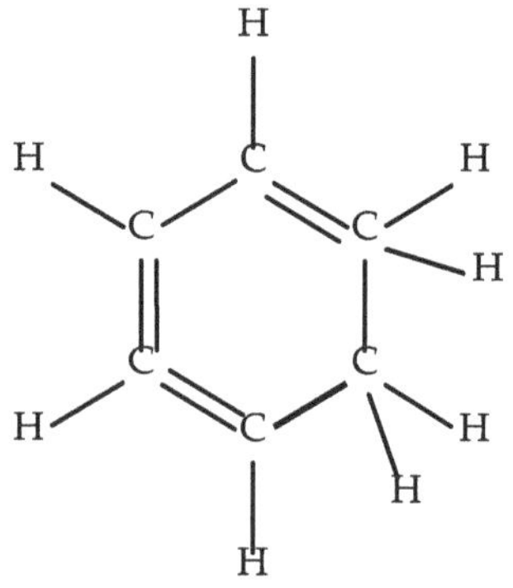

Answer(c)

Question 8

Photosynthesis is a

(a) Catabolic process

(b) Parabolic process

(c) Amphibolic process

(d) Photochemical process

Ans (d) Photochemical process

Question 9

Opening and closing of pores is a function performed by

(a) Stomata

(b) Chlorophyll

(c) Chloroplast

(d) Guard cells

Answer(d) Guard cells

Question 10

Which element is used in the synthesis of proteins?

(a) Hydrogen

(b) Oxygen

(c) Nitrogen

(d) Carbon dioxide

Answer(c) Carbon dioxide

Question 11

Temporary finger like extensions on amoeba are called

(a) Cell membrane

(b) Cell wall

(c) Pseudopodia

(d) Cilia

Answer(c) Pseudopodia

Question 12

Bile juice is secreted by

(a) Stomach

(b) Pancreas

(c) Small intestine

(d) Liver

Answer(d) Liver

Question 13

A rectangular coil is kept in a uniform magnetic field with its plane in the direction of magnetic field The magnetic lines field linked with the coil is

(a) Maximum

(b) Minimum but not zero

(c) Zero

(d) Infinite

Answer(b) Minimum but not zero

Question 14

Which one of the following is correct?

(a) $\frac{1 \text{ volt}}{1 \text{ ampere}} = 1\Omega$

(b) $\frac{1 \text{ volt}}{1 \text{ ampere}} = 1 \text{ J}$

(c) $\frac{1\text{volt}}{1 \text{ ampere}} = \text{Siemen}$

(d) $\frac{1 \text{ volt}}{1 \text{ ampere}} = 1\Omega - \text{m}$

Answer(a) $\frac{1 \text{ volt}}{1 \text{ ampere}} = 1\Omega$

Question 15

Which of the following shows the bending of light from rarer (R) into denser (D) medium?

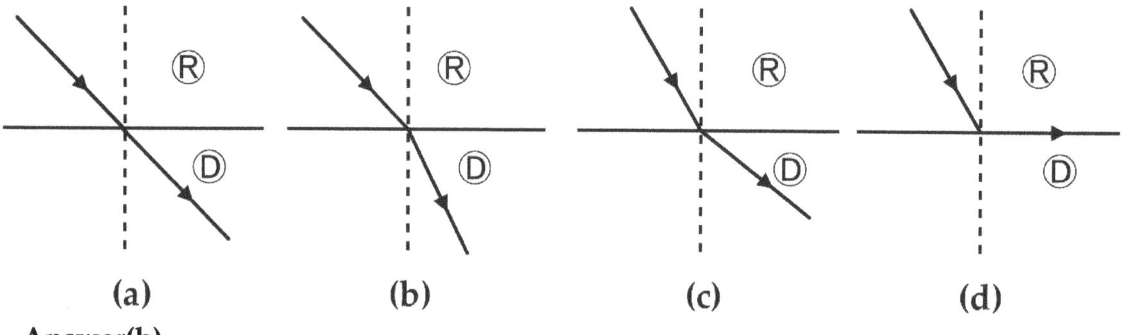

Answer(b)

Question 16

To obtain a magnified, inverted image in a concave mirror, an object should be held

(a) At pole

(b) At focus

(c) Between P and F

(d) Beyond F and C

Answer(c) Beyond F and C

Q. no 17 to 20 are Assertion - Reasoning based questions. These consist of two statements – Assertion (A) and Reason (R). Answer these questions selecting the appropriate option given below: (a) Both A and R are true and R is the correct explanation of A (b) Both A and R are true and R is not the correct explanation of A (c) A is true but R is false (d) A is False but R is true

Question 17

Assertion : One should clean the mouth after eating sugary foods.

Reason : HCl is secreted by stomach glands to aid digestion.

Answer(b)

Question 18
Assertion(A) : Bile is essential for digestion of lipids.
Reason (R) : Bile juice contains enzymes.
Answer(c)

Question 19
Assertion(A) : In plants there is no need of specialised respiratory organs.
Reason (R) : Plants do not have great demands of gaseous exchange.
Answer(c)

Question 20
Assertion: Linear magnification of a mirror has no unit.
Reason: The ratio of the height of the image to the height of the object is the linear magnification produced by the mirror.
Answer(A)

Section B

Section B has 5 questions carrying 02 marks each.

Q. no. 21 to 26 are very short answer questions

Question 21 **[2]**

Draw the electron dot structure of ethyne and draw its structural formula.

Answer. Electron dot structure: $H:C::C:H$

Structural formula: $H-C\equiv C-H$

OR

State the chemical change that takes place when limestone is heated

Answer. When limestone is heated, it decomposes to form calcium oxide and carbon dioxide gas.

$$CaCO_3(s) \longrightarrow CaO(s) + CO_2(g)$$

Question 22

How are fats digested in our boclien? Where does this process take place?

Answer:

Fats are first emulsified with the help of bile salts followed by their breakdown in fatty acids and glycerol due to the action of lipase. All these events take place in first part of stuall intertine-duodenum. Saprophytic

Question 23

Differentiate between saprophytic nutrition and parasitic nutrition based on the type of food and manner of obtaining it.

Answer:

	Saprophytic Nutrition	Parasitic Nutrition
1.	Taking dead decay organic matter in the form of food is called saprophytic nutrition.	Living ou or inside other organisms and deriving their food from tlem without killing them.
2.	It shows extracellular digestion.	It lass intrucellular digestion.
3.	It does not depend on living host.	It causes larm to the organism.
4.	E.g., fungi and bacteria.	E.g., lice, tapeworm, leech.

Question 24

How do plants exchange gases?

Answer:

Plants exchange gases through stomata. Large intercellular spaces ensure that ench cell is in contact with air. Carbon dioxide and oxygen are exchanged here.

Question 25

Calculate the equivalent resistance across A and B in the circuit shown in Fig.

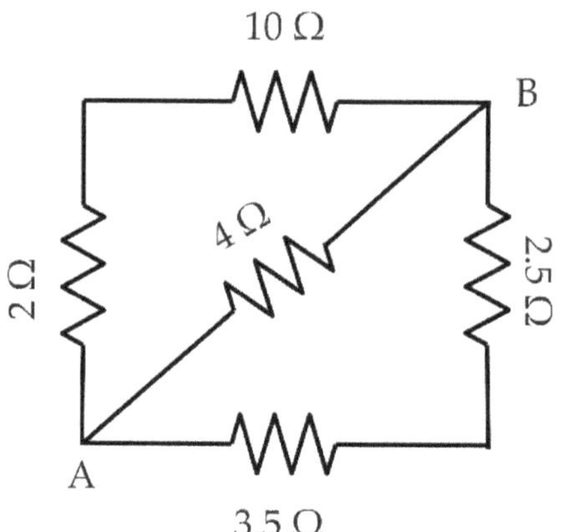

R_1 & R_2 are in series

$R' = R_1 + R_2$

$= 2 + 10 = 12\Omega$

R_3 & R_4 are in series

$R^{11} = R_3 + R_4$

$\Rightarrow 3.5 + 2.5 = 6\Omega$

$R^1, R^{11} \& R_5$ *are in* 11^{al} *combination*

$$\frac{1}{Req} = \frac{1}{R^1} + \frac{1}{R_5} + \frac{1}{R^{11}}$$

$$= \frac{1}{12} + \frac{1}{4} + \frac{1}{6} = 0.5\Omega$$

OR

An erect diminished and virtual image is formed when an object is placed between the optical centre and the principal focus of a lense

(i) Name the type of lens, which forms that above image.

(ii) Draw a ray diagram to show the formation of the image with the above characteristics.

Answer:

(i) Concave lens.

(ii)

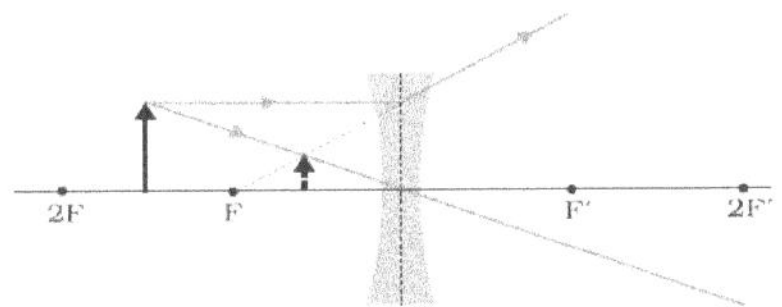

Question 26

List two functions which decide direction of diffusion of oxygen and carbon dioxide.

Answer:

Environmental conditions ned requirement of the plants decide direction of diffitsion of oxygen and carbon dioxide.

Section - C

Q.no. 27 to 33 are short answer questions

Question 27

In column-I are given different methods of extraction. Nants extraction. Name the methods for the extraction of metals to give in column II:

Column-I	Column. II
(i) Reduction with carbon	Al, Zn, Na
(ii) Electrolytic reduction	Fe, Mn, Pb
(iii) Reduction with aluminium	

AnswerAl – (ii), Zn – (i), Na – (ii). Fe – (i), Mn – (iii), Pb – (i)

Question 28

(i) Name the raw materials used in the manufacture of sodium carbonate by the Solvay process.

(ii) How is the sodium hydrogen carbonate formed during the Solvay process separated from a mixture of NH_4Cl and $NaHCO_3$?

(iii) How is sodium carbonate obtained from sodium hydrogen carbonate?

Answer.

(i) The raw materials are brine solution ($NaCl + H_2O$), ammonia (NH_3) and carbon dioxide (CO_2).

(ii) $NaHCO_3$ is insoluble and forms a precipitate. Therefore, it can be separated by filtration.

(iii) By heating $NaHCO_3$ as follows

$$2NaHCO_3 \xrightarrow{\Delta} Na_2CO_3 + H_2O + CO_2$$

Question 29

(i) What is sequence of steps in photosynthesis? How is it different in desert plants and those in temperate regions?

Answer:

Chloroplast (chlorophyll), on exposure to light energy, becomes activated by absorbing light energy, and splits water (photolysis of water) to oxygen and hydrogen. Ilydrogen reluces CO_2, and synthesizes glucose.

In plants of temperate regions, stomata open during day to take in CO_2 and release O_2.

Desert plants open stomata at night to check excessive loss of water hence sequence of steps of photosynthesis are slightly different.

Tliese plants take up carbon dioxide at night and prepare an internediate which is acted upon by the energy absorbed by the chlorophyll during the day.

OR

(i) What is the role of mucus in stomach?

(ii) What are the two vital functions of human kidney?

Answer:

(i) To protect the stomach lining from the action of acid and pepsin.

(ii) The two vital functions of human kidney are:

Kidney's act as an excretory organ in the human body to remove toxic wastes from the body.

Kidneys also control and maintain water levels in the body.

Question 30

Why does the rising sun appear bigger?

Answer Light from the rising sun reaches obliquely through the atmosphere due to atmospheric refraction. Rays from different parts of the sun pass through different parts of the earth's atmosphere. Obviously, due to unequal refraction of light rays, the horizontal diameter of the sun appears bigger and the vertical diameter appears shorter. This is why the rising sun appears bigger.

Question 31

An electric bulb is marked 200 V, 100 W. The bulb is connected to a 200 V supply. Calculate

(i) The resistance of the filament, and

(ii) The current flowing through the filament.

Answer:

$$V = 200V$$
$$P = 100W$$

(i) $R = \frac{V^2}{P}$

$$= \frac{(200)^2}{100}$$

$$= \frac{40000}{100} = 400\Omega$$

(ii) $P = V \times I$

$$I = \frac{P}{V} = \frac{100}{200} = 0.5A.$$

Question 32

Should the heating element of an electric iron be made of iron, silver or nichrome wire. Why?

Answer: The heating element of an electric iron should be made of nichrome wire because

(i) Resistivity of nichrome is greater than that of iron and silver, so more heat is produced in the nichrome wire doe to the flow of current.

(ii) Nichrome wire does thot oxides (of burn) easily even at higher temperature.

(iii) Nichrome wire does not oxides (or bum) easily even at higher temperature.

Or

Four resistances 2.0Ω of each are joined end to that of iron and silver. resistance of the combination between two adjecent to form a square ABCD. Calculate the equivalent resistance of the combination between two adjacent concern.

Answer: Effective resistance between ADCB $= 2 + 2 + 2 = 6\Omega$

∴ Equivalent resistance between two adjacent corners A and B

$$\frac{1}{R_{AB}} = \frac{1}{R_1} + \frac{1}{R_2} = \frac{1}{6} + \frac{1}{2} = \frac{1+3}{6} = \frac{2}{3}$$

Thus, $R_{AB} = \frac{3}{2\Omega} = 1.5\Omega$

Question 33

(i) How is oxygen and carbon dioxide exchanged between blood and tissue? How are the gases transported in human being?

(ii) What is haemoglobinate?

Answer:

(a) Exchange of grues in tissues occurs through diffusion. Oxygen is curried as oxyluemoglobin from lungs to twister. It dissociates and carbon dioxide diffusion not into blood from tithes. It is transported in dissolved form and reaches lungs where again it diffusion to alveoli.

(b) Respiratory pigment: Haemoglobin is a red coloured protein present in red blood cells. Macroglossia has affinity for O_2.

Section - D

Q.no. 34 to 36 are Long answer questions

Question 34

An organic compound A on heating with concentrated H_2SO_4 forms a compound B which on addition of one mole of hydrogen in presence of Ni forms a compound C. One mole of compound C on combustion forms two moles of CO_2 and 3 moles of H_2O. Identify compounds A, B, and C and write the cher equations of the reactions involved.

Answer. A should be an alcohol and B an alkene which can add one mole of H_2 to form C. Since ' C ' on combustion gives two moles of CO_2, ' C ' contains two carbon atoms and the same should be with ' B ' and ' A '. Therefore, A should be ethanol B ethene and ' C ' ethane.

The reactions involved are.

(i) $CH_3CH_2OH \xrightarrow[443\ K]{conc.\ H_2SO_4} H_2C = CH_2 + H_2O$

(ii) $H_2C = CH_2 + H_2 \underset{Catalyst}{\overset{Ni}{\longrightarrow}} C_2H_6$

(B) (C) Ethane

(iii) $2C_2H_6 + 7O_2 \longrightarrow 4CO_2 + 6H_2O$ + Heat and light

2 moles or 1 mole | 4 moles or 2 moles | 6 moles or 3 moles

OR

Write balanced chemical equations for the following statements:

(a) NaOH solution is heated with zinc granules.

(b) Excess carbon dioxide gas is passed through lime water.

(c) Dilute sulphuric acid reacts with sodium carbonate.

(d) Egg shells are dropped in hydrochloric acid.

(e) Copper (II) oxide reacts with dilute hydrochloric acid.

Answer.

(a) $2NaOH(aq) + Zn(s) \longrightarrow Na_2ZnO_2(aq) + H_2(g)$

(b) $Ca(OH)_2(aq) + CO_2(g) \longrightarrow CaCO_3(s) + H_2O(l)$

$CaCO_3(s) + CO_2(g) + H_2O(l) \longrightarrow Ca(HCO_3)_2$

soluble in water

(c) $Na_2CO_3(s) + H_2SO_4(\text{dil}) \longrightarrow Na_2SO_4(aq) + CO_2(g) + H_2O(l)$

(d) $CaCO_3(s) + 2HCl(aq) \longrightarrow CaCl_2(aq) + H_2O(l) + CO_2(g)$

(e) $CuO(s) + 2HCl(aq) \longrightarrow CuCl_2(aq) + H_2O(l)$

Question 35

Describe structure and functioning of nephron.

Answer:

Within the kidney are small functional units called nephrons, which are male up of glomeruli, Bowman's capsiule, proximal convoluted tubule, loop of Henleyl s loop, distal convoluted loop, and collecting duct. Stepy of urine formution: Each kidney is macle of millions of nephron. Each nephron lats a hollow cup like Bowman's capsulule and a long tubule system following it. Arteriole branching from remal artery make bunches of capillaries, one of which is called a Glotnerulus. The first step in the filtrution process is when the blood enters the Glomerulus, where it is then pumped through the porous walls into the Bowman's space, This filtered plasma is mainly water, various salts, urea and glucose. The "glomerular filtrate" then passes through the proximal convolutel tubule, Loop of Henle, the clistal convoluterl tubule so that useful sulsitances are re-alsorbed by blood present in the capillaries around them.

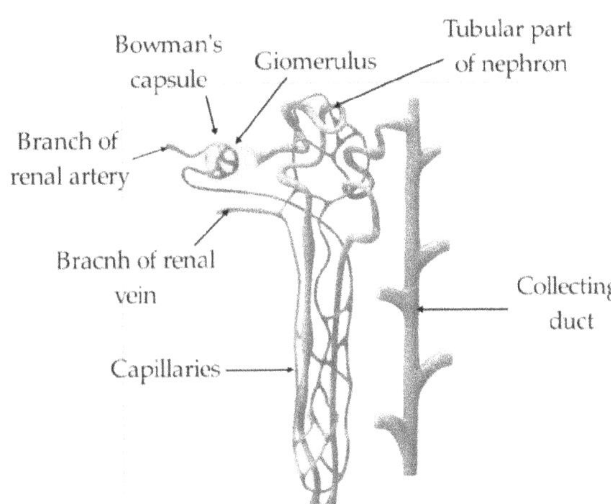

The liquicl is now called urine is concentrated and collected in collecting duct und poured in uretern to be carriecl to urimary blacker. Urine is passecl ont throngh urethra, when the urinary bladeler is full and due to pressure there is an urge to clo so. Sphincter muscles regulate this process

Osmeregulation und excretion are intimately related, these processes together maintain homeostsesis (i.e. Ntaying the same), and are performed by the sane set of organs. The kichey is the major organ of osmoregulation and excretion in vertelsates.

OR

Usman collected her saliva and mixed it with liquid A in the test tulse. In mother test tube she took only liquid A nfter abont 10 minutes, she adtled n few drops of iocline solntion to the mixture in the first test tube. It did not show any colour hit when she rented the other test tube with iodine, a blue black colour appearel. Now answer the following questions:

(i) What is the aim of this activity?
(ii) What is liquid A'?
(iii) Why did the first test tube not show may colour change with iodine while the record one diel?
(iv) Which enzyme is responsible for such a result?
(v) Why deos a piece of bread chewed for a long time tasted sweet?

Answer:

(i) To show the action of salivary amylase on starch.
(ii) Liquid A is starch.
(iii) The first text tube did not show any colour change with iodine because starch was not present anymore in it. It was already digested by salivary amylase present in saliva. The colonel of liquid in the second one changed to blue black as the starch was still unchanged clue to absence of the enzyme.
(iv) Salivary analyse enzyme is responsible for such a result.
(v) A piece of bread chewed for a long time tastes sweet because the stacks is broken down by salivary amylase to maltosc sugar.

Question 36

An object 0.2m high is placed at a distance of 0.4m front a concave of radius of curvature 0.3m
Find the position, nature, and size of the image forward.

Answer. The focal length $f = \frac{R}{2} = -0.15\ m = -15cm$, $h_O = 0.2\ m = 20\ cm$

The object distance $u = -0.4\ m = -40\ cm.$

using mirror formula, $\frac{1}{f} = \frac{1}{v} + \frac{1}{u}$

We have $\frac{1}{-15} = \frac{1}{v} + \frac{1}{-40}$ or $-\frac{1}{15} + \frac{1}{40} = \frac{1}{v}$

OR $v = -\frac{40 \times 15}{25} = -24\ cm = -1.24\ m$

The image is formed in front of mirror (because vis negative).

For height of image, using the relation $\frac{h_i}{h_o} = -\frac{v}{u}$.

$$\frac{h_i}{20} = \frac{-(-2u)}{-40}$$

$$h_i = -12\ cm$$

Negative sign implies that the image will be inverted.

OR

A concave lens has a focal length of 20cm. At what distance should an object from the lens be placed so that it forms an image at 15cm from the lens? Also find the magnification of the lens.

Answer. Given that, $v = -15cm$, $f = -20cm$

using lens formula $\frac{1}{f} = \frac{1}{v} - \frac{1}{u}$

$\frac{1}{-20} = \frac{1}{-15} - \frac{1}{u}$ OR $\frac{1}{u} = \frac{1}{20} - \frac{1}{15}$

$u = -60cm$

∴ Object should be placed at a distance of 60cm from the lens

Magnification $m = \frac{v}{u} = \frac{-15}{-60} = \frac{1}{4}$

Section - E

Q.no. 37 to 39 are case - based/data -based questions with 2 to 3 short sub - parts. Internal choice is provided in one of these sub-parts

Question 37

Answer the following questions based on your understanding of the following paragraph and the related studied concepts.

During summer break, Rohan's house was being whitewashed. Being the observant kid that he is, he observed everything done by the workers. This is how he saw one of them adding copper sulfate to the solution of slaked lime. After using the needed amount, they dumped the remaining copper sulphate into an iron pot. A few days later, Rohan found the iron pot has holes in it. This left him confused. So, after the summer break was over, he asked his science teacher the reason behind those holes.

K	Potassium	Most reactive
Na	Sodium	
Ca	Calcium	
Mg	Magnesium	
Al	Aluminium	
Zn	Zinc	
Fe	Iron	
Sn	Tin	
Pb	Lead	
H	Hydrogen	
Cu	Copper	
Ag	Silver	
Au	Gold	Least reactive
Pt	Platinum	
K	Potassium	

(i) What is activity series?
(ii) What is displacement reaction?
(iii) What explanation must Rohan's teacher have given him?
(iv) What happens when $FeSO_4$ (aq) is present in a copper vessel?

Answer

(i) A type of ordering system for elements, which ranks how reactive a certain element is in relation to other elements.
(ii) The one wherein the atom or a set of atoms is displaced by another atom in a molecule.
(iii) Iron (Fe) displaced copper (cu) from its solution as (Fe) is placed above in reactivity series than cu

$$Fe_{(s)} + CuSO_{4(ag.)} \rightarrow FeSO_{4aq.} + Cu_{(s)}$$

(iv) Since Cu is less reactive than Fe, there will be no reaction on the solution $FeSO_4$ can be stored in copper vessel.

OR

Kabir and Nayak went on a school trip to Qutub Minor. There, they learned a lot about its history and were awe-struck at its beauty. Kabir was particularly amazed by the fact that an ancient iron pillar of Qutub Minar stands without a hint of rust on it. While he was appreciating its beauty.

(i) What is corrosion?
(ii) What is rusting?
(iii) How could the technicians of that era make such a minar which does not rust?
(iv) What is galvanization?

Answer

(i) Corrosion is the deterioration of a material as a result of its interaction with its surroundings.

(ii) The interaction of Iron with air and water produces rust.

(iii) The rusting has been prevented because of the formation of a thin film of magnetic oxide of iron (Fe_3O_4) on the surface as a result of finishing treatment given to the pillar.

(iv) The process of applying a protective zinc coating to iron or steel, to prevent rusting.

Question 38

(i) Name the part marked A in the cliagram.

(ii) How does "A" reaches part B ?

(iii) State the importance of , the part C.

(iv) What happens to the part marked D after fertilization is over?

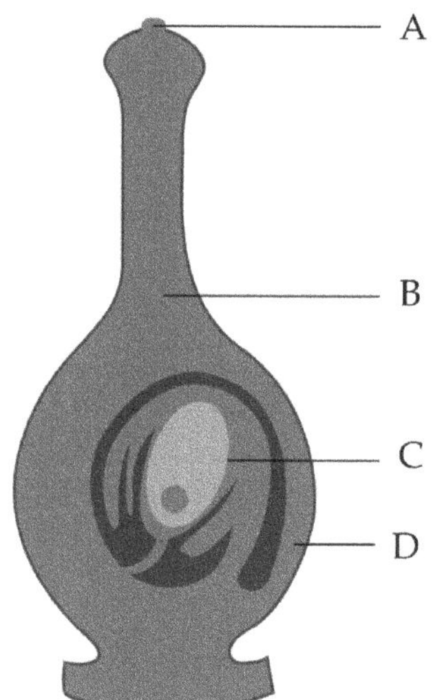

Answer:

(i) Pollen

(ii) Pollination

(iii) Pollen tube carries male gametes to the ovule in ovary:

(iv) Ovule turns into seeds,

OR

How does vegetative propagation occur in nature? Explain with four different examples.

Answer:

There are many plants in which parts like the root, stem and leaves develop into new plants under appropriate conditions. This is called as vegetative propagation. Examples of vegetative propagation:

(a) Adventitious buds: In Bryophyllum, adventitious buck grow in the notches along the leaf margin,

(b) which when fall on the soil, develop into new plants.

(c) Cutting: A piece of stem, root, leaf or even a bulb scale is placed partly under moist soil which grows into a new plant, e.g.. rose.

(d) Layering: A part of the stem is pulled out and buried in the soil. The layered stem grows into a new plant, e.g.. Pudina.

(e) Grafting: In grafting, two parts from two different plants are joined together so that they can unite and grow into a new plant, e.g., sugarcane.

Question 39

The spherical mirror forms different types of images when the object is placed at different locations. When the image is formed on the screen, the image is real and when the image does not form on the screen, the image is virtual. When the two reflected rays meet actually, the image is real and when they appear to meet, the image is virtual.

A concave mirror always forms a real and inverted image for different positions of the object. But if the object is placed between the focus and pole. The image formed is virtual and erect.

A convex mirror always forms a virtual, erect, and diminished image. A concave mirror is used as a doctor's head mirror to focus light on body parts like eyes, ears, nose, etc., to be examined because it can form an erect and magnified image of the object. The convex mirror is used as a rearview mirror in automobiles because it can form a small and erect image of an object.

(i) When an object is placed at the center of the curvature of a concave mirror, the image formed is

(a) Larger than the object

(b) Smaller than the object

(c) Same size as that of the object

(d) Highly enlarged.

Answer(c) Same size as that of the object

(ii) No matter how far you stand from a mirror, your image appears erect. The mirror is likely to be

(a) Plane

(b) Concave

(c) Convex

(d) Either plane or convex.

Answer(d) Either plane or convex.

(iii) A child is standing in front of a magic mirror. She finds the image of her head bigger, the middle portion of her body of the same size, and that of the legs smaller. The following is the order of combinations for the magic mirror from the top.

(a) The plane, convex and concave

(b) Convex, concave, and plane

(c) Concave, plane, and convex

(d) Convex, plane, and concave

Answer(c) Concave, plane, and convex

(iv) To get an image larger than the object, one can use

(a) Convex mirror but not a concave mirror

(b) A concave mirror but not a convex mirror

(c) Either a convex mirror or a concave mirror

(d) A plane mirror.

Answer(b) A concave mirror but not a convex mirror

(v) A convex mirror has a wider field of view because

(a) The image formed is much smaller than the object and a large number of images can be seen.

(b) The image formed is much closer to the mirror

(c) Both (a) and (b)

(d) None of these.

Answer(c) Both (a) and (b)

OR

If two or more resistances are connected in such a way that the same potential difference gets applied to each of them, then they are said to be connected in parallel. The current flowing through the two resistances in parallel is, however, not the same. When we have two or more resistances joined in parallel to one another, then the same current gets additional paths to flow and the overall resistance decreases. The equivalent resistance is given by $\frac{1}{R_p} = \frac{1}{R_1} + \frac{1}{R_2} + \frac{1}{R_3}$

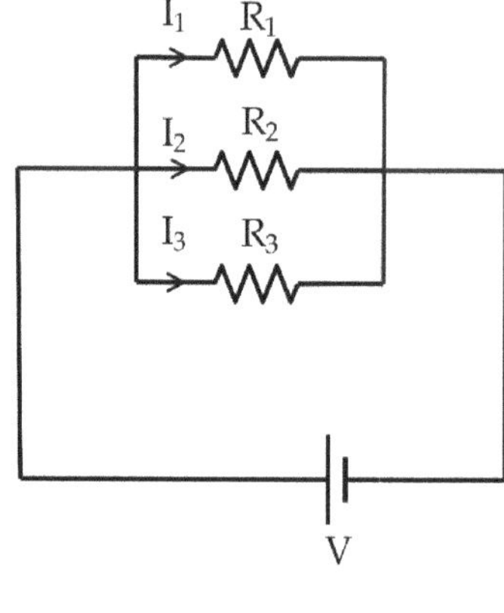

(i) Three resistances, 2Ω, 6Ω, and 8Ω are connected in parallel, then the equivalent resistance is

(a) Less than 6Ω but more than 2Ω

(b) Less than 8Ω but more than 6Ω

(c) Less than 2Ω

(d) More than 8Ω

Answer(a) Less than 6Ω but more than 2Ω

(ii) A wire of resistance 12Ω is cut into three equal pieces and then twisted their ends together, the equivalent resistance is

(a) $\frac{3}{8}\Omega$

(b) $\frac{4}{3}\Omega$

(c) $\frac{3}{4}\Omega$

(d) $\frac{5}{6}\Omega$

Answer(b) $\frac{4}{3}\Omega$

(iii) Three resistances are connected as shown. The equivalent resistance between *A* and *B* is

(a) $\frac{2}{3}\Omega$

(b) $\frac{3}{2}\Omega$

(c) $\frac{4}{3}\Omega$

(d) $\frac{3}{4}\Omega$

Answer(a) $\frac{2}{3}\Omega$

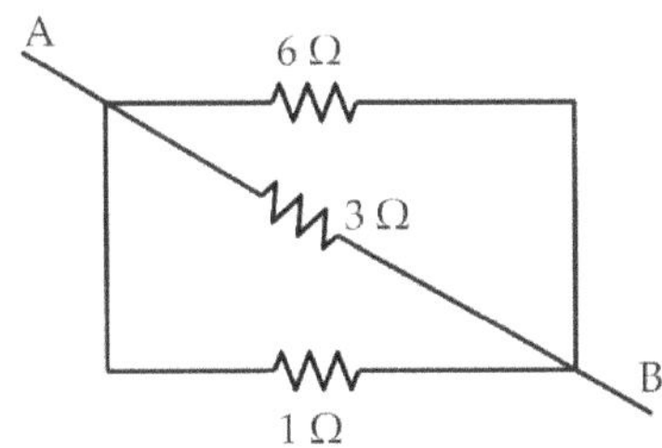

(iv) Which of the following relation is correct?

(a) $I_1 = 2I_2 = 3I_3$

(b) $I_1 = 4I_2 = 3I_3$

(c) $2I_1 = I_2 = 3I_3$

(d) $3I_1 = 2I_2 = I_3$

Answer(a) $I_1 = 2I_2 = 3I_3$

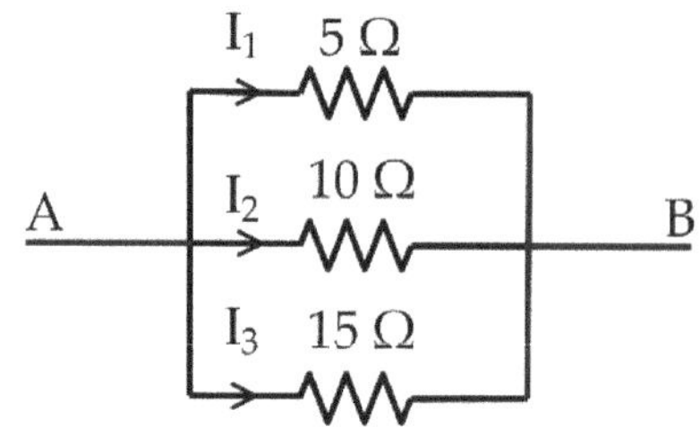

(v) Find the current in each resistance.

(a) 1 A

(b) 2 A

(c) 3 A

(d) 0.25 A

Answer(c) 3 A

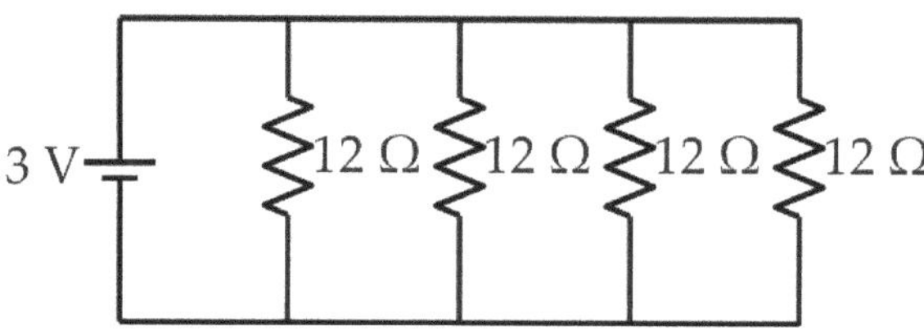

UNSOLVED SAMPLE TEST PAPER

Class- X Session- 2022-23

Science

SAMPLE TEST PAPER-1

Time Allowed: 3 Hrs. **Maximum Marks: 80**

General Instructions:

1. This Question Paper has 5 Sections A-E.
2. Section **A** has 20 MCQs carrying 1 mark each
3. Section **B** has 5 questions carrying 02 marks each.
4. Section **C** has 6 questions carrying 03 marks each.
5. Section **D** has 4 questions carrying 05 marks each.
6. Section **E** has 3 case-based integrated units of assessment (04 marks each) with subparts of the values of 1, 1, and 2 marks each respectively.
7. All Questions are compulsory. However, an internal choice in 2 Qs of 5 marks, 2 Qs of 3 marks, and 2 Questions of 2 marks has been provided. An internal choice has been provided in the 2marks questions of Section E
8. Draw neat figures wherever required. Take π =22/7 wherever required if not stated

Section A

Section A consists of 20 questions of 1 mark each

Question 1

In which form zinc metal is used from laboratory to prepare hydrogen?

(a) Rod

(b) Powder

(c) Filling

(d) Granules

Answer. (d)

Question 2

In an attempt to demonstrate electrical conductivity through an electrolyte, the following apparatus (Figure) was set up.

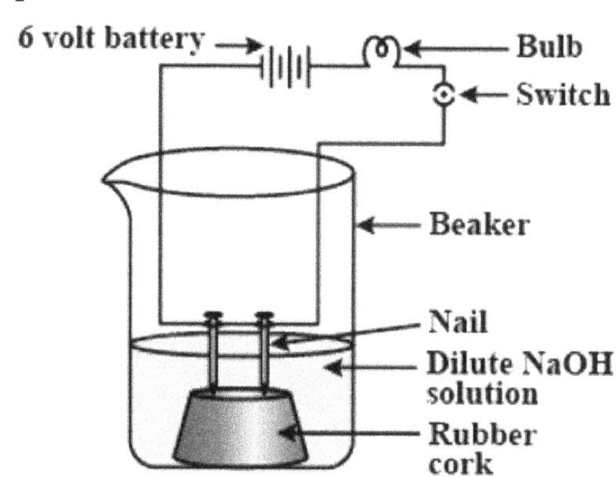

Which among the following statement (s) is (are) correct?

(i) Bulb will not glow because electrolyte is not acidic.

(ii) Bulb will glow because NaOH is a strong base and furnishes ions for conduction.

(iii) Bulb will not glow because circuit is incomplete.

(iv) Bulb will not glow because it depends upon the type of electrolytic solution.

(a) (i) and (iii)

(b) (ii) and (iv)

(c) (ii) only

(d) (iv) only

Answer(c) (ii) only

Question 3

Identify the correct representation of reaction occurring during chlor-alkali process

(a) $2NaCl(l) + 2H_2O(l) \longrightarrow 2NaOH(l) + Cl_2(g) + H_2(g)$

(b) $2NaCl(aq) + 2H_2O(aq) \longrightarrow 2NaOH(aq) + Cl_2(g) + H_2(g)$

(c) $2NaCl(aq) + 2H_2O(l) \longrightarrow 2NaOH(aq) + Cl_2(aq) + H_2(aq)$

(d) $2NaCl(aq) + 2H_2O(l) \longrightarrow 2NaOH(aq) + Cl_2(g) + H_2(g)$

Answer(d) $2NaCl(aq) + 2H_2O(l) \longrightarrow 2NaOH(aq) + Cl_2(g) + H_2(g)$

Question 4

Two beakers A and B contain an aqueous solution of $FeSO_4$. In beaker A zinc granules and in beaker B copper turnings have been placed. A grey ccating was observed on zinc but not on copper. From the above observations we can conclude.

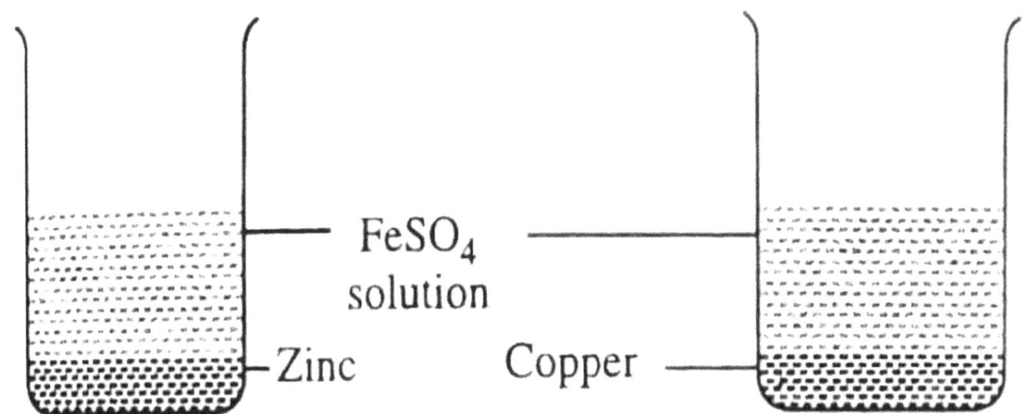

(a) Zinc is more reactive than iron and copper.

(b) Iron is more reactive than zinc and copper.

(c) Iron is more reactive than zinc but less than copper.

(d) Copper is more reactive than iron but less than zinc.

Answer. (a)

Question 5

Which of the following reactions will not proceed?

(a) Copper + copper sulphate

(b) Iron + copper sulphate

(c) Zinc + copper sulphate

(d) Aluminum + copper sulphate

Answer. (a)

Question 6

In which of the following compounds, −OH is the functional group?

(a) Butanone

(b) Butanol

(c) Butanoic acid

(d) Butanal

Answer. (b)

Question 7

Vinegar is a solution of

(a) 50% – 60% acetic acid in alcohol

(b) 5% – 8% acetic acid in alcohol

(c) 5% – 8% acetic acid in water

(d) 50% – 60% acetic acid in water

Answer (c)

Question 8

Which of these juices is secreted by pancreas?

(a) Trypsin

(b) Pepsin

(c) Bile juice

(d) Both I and II

Answer. (d)

Question 9

Lipase acts on

(a) Amino acids

(b) Fats

(c) Carbohydrates

(d) All of these

Answer. (b)

Question 10

Respiratory pigment in human body is

(a) chlorophyll

(b) Water

(c) Blood

(d) haemoglobin

Answer. (d)

Question 11

Blood consists of what fluid medium?

(a) Lymph
(b) Platelets
(c) Plasma
(d) All of these

Answer. (c)

Question 12

One cell-thick vessels are called

(a) Arteries
(b) Veins
(c) Capillaries
(d) Pulmonary artery

Answer. (c)

Question 13

Which of the following graph represents an ohmic conductor?

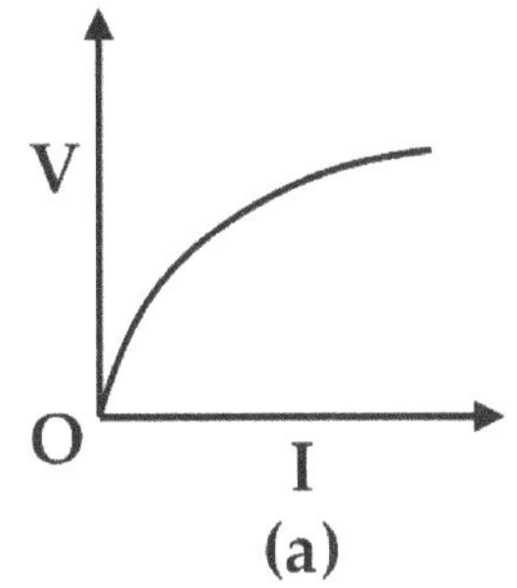

(a)

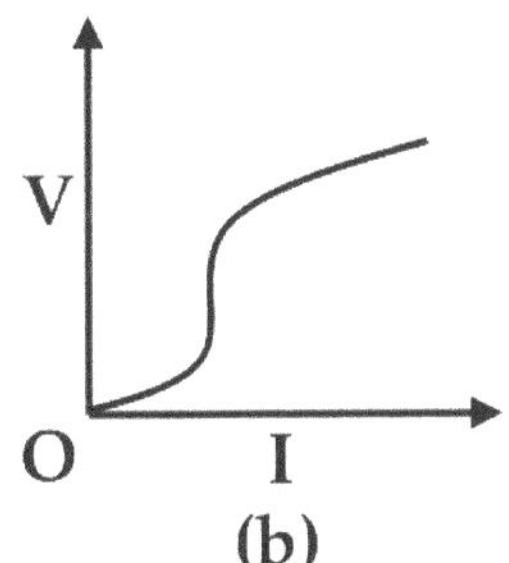

(b)

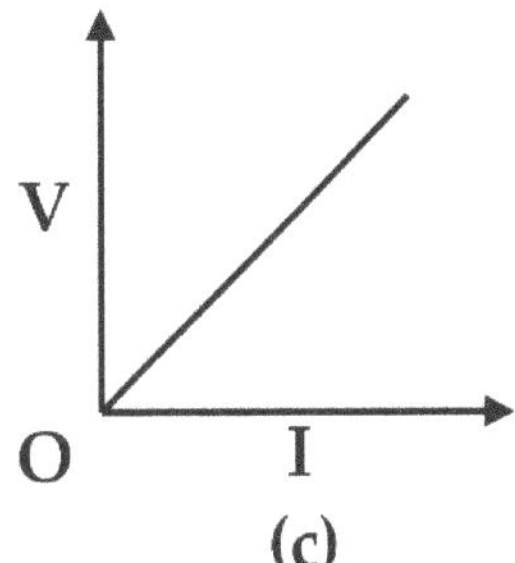

(c)

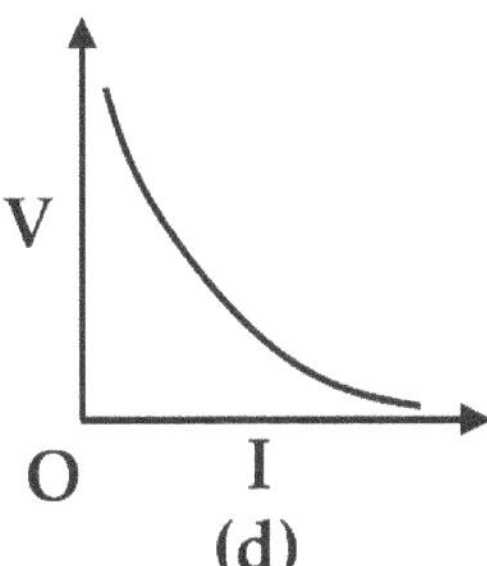

(d)

(a) Germanium
(b) Diode
(c) Diamond
(d) Nichrome

Answer(c)

Question 14

A motor converts ________energy into __________energy .

(a) Electrical, mechanical
(b) Mechanical, electrical
(c) Thermal, mechanical
(d) None of these

Answer(a) Electrical, mechanical

Question 15

The angle of incidence of a ray passing through the centre of curvature of a spherical mirror is

(a) 90°

(b) 0°

(c) 45°

(d) 180°

Answer(a) 90°

Question 16

Which of the following diagrams shows the refraction of a ray of light through a concave lens?

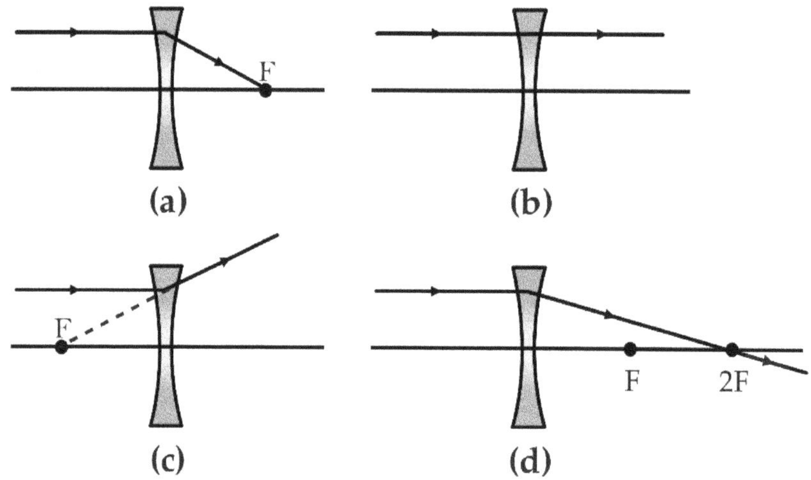

Answer(c)

Q. no 17 to 20 are Assertion - Reasoning based questions. These consist of two statements – Assertion (A) and Reason (R). Answer these questions selecting the appropriate option given below: (a) Both A and R are true and R is the correct explanation of A (b) Both A and R are true and R is not the correct explanation of A (c) A is true but R is false (d) A is False but R is true

Question 17

Assertion : Silver and gold do not react with oxygen.

Reason : Sodium and potassium react with oxygen even below room temperature and therefore stored in kerosene.

Answer(b)

Question 18

Assertion(A) : Carbohydrate digestion mainly takes place in small intestine.

Reason (R) : Pancreatic juice contains the enzyme lactase.

Answer(c)

Question 19

Assertion (A) : The walls of the ventricle are thicker than the walls of the auricles.

Reason (R) : The ventricles have to pump blood to long distances and various org

Answer(A)

Question 20
Assertion: Light is able to reach earth from the sun.
Reason: Light rays can travel in a vacuum.
Answer(A)

Section B

Section B has 5 questions carrying 02 marks each.

Q. no. 21 to 26 are very short answer questions

Question 21

A person is suffering from indigestion due the intake of hot spicy food. What remedy will you prescribe to the patient? Give the name a chemical that can give relief to him?

OR

What are amphoteric oxides? Choose the amphoteric oxides from amongst the following oxides :

$$Na_2O, ZnO, Al_2O_3, CO_2, H_2O$$

Question 22

State the changes that take place in the uterus when

(a) Implantation of embryo has occurred

(b) Female gamete/egg is not fertilized

Question 23

Give reasons as to why the following processes are different from each other:

(i) Fission in Amoeba and Plasmodium.

(ii) Binary fission and Fragmentation.

Question 24

(i) What is the location of the following:

(a) DNA in a cell

(b) Gene

(ii) Expand DNA.

Question 25

Two wires of the same material and same length have their radii r_1 and r_2. Compare their

(i) Resistances,

(ii) And resistivities.

OR

A ray of light after refraction through a concave lens emerges parallel to the principal axis. Draw a ray diagram to show the incidental and its corresponding emergent ray.

Question 26

Explain how organisms create an exact copy of themselves.

Section – C

Section C has 6 questions carrying 03 marks each.

Q.no. 27 to 33 are short answer questions

Question 27

Five solutions A, B, C, D and E when tested with universal indicator showed pH as 4,1,11,7 and 9 respectively. Which solution is:

(i) Neutral?

(ii) Strongly alkaline?

(iii) Strongly acidic?

(iv) Weakly acidic?

(v) Weakly alkaline?

(vi) Arrange the pH in increasing order of hydrogen ion concentration.

OR

Solid calcium oxide was taken in a container and water was slowly added to it.

(i) State the two observations made in the experiment.

(ii) Write the name and chemical formula of the product formed.

Question 28

Write the name and molecular formula of an organic compound having its name suffixed with '-ol' and having two carbons in the molecule. With the help of balanced chemical equation indicate what happens when it is heated with excess of conc. H_2SO_4.

Question 29

(i) List five distinguishing features between sexual and asexual types of reproductions in tabular form.

OR

(ii) **(a)** Name the human male reproductive organ that produces sperms and abo secretes a hormone. Write the functions of the secreted hormone.

(b) Name the parts of the human female reproductive system where

i. Fertilization takes place.

ii. Implantation of the fertilized egg occurs. Explain how the embryo gets nourishment inside the mother's body.

Question 30

In object is placed at a distance of 15 cm from a conver len of focal length 10 cm. Find the position and nature of image formed.

Answer :(v=30cm)

Question 31

An electric heater is marked 500KW, 220 V. If the heater is operated for 1 hour, calculate the energy consumed in kWh and in J.

Answer(500kWh $= 1.8 \times 10^9$ **J)**

Question 32

A wire of length I and resistance R is stretched so that its length is doubled, and the area of cross-Section is halved. How will its

(i) resistance change?

(ii) resistivity change?

Answer: (i) For first wire $R = \frac{\rho l}{A}$

Now for second wire $R' = \frac{\rho(2l)}{\frac{A}{2}} = \frac{4\rho l}{A}$

Thus, the resistance of the wires becomes 4 times its original resistance.

(ii) $P_1 : P_2 = 1 : 1$

OR

(i) Identify the V - I graphs for ohmic and non-ohmic materials.

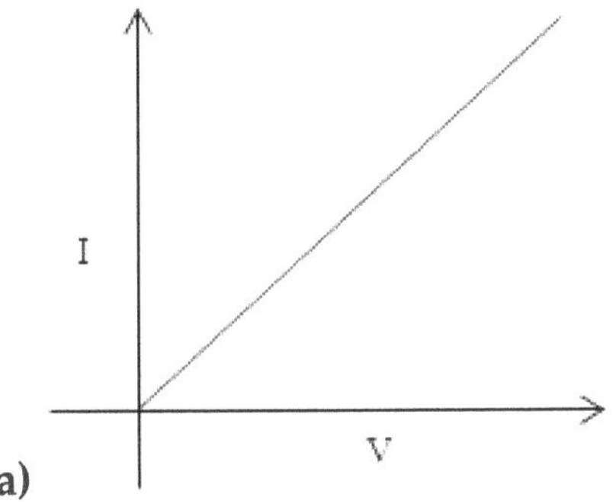

(a)

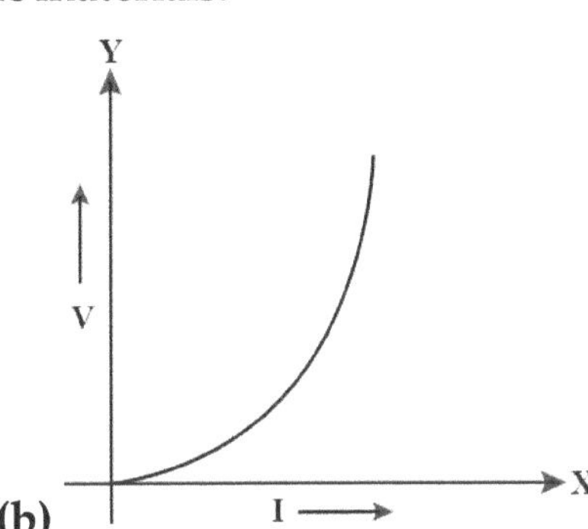

(b)

(ii) Give one example for each.

Answer:

(i) Figure (a) is the V – I graphs for ohmic material.
Figure (b) is the V - I graphs for non-ohmic material.

(ii) Copper is a ohmic material Electrolyte is a non-ohmic material.

Question 33

Write the functions of the following in human female reproductive system: Ovary, oviduct, uterus How does the embryo get nourishment inside the mother's body? Explain in brief.

Section - D

Q.no. 34 to 36 are Long answer questions

Question 34

Account for the following:

(a) Melting and boiling points of ionic compounds are high.

(b) Aluminium is more active than iron. yet there is less crosion of aluminium when both are exposed to air.

(c) Solder is used for welding electrical wires together.

(d) A sulphide ore is converted into its oxide to extract the metal.

(e) Tarnished copper vessels are cleaned with tamarind juice.

OR

(i) Name the following compounds

(a) $CH_3 - CH_2 - OH$

(b)

$$H-\overset{\displaystyle H}{\underset{\displaystyle H}{\overset{|}{\underset{|}{C}}}}-\overset{\displaystyle O}{\overset{\|}{C}}-H$$

(ii) How will you convert

(a) Methane to Carbon dioxide

(b) Methane to chloroform

(iii) What happens when 5% alkaline potassium permanganate solution is added drop by drop to warm propyl alcohol (propanol) taken in a test tube? Explain with the help of a chemical equation.

Question 35

(i) Differentiate between:

(a) Pollen tube and Style

(b) Fission of Amoeba and Plasmodium

(c) Fragmentation and regeneration

(d) Bud of Hydra and bud of Podophyllum

(e) Vegetative propagation and spore formation.

OR

(ii) What happens when

(a) Testosterone is released in the male reproductive system.

(b) Pollen grain falls on the stigma of flower.

(c) Egg fuses with the sperm cell.

(d) A Planaria is cut into three different pieces.

(e) Buds are formed on the notches of leaf of the Podophyllum.

Question 36

Why is pure iron not used for making permanent magnets? Name one material used for making permanent magnets. Describe how permanent magnet are made electrically. State two examples of electrical appliance made by using permanent magnets.

OR

Why does a current- carrying conductor kept in a magnetic field experience force? On what factors does the direction of this force depends? Name and state the rule used for determination of the direction of this force.

Section - E

Q.no. 37 to 39 are case - based/data -based questions with 2 to 3 short sub - parts. Internal choice is provided in one of these sub-parts

Question 37

(i) the figure and answer the following questions.

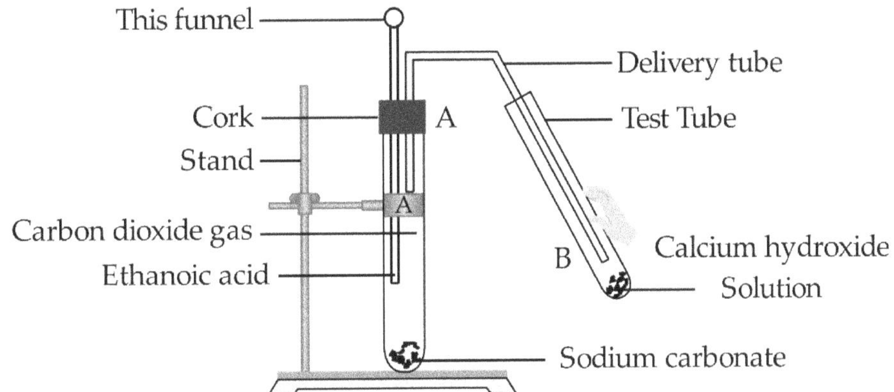

(a) What change would you observe in the calcium hydroxide solution taken in ate B ?

(b) Write the reaction involved in test tubs: A and B respectively.

(c) If ethanol is given instead of ethanoic acid would you expect the same change?

(d) How can a solution of lime water be prepared in the laboratory?

OR

A metal carbonate X on reacting with an acid gives a gas which when passed through a solution Y gives the carbonate back. On the other hand, a gas G that is obtained at anode during electrolysis of brine is passed on dry Y, it gives a compound Z. used for disinfecting drinking water. Identify X, Y, G and Z.

Question 38

How do Mendel's experiment show that traits are inherited independently?

OR

Define evolution. How does it occur? Describe how fossils provide us evidence in support of evolution.

Question 39

The relation between the distance of an object from the mirror (u), the distance of the image from the mirror (v), and the focal length (F) are called the mirror formula. This formula is valid in all situations for all spherical mirrors for all positions of the object. The size of the image formed by a spherical mirror depends on the position of the object from the mirror. The image formed by a spherical mirror can be bigger than the object, equal to the object, or smaller than the object. The size of the image relative to the object is given by the linear magnification (m). Thus, the magnification is given by the ratio of the height of an image to the height of an object. If magnification is negative, the image is real and if it is positive, the image is virtual.\

(i) What is the position of an image when an object is placed at a distance of 20 cm from a concave mirror of a focal length of 20 cm?

(a) 5 cm
(b) 20 cm
(c) 10 cm
(d) Infinity

Answer(d) Infinity

(ii) Which of the following ray diagrams is correct for the ray of light incident on a concave mirror as shown in the figure?

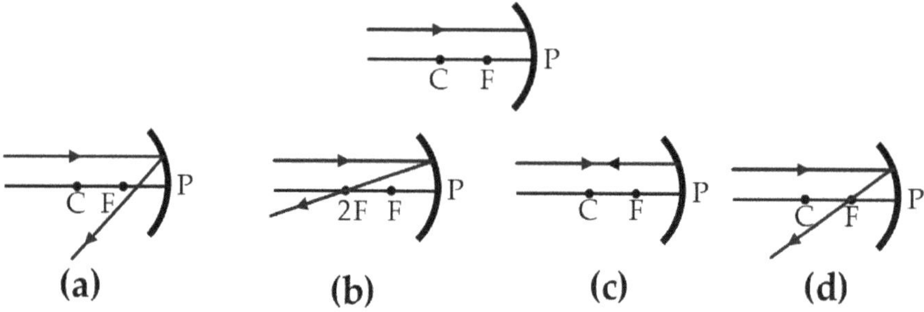

(a) Figure A
(b) Figure B
(c) Figure C
(d) Figure D

Answer(d) Figure D

(iii) If the magnification of an image is −2, the characteristic of the image will be

(a) Real and inverted
(b) Virtual and enlarged
(c) Virtual and inverted
(d) Real and Small

Answer(a) Real and inverted

(iv) A parallel beam of light is made to fall on a concave mirror. An image is formed at a distance of 7.5 cm from the mirror. The focal length of the mirror is

(a) 15 cm
(b) 7.5 cm
(c) 3.75 cm
(d) 10 cm

Answer(b) 7.5 cm

OR

Several resistors may be combined to form a network. The combination should have two endpoints to connect it with a battery or other circuit elements. When the resistances are connected in series, the current in each resistance is the same but the potential difference is different in each resistor. When the resistances are connected in parallel, the voltage drop across each resistance is the same but the current is different in each resistor.

(i) The household circuits are connected in

(a) Series combination

(b) Parallel combination

(c) Both and (b)

(d) None of these

Answer(b) Parallel combination

(ii) The two wires of each resistance *R*, are initially connected in series and then in parallel. The graph it shows the resistance in series and in parallel. Which of the following is correct?

(a) A denotes a parallel combination.

(b) *B* denotes series combination.

(c) A denotes series combination and *B* denotes parallel combination.

(d) None of these.

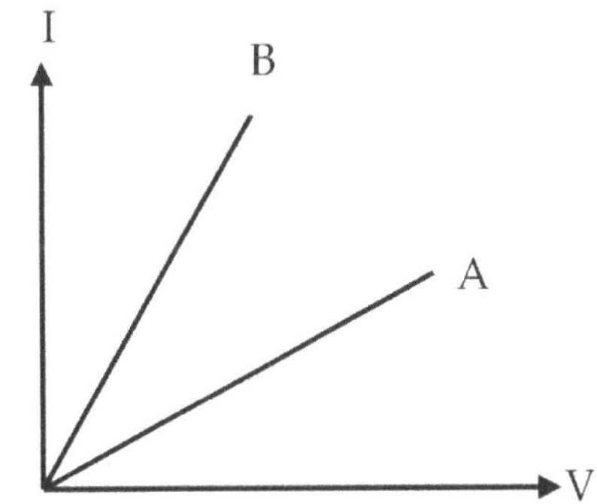

Answer(c) A denotes series combination and *B* denotes parallel combination.

(iii) The equivalent resistance of r_1 and r_2, when connected in series is R_1 and when they are connected in parallel is R_2. Then the ratio is

(a) $\frac{r_1}{r_2}$

(b) $\frac{r_1+r_2}{r_1 r_2}$

(c) $\frac{(r_1+r_2)^2}{r_1 r_2}$

(d) $\frac{r_1 r_2}{2r_1+2r_2}$

Answer(c) $\frac{(r_1+r_2)^2}{r_1 r_2}$

(iv) The equivalent resistance between *A* and *B* is

(a) 6Ω
(b) 9Ω
(c) 3Ω
(d) 12Ω

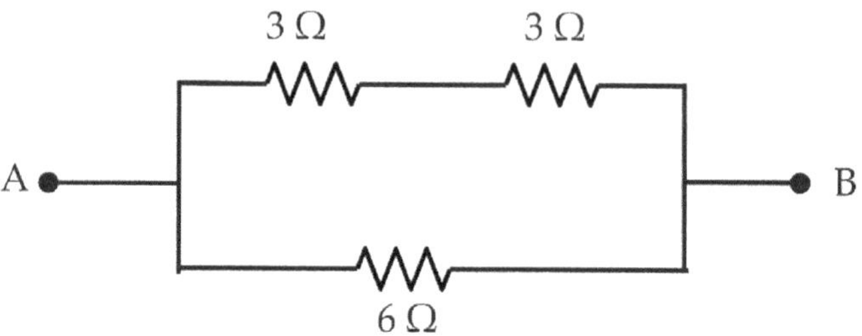

Answer(c) 3Ω

Class- X Session- 2022-23

Science

SAMPLE TEST PAPER-2

Time Allowed: 3 Hrs. **Maximum Marks: 80**

General Instructions:

1. This Question Paper has 5 Sections A-E.
2. Section **A** has 20 MCQs carrying 1 mark each
3. Section **B** has 5 questions carrying 02 marks each.
4. Section **C** has 6 questions carrying 03 marks each.
5. Section **D** has 4 questions carrying 05 marks each.
6. Section **E** has 3 case-based integrated units of assessment (04 marks each) with subparts of the values of 1, 1, and 2 marks each respectively.
7. All Questions are compulsory. However, an internal choice in 2 Qs of 5 marks, 2 Qs of 3 marks, and 2 Questions of 2 marks has been provided. An internal choice has been provided in the 2marks questions of Section E
8. Draw neat figures wherever required. Take π =22/7 wherever required if not stated

Section A

Section A consists of 20 questions of 1 mark each

Question 1

Aqueous solution of which of the following is colourless?

(a) $FeSO_4$

(b) $ZnSO_4$

(c) $Al_2(SO_4)_3$

(d) Both (b) and (c)

Answer. (d)

Question 2

Match the chemical substances given in Column (A) with their appropriate application given Column (B),

Column (A)	Column (B)
(a) Bleaching powder	(i) Preparation of glass
(b) Baking soda	(ii) Production of H_2 and Cl_2
(c) Washing soda	(iii) Decolourisation
(d) Sodium chloride	(iv) Antacid

(a) A – (ii), B – (i), C – (iv), D – (iii)

(b) A – (iii), B – (ii), C – (iv), D – (i)

(c) A – (iiii), B – (iv), C – (i), D – (ii)

(d) A – (ii), B – (iv), C – (i), D – (iii)

Answer. (c)

Question 3

Equal volumes of hydrochloric acid and sodium hydroxide solutions of same concentration at mixed and the pH of the resulting solution checked with a pH paper. What would be the colour obtained?

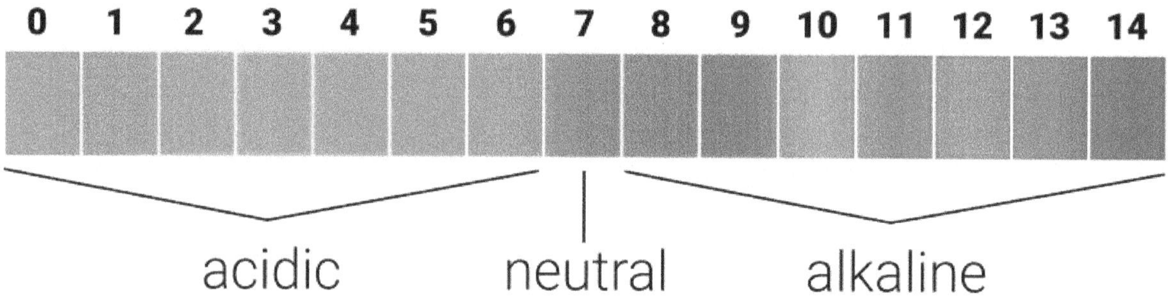

(a) Red
(b) Yellow
(c) Yellowish green
(d) Blue
Answer. (c)

Question 4

A thin plate of zinc metal is placed in a beaker containing aqueous ferrous sulphate solution. The zinc plate is taken out after 15 mins. The colour of solution changes to :
(a) Deep yellow
(b) Deep green
(c) Light blue
(d) Colourless
Answer. (d)

Question 5

The non-metal which is a good conductor of electricity is :
(a) Arsenic
(b) Bromine
(c) Sulphur
(d) Graphite
Answer. (d) Graphite

Question 6

Which of the following statements are usually correct for carbon compounds? These
(i) Are good conductors of electricity
(ii) Are poor conductors of electricity
(iii) Have strong forces of attraction between their molecules.
(iv) Do not have strong forces of attraction between their molecules.

(a) (i) and (iii)
(b) (ii) and (iii)
(c) (i) and (iv)
(d) (ii) and (iv)
Answer(d) (ii) and (iv)

Question 7

Which among the following is/are unsaturated hydrocarbons?

(i) $CH_3 - CH_2 - CH_2 - CH_3$

(ii)

$$CH_3 - CH_2 - \underset{\substack{| \\ CH_2 - CH_3}}{CH} - CH_3$$

(iii) $CH_3 - CH = CH - CH_2 - CH_3$

(iv) $CH_3 - C \equiv C - CH_2 - CH_3$

(a) (i) and (ii)
(b) (ii) and (iii)
(c) (iii) and (iv)
(d) (ii) and (iv)
Answer(c) (iii) and (iv)

Question 8

A student setup an experiment to study the human respiratory system. In the experiment, the student places candle, and a living cockroach in the flask A, while a candle and a dead cockroach in flask B. The burning of candle needs oxygen.

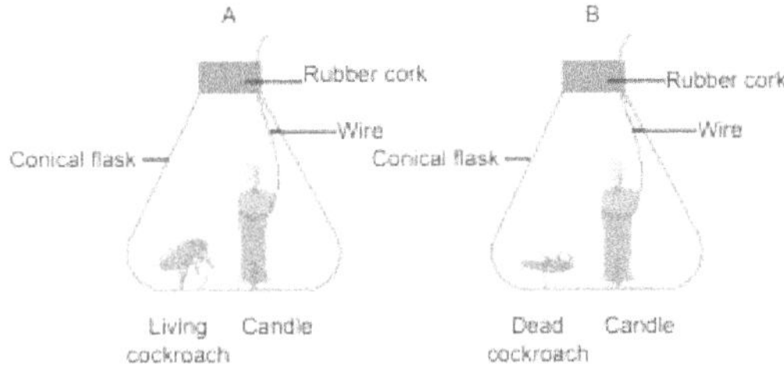

After 10 minutes, the student observes that the candle in flask A extinguish faster while car in flask B keeps burning for a longer time. What can be evaluated from this experiment?

(a) Water vapours produced by living beings prevents burning of candle.
(b) Living beings consumes oxygen during respiration.
(c) Burning of candle decreases the life span of cockroach.
(d) Candle produces high amount of carbon dioxide.
Answer. (b)

Question 9

Which of the following is an incorrect statement?

(a) Organisms grow with time

(b) Organisms must repair and maintain their structure

(c) Movement of molecules does not take place among cells

(d) Energy is essential for life processes

Answer: (c)

Question 10

Which of the following equations is the summary of photosynthesis?

(a) $6CO_2 + 12H_2O \rightarrow C_6H_{12}O_6 + 6O_2 + 6H_2O$

(b) $6CO_2 + H_2O + \text{Sunlight} \rightarrow C_6H_{12}O_6 + O_2 + 6H_2O$

(c) $6CO_2 + 12H_2O + \text{Chlorophyll} + \text{Sunlight} \rightarrow C_6H_{12}O_6 + 6O_2 + 6H_2O$

(d) $6CO_2 + 12H_2O + \text{Chlorophyll} + \text{Sunlight} \rightarrow C_6H_{12}O_6 + 6CO_2 + 6H_2O$

Answer: (c)

Question 11

Choose the event that does not occur in photosynthesis

(a) Absorption of light energy by chlorophyll

(b) Reduction of carbon dioxide to carbohydrates

(c) Oxidation of carbon-to-carbon dioxide

(d) Conversion of light energy to chemical energy

Answer: (c)

Question 12

Choose the forms in which most plants absorb nitrogen

(i) Proteins

(ii) Nitrates and Nitrites

(iii) Urea

(iv) Atmospheric nitrogen

(a) (i) and (ii)

(b) (ii) and (iii)

(c) (iii) and (iv)

(d) (i) and (iv)

Answer(b) (ii) and (iii)

Question 13

There are three resistors of values 2Ω, 3Ω, and 5Ω respectively. To get total resistance less than 2Ω these resistances wall have to join in

(a) Series

(b) Parallel

(c) Series as well as parallel

(d) None of the above

Answer(b) Parallel

Question 14

The fuse wire is made of a/an

(a) Tin-lead alloy

(b) Iron-lead alloy

(c) Copper-tin alloy

(d) None of these

Answer(a) Tin-lead alloy

Question 15

As per New Cartesian Sign Conventions,

(a) Focal length of a concave mirror is positive and that of a convex mirror is negative.

(b) Focal length of both, convex and concave mirrors is positive.

(c) Focal length of both. Convex and concave mirror is negative.

(d) Focal length of a concave mirror is negative and that of a convex mirror is positive.

Answer(d) Focal length of a concave mirror is negative and that of a convex mirror is positive.

Question 16

The term 'bending of light when it passes from one medium into another medium of different refractive index is called

(a) Dispersion

(b) Reflection

(c) Refraction

(d) Scattering

Answer(c) Refraction

Q. no 17 to 20 are Assertion - Reasoning based questions. These consist of two statements – Assertion (A) and Reason (R). Answer these questions selecting the appropriate option given below:

(a) Both A and R are true and R is the correct explanation of A

(b) Both A and R are true and R is not the correct explanation of A

(c) A is true but R is false

(d) A is False but R is true

Question 17

Assertion(A) :Soap is non-biodegradable.

Reason (R) : Detergent is biodegradable.

Answer(d)

Question 18

Assertion(A)) : Photosynthesis is considered as an endothermic reaction.

Reason (R) : Energy gets released in the process of photosynthesis.

Answer(c)

Question 19

Assertion (A) : The concentration of harmful substances is more in human being.

Reason (R) : humans are at the apex of the food chain.

Answer(a)

Question 20

Assertion: The property of converging a convergent lens does not remain the same in all media.

Reason: The property of the lens whether the ray is diverging or converging is independent of the surrounding medium.

Answer(a)

Section B

Section B has 5 questions carrying 02 marks each

Q. no. 21 to 26 are very short answer questions

Question 21

(i) A student dropped a few pieces of marble in dil. hydrochloric acid contained in a test tube. The evolved gas was passed through lime water? Write the balanced chemical equations for both the changes observed

OR

Write the electron dot structure of magnesium and chlorine and show the formation of magnesium chloride by transfer of electrons.

Question 22

"The chromosomal number of the sexually producing parents and their offspring is the same." Justify this statement.

Question 23

Why is vegetative propagation practiced for growing some types of plant? List two plants which are grown by this method.

Question 24

Define variation in relation to a species. Why is variation beneficial to the species?

Question 25

Calculate the equivalent resistance between A and B from figure.

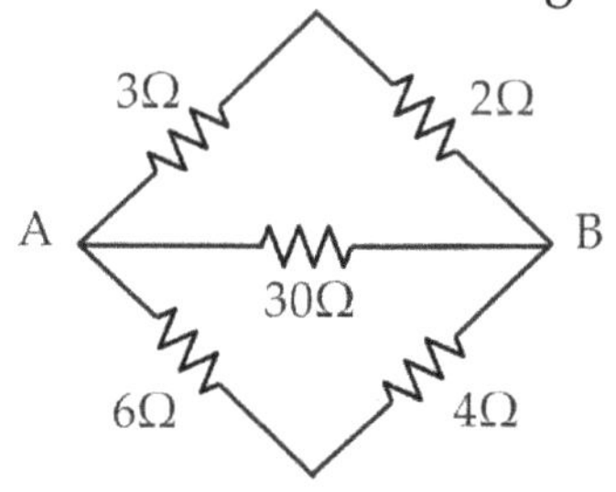

Answer(R = 3Ω)

OR

Copy and complete the following table:

Type of Lens	Position of object	Nature of Image	Size of image
Convex	At F		
Concave	At infinity		

Question 26

Label any four parts.

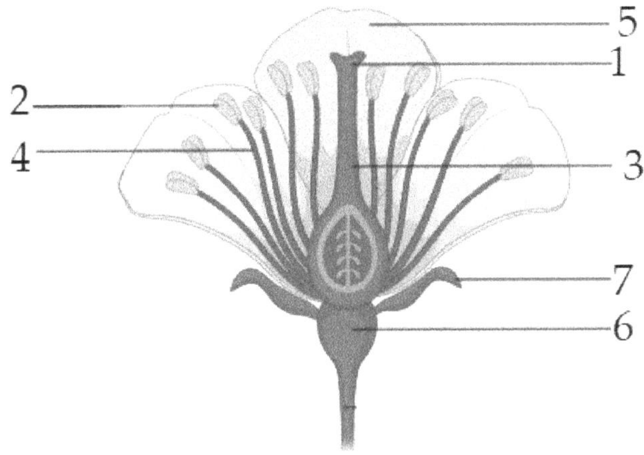

Answer:

1. Stigma
2. Anther
3. Style
4. Filament
5. Petal
6. Ovary
7. Sepal (any four)

Section - C

Q.no. 27 to 33 are short answer questions

Question 27

Why is the amount of gas collected in one of the test tubes in diagram given below is double of the amount collected in the other? Name this gas.

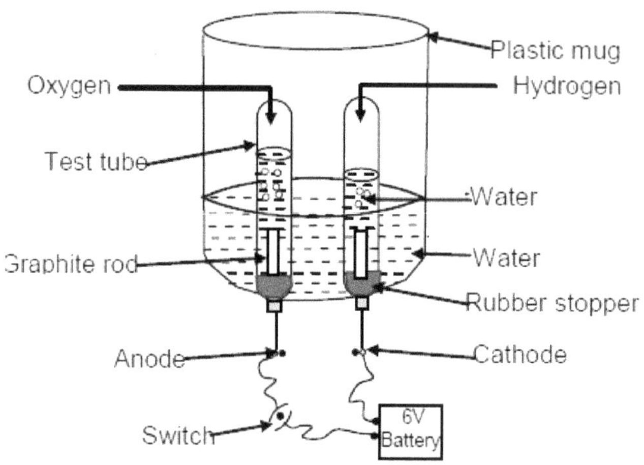

Question 28

What is methane? Draw its electron dot structure. Name the type of bonds formed in this compound. Why are such compounds:

(a) Poor conductors of electricity? And

(b) Have low melting and boiling points? What happens when this compound burns in oxygen?

Question 29

(i)) Identify A.B.C and D in the given diagram and write their names.

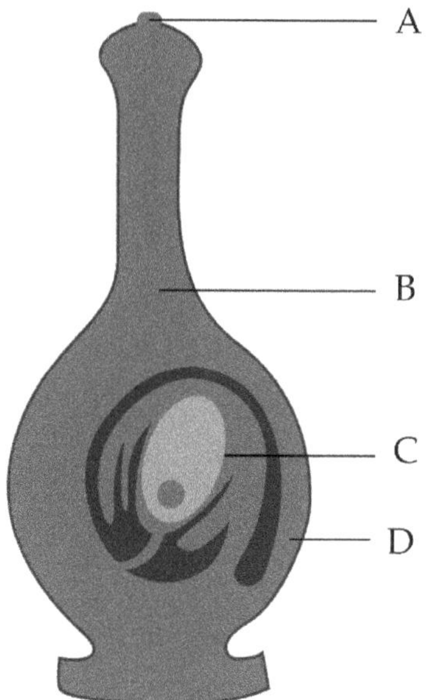

(b) What is pollination? Explain its significance.

(c) Explain the process of fertilization in flowers. Name the parts of flower that develop after fertilization into (i) seed (ii) fruit

OR

(ii) Differentiate between:

(a) Pollen tube and Style

(b) Fission of Amoeba and Plasmodium

(c) Fragmentation and regeneration

(d) Bud of Hydra and bud of Podophyllum
(e) Vegetative propagation and spore formation.

Question 30

The refractive index of dense flint glass is 1.65 and for alcohol is 1.36 w.r.t air. Find the refractive index of dense flint glass with respect to alcohol.

Answer(1.21)

Question 31

There are three pins in an electric plug.

(i) How would you identify the earth pin?
(ii) In which of the three connecting wires (lines) should a switch be connected?

Question 32

What is meant by the term "Magnetic field Lines"? List three properties of magnetic field lines.

OR

Draw the pattern lines of force due to a magnetic field associated with a current-carrying conductor. State how the magnetic field produced changes

(i) with an increase in current in the conductor and
(ii) the distance from the conductor.

Question 33

(a) Identify the organisms A. B and the mocle of asexual reproduction exhibited by them.

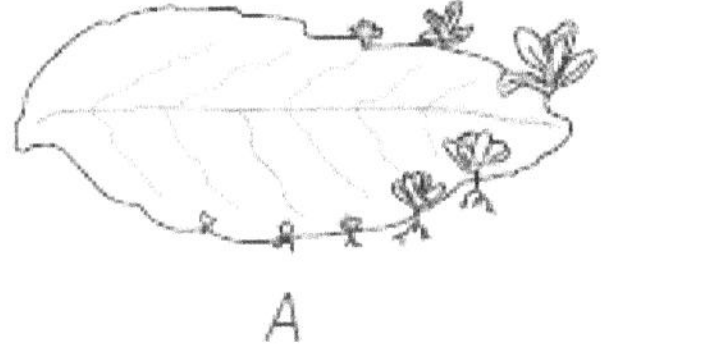

B

(b) How will an organism be benefitted if it reproduces through spores?
(c) Mention the two asexual methods by which hydra can reproduce. Explain briefly any one such method.

Section - D

Q.no. 34 to 36 are Long answer questions

Question 34

(i) **(a)** What is the importance of pH in every day life?
(b) How is sodium hydroxide and Cl_2 (Chlorine) gas produced from common salt? What is this process called.

OR

(ii) 2 g of ferrous sulphate crystals were heated in a hard glass tube and observations recorded.
(a) What is the successive colour change?

(b) Identify the liquid droplets collected on the cooler parts of the test-tube.
(c) What type of odour is observed on heating ferrous sulphate crystals?
(d) Name the products on heating ferrous sulphate crystals.
(e) What type of reaction is taking place?

Question 35

(i) Define the following processes:
(a) Fertilization
(b) Menstruation
(c) Binary fission
(d) Vegetative propagation

OR

(ii) (a) Identify the organisms in figure A, B, C and D.

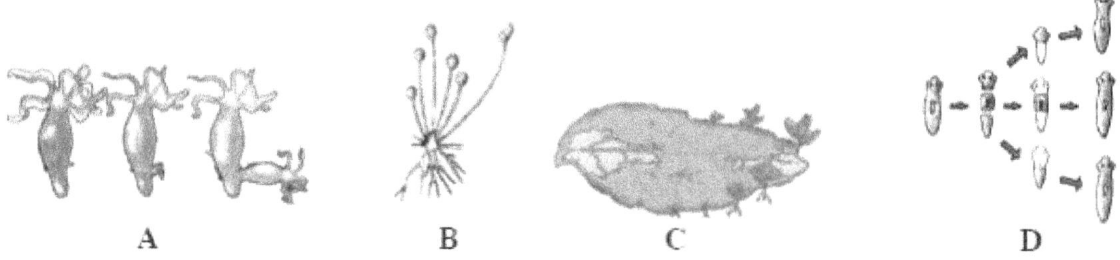

(a) Identify the life process commonly shown in all the figures,
(b) How is this life process advantageous to the organisms? Mention any two advantages.

Question 36

Name the two major defects of vision.
Explain their cause and discuss their removal.

OR

Draw a block diagram of human eye and name all its important parts.

Section - E

Q.no. 37 to 39 are case - based/data -based questions with 2 to 3 short sub - parts. Internal choice is provided in one of these sub-parts

Question 37

The metals extracted from their ores are not very pure. They contain impurities, which can be removed by the process of refining. Name the most widely used process of refining impure metals. Draw a diagram of the apparatus used for refining of copper metal and state :
(a) The name of the rods which are used as cathode and anode.
(b) The electrolyte used during the process.
(c) What happens to the pure metal when current passes through the electrolyte?
(d) What happens to the soluble and insoluble impurities present in the impure copper?

OR

(a) What is a neutralization reaction? Give two examples.

(b) Give two important uses of washing soda and baking soda

Question 38

How do Mendel's experiment show that traits are inherited independently?

OR

(a) What are monohybrid and dihybrid cross?

(b) How Mendel proved that tallness is the dominant trait and dwarfness is recessive in a pea plant? Explain with the help of a monohybrid cross.

Question 39

When the rays of light travel from one transparent medium to another, the path of light are deviated. This phenomenon is called the refraction of light. The bending of light depends on the optical density of the medium through which the light pass.

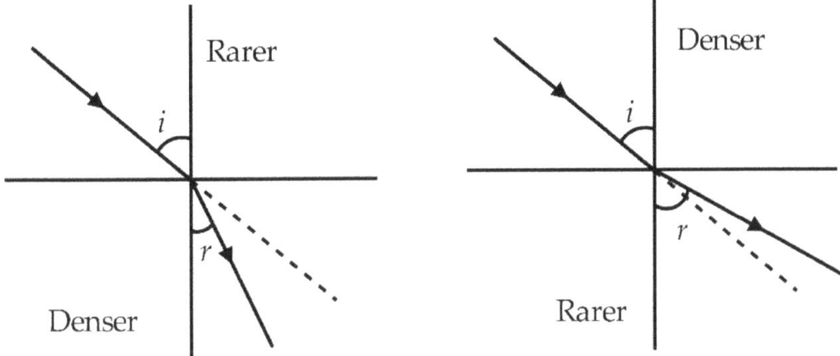

The speed of light varies from medium to medium. A medium in which the speed of light is more is an optically rarer medium whereas in which the speed of light is less is an optically denser medium. Whenever light goes from one medium to another, the frequency of light does not change however, speed and wavelength change. It concluded that change in speed of light is the basic cause of refraction.

(i) When light travels from air to glass, the ray of light bends

(a) Towards the normal

(b) Away from normal

(c) Anywhere

(d) None of these

Answer(a) Towards the normal

(ii) A ray of light passes from a medium A to another medium B. No bending of light occurs if the ray of light hits the boundary of medium B at an angle of

(a) 0°

(b) 45°

(c) 90°

(d) 120°

Answer(a) 0°

(iii) When light passes from one medium to another, the frequency of light

(a) Increases

(b) Decreases

(c) Remains same

(d) None of these

Answer(c) Remains same

OR

The heating effect of current is obtained by the transformation of electrical energy into heat energy. Just as mechanical energy used to overcome friction is covered into heat, in the same way, electrical energy is converted into heat energy when an electric current flows through a resistance wire. The heat produced in a conductor, when a current flows through it is found to depend directly on (a) the strength of the current and (b)resistance of the conductor, and (c) the time for which the current flows.

The mathematical expression is given by $H = I^2Rt$.

The electrical fuse, electrical heater, electric iron, electric geyser, etc. all are based on the heating effect of current.

(i) What are the properties of an electric fuse?

(a) Low resistance, low melting point

(b) High resistance, high melting point.

(c) High resistance, low melting point

(d) Low resistance, high melting point

Answer(c) High resistance, low melting point

(ii) When the current is doubled in a heating device and time is halved, the heat energy produced is

(a) Doubled

(b) Halved

(c) Four times

(d) One fourth time

Answer(a) Doubled

(iii) A fuse wire melts at 5 A. It is desired that the fuse wire of the same material melt at 10 A. The new radius of the wire is

(a) 4 times

(b) 2 times

(c) $\frac{1}{2}$ times

(d) $\frac{1}{4}$ times

Answer(b) 2 times

(iv) When a current of 0.5 A passes through a conductor for 5 min and the resistance of a conductor is 10Ω, the amount of heat produced is

(a) 250 J

(b) 5000 J

(c) 750 J

(d) 1000 J

Answer(c) 750 J

Class- X Session- 2022-23

Science

SAMPLE TEST PAPER-3

Time Allowed: 3 Hrs. **Maximum Marks: 80**

General Instructions:

1. This Question Paper has 5 Sections A-E.
2. Section **A** has 20 MCQs carrying 1 mark each
3. Section **B** has 5 questions carrying 02 marks each.
4. Section **C** has 6 questions carrying 03 marks each.
5. Section **D** has 4 questions carrying 05 marks each.
6. Section **E** has 3 case-based integrated units of assessment (04 marks each) with subparts of the values of 1, 1, and 2 marks each respectively.
7. All Questions are compulsory. However, an internal choice in 2 Qs of 5 marks, 2 Qs of 3 marks, and 2 Questions of 2 marks has been provided. An internal choice has been provided in the 2marks questions of Section E
8. Draw neat figures wherever required. Take π =22/7 wherever required if not stated

Section A

Section A consists of 20 questions of 1 mark each

Question 1

Four students were asked to study the reaction between aqueous solutions of barium chloride and sodium sulphate. On mixing the solutions of the two salts in a test tube, they reported their experiment as follows:

(i) The colour of the mixture becomes brown

(ii) The solutions form a separate layer.

(iii) A colourless mixture is obtained.

(iv) A white substance settles at the bottom.

The correct report is

(a) (i)

(b) (ii)

(c) (iii)

(d) (iv)

Answer. (d)

Question 2

Sapna added a strip of aluminum to 50 mL of 3 solutions of $FeSO_4$ in a test tube, The correct observation for change in color of a solution made by her is

(a) The pale green coloured solution turned colourless

(b) The colourless solution turned pale green

(c) Pale green coloured solution remained pale green.

(d) The colourless solution turned blue.

Answer. (a)

Question 3

Which of the following gives the correct increasing order of acidic strength?

(a) Water < Acetic acid < Hydrochloric acid

(b) Water < Hydrochloric acid < Acetic acid

(c) Acetic acid < Water < Hydrochloric acid

(d) Hydrochloric acid < Water < Acetic acid

Answer. (a)

Question 4

Common salt besides being used in kitchen can also be used as the raw material for making

(i) Washing soda

(ii) Bleaching powder

(iii) Baking soda

(iv) Slaked lime

(a) (i) and (ii)

(b) (i), (ii) and (iv)

(c) (i) and (iii)

(d) (i), (iii) and (iv)

Answer. (c)

Question 5

Mrignayani was experimenting with comparing the reactivity of metals in the laboratory She was given aluminum metal and was told to check reactivity by using four solutions as shown below. She would observe that reaction takes place in

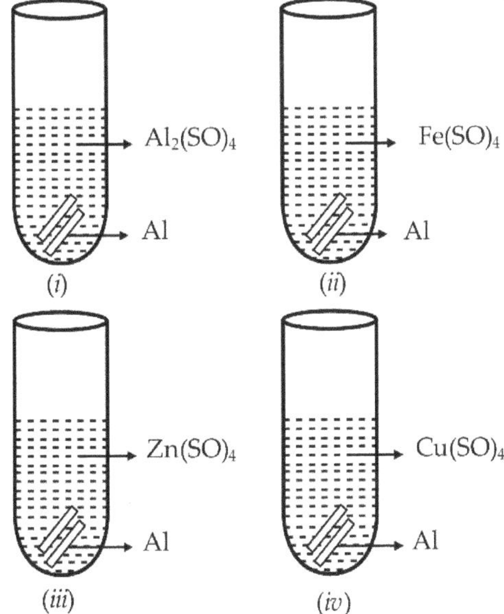

Answer. (b)

Question 6

For preparing soap in the laboratory, we require oil and a base. Which of the following combinations of an oil and a base would be best suited for the preparation of soap?

(a) Castor oil and calcium hydroxide

(b) Turpentine oil and sodium hydroxide

(c) Castor oil and sodium hydroxide

(d) Mustard oil and calcium hydroxide

Answer. (c)

Question 7

A student prepared a 20% sodium hydroxide solution in a breaker to study the saponification reaction. Some observations related to this are given below:

(i) Sodium hydroxide solution turns red litmus blue.

(ii) Sodium hydroxide readily dissolves in water.

(iii) The beaker containing the solution appears cold when touched from the outside.

(iv) The blue litmus paper turns red when dipped into the solution.

The correct observations are:

(a) (i), (ii) and (iv)

(b) only iii and iv

(c) (i), (ii) and (iii)

(d) only (i) and (ii)

Answer. (a)

Question 8

In which of the following groups of organisms, food material is broken down outside the body and absorbed?

(a) Mushroom, green plants, Amoeba

(b) Yeast, mushroom, bread mould

(c) Paramecium, Amoeba, Cuscuta

(d) Cuscuta, lice, tapewor

Answer. (B)

Question 9

Select the correct statement

(a) Heterotrophs do not synthesise their own food

(b) Heterotrophs utilise solar energy for photosynthesis

(c) Heterotrophs synthesise their own food

(d) Heterotrophs are capable of converting carbon dioxide and water into carbohydrateS

Answer. (A)

Question 10

Which part of alimentary canal receives bile from the liver?

(a) Stomach

(b) Small intestine
(c) Large intestine
(d) Oesophagus
Answer. (b)

Question 11

Choose the function of the pancreatic juice from the following
(a) trypsin digests proteins and lipase carbohydrates
(b) trypsin digests emulsified fats and lipase proteins
(c) trypsin and lipase digest fats
(d) trypsin digests proteins and lipase emulsified fats
Answer. (d)

Question 12

The filtration units of kidneys are called
(a) Ureter
(b) Urethra
(c) Neurons
(d) Nephrons
Answer. (d)

Question 13

The direction of lines of force of the magnetic fieldε produced by a straight wire carrying current can be obtained by using
(a) Maxwell's right hand grip rule
(b) Maxwell's right hand rule
(c) Maxwell's left hand rule
(d) Lenz's law
Answer(b) Maxwell's right hand rule

Question 14

Which of the following combinations of resistances is different from others?

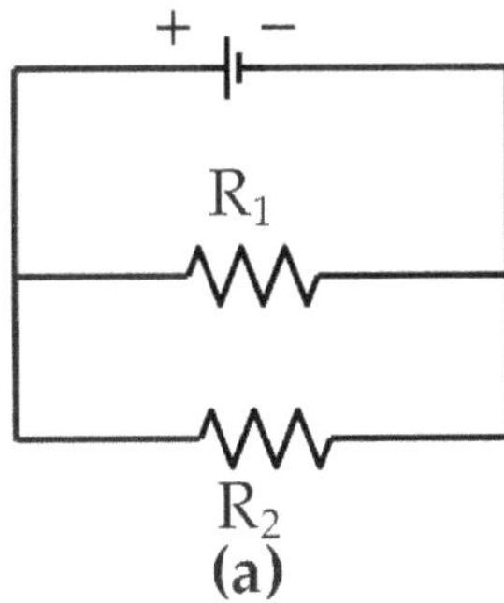

(a)

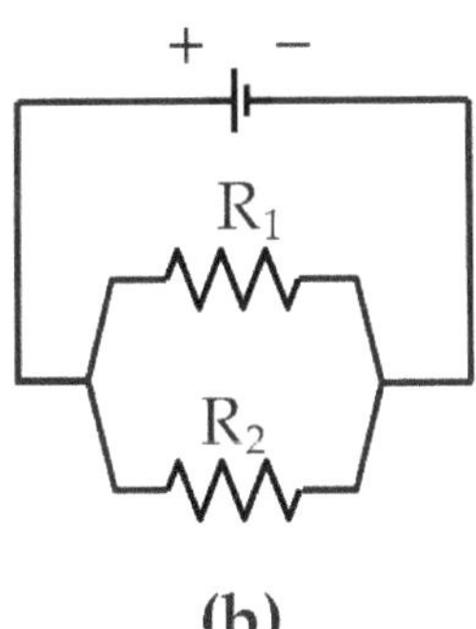

(b)

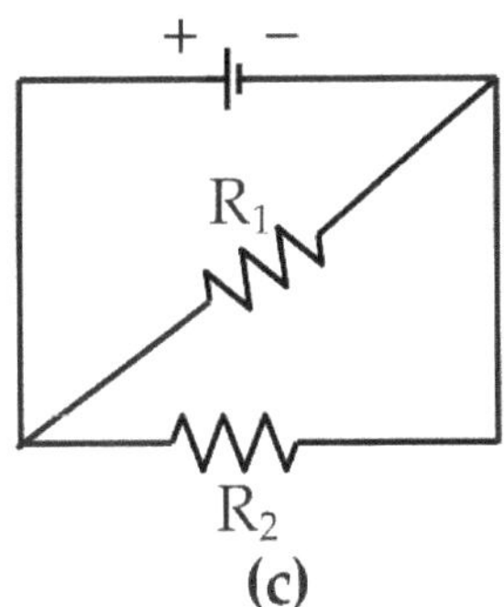

(c)

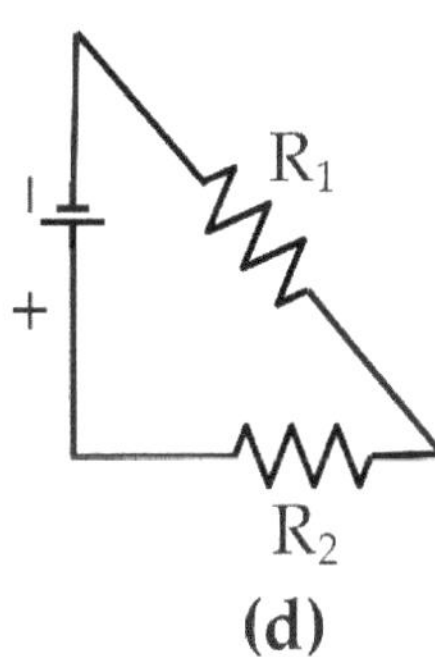

(d)

Answer(d)

Question 15

The image formed by a spherical mirror is virtual, erect, and smaller the size. Whatever be the position of the object. The mirror is

(a) Convex

(b) Concave

(c) Either convex or concave

(d) Cannot say

Answer(a) Convex

Question 16

Which of the following shows the bending of light from a denser (D) medium into a rarer ® medium?

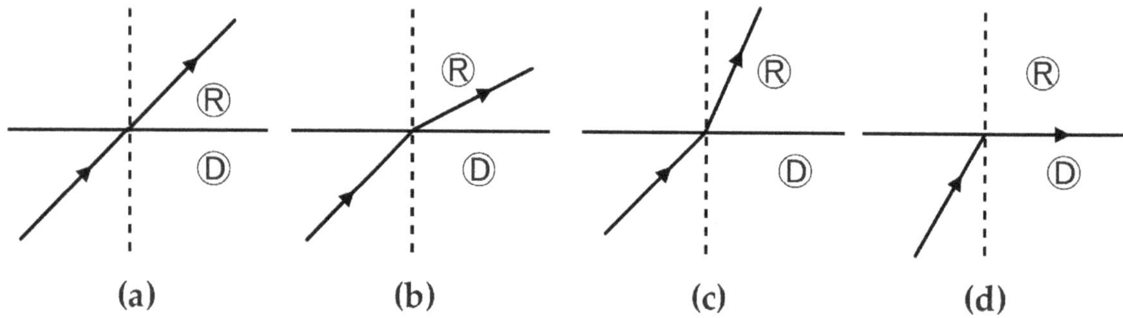

Answer(b)

Q. no 17 to 20 are Assertion - Reasoning based questions. These consist of two statements – Assertion (A) and Reason (R). Answer these questions selecting the appropriate option given below:

(a) Both A and R are true and R is the correct explanation of A

(b) Both A and R are true and R is not the correct explanation of A

(c) A is true but R is false

(d) A is False but R is true

Question 17

Assertion(A)) :Bleaching powder is $NaHCO_3$.

Reason (R) : Sodium hydroxide is NaOH.

Answer(a)

Question 18

Assertion(A)) : Photosynthesis is considered as an endothermic reaction.

Reason (R) : Energy gets released in the process of photosynthesis.

Answer(c)

Question 19

Assertion (A) : The concentration of harmful substances is more in human being.

Reason (R) : humans are at the apex of the food chain.
Answer(a)

Question 20
Assertion: We can decide the nature of a mirror by observing the size of the erect image in the mirror.

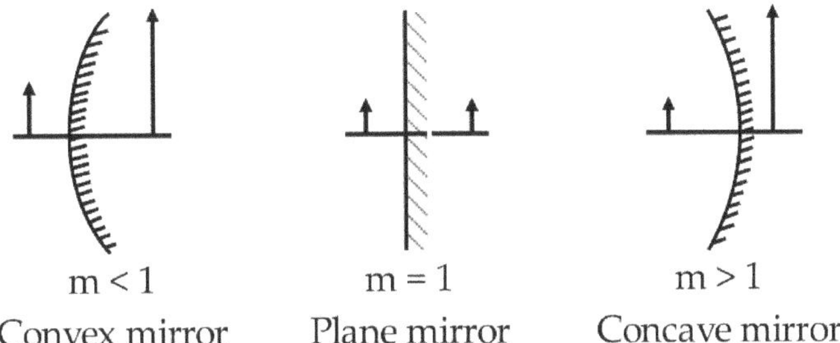

Reason: The minimum distance between a real object and its real image in a concave mirror is non-zero.
Answer(c)

Section B

Section B has 5 questions carrying 02 marks each

Q. no. 21 to 26 are very short answer questions

Question 21 **[2]**

Match the reactions given in Column (A) with the names given in Column (B).

Column (A)	**Column (B)**
(a) $CH_3OH + CH_3COOH \xrightarrow{H^+} CH_3COOCH_3 + H_2O$	(i) Addition reaction
(b) $CH_2 = CH_2 + H_2 \xrightarrow{Ni} CH_3 - CH_3$	(ii) Substitution reaction
(c) $CH_4 + Cl_2 \xrightarrow{Sunlight} CH_3Cl + HCl$	(iii) Neutralisation reaction
(d) $CH_3COOH + NaOH \longrightarrow CH_2COONa + H_2O$	(iv) Esterification reaction

Answer. A – (iv), B – (i), C – (ii), D – (iii),

OR

Why does the colour of copper sulphate solution change when an iron nail is dipped in it?

Question 22

What are the functions of the following in male reproductive system?

(i) Seminal vesicles
(ii) Prostate gland

Question 23

Differentiate between plumule and radicle.

Question 24 **[2]**

Write two differences between binary fission and multiple fission in a tabular form as observed in the cells of the organisms.

Question 25

The equivalent resistance of the circuit shown in Fig. is 4Ω. Calculate the value of x.

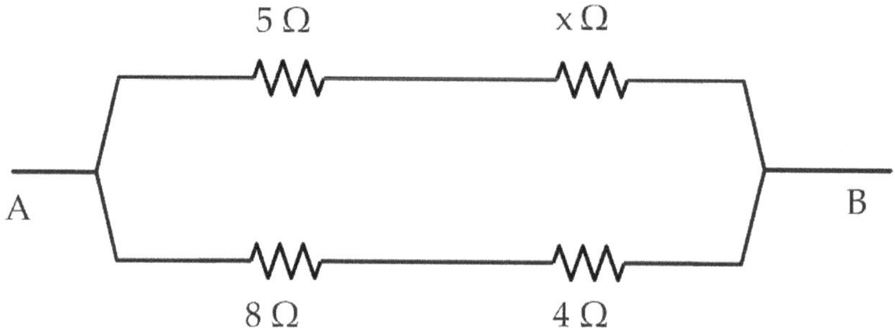

Answer(X = 1Ω)

OR

An erect, magnified, and virtual image is formed, when an object is placed between the optical center and principal focus of a lens.

(i) Name the lens

(ii) Draw a ray diagram to show the formation of the image with the above stated characteristics.

Question 26

What is the functions of copper-T used by some women? What is its effect?

Section - C

Q.no. 27 to 33 are short answer questions

Question 27

Metal E is stored under kerosene. When a small piece of it is left open in the air, it catches fire. When the product formed is dissolved in water it turns red litmus to blue:

(i) Name the metal E.

(ii) Write the chemical equation for the reaction when it is exposed to air and when the product is dissolved in water.

(iii) Explain the process by which the metal is obtained from its molten chloride.

Question 28

Identify the compound X based on the reactions given below.
Also, write the name and chemical formulae of A, B, and C.

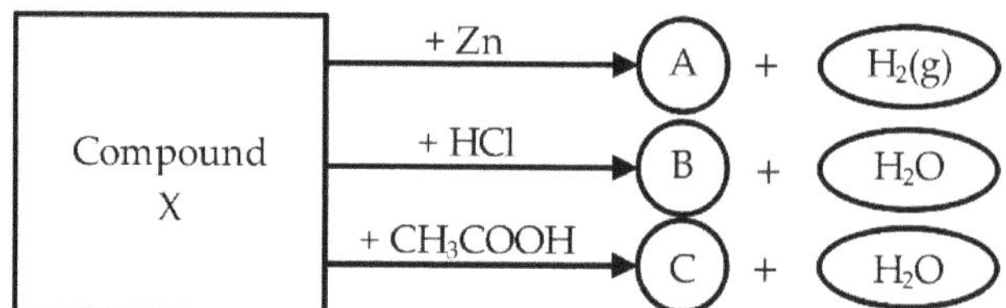

Question 29

What are monohybrid and dihybrid cross?

How Mendel proved that tallness is the dominant trait and dwarfness is recessive in a pea plant?. Explain with the help of a monohybrid cross.

OR

How many pairs of chromosomes are present in human beings? Out of these how many are sex chromosomes? How many types of sex chromosomes are found in human beings?

Question 30

Draw the magnetic field lines due to a current-carrying circular coil. State the clock rule to find the polarities of the faces of the coil.

Question 31

The speed of light in diamond is 125,000kms^{-1} And in air is 3×10^8 ms^{-1}. Find the refractive index of a diamond.

[**Answer**2.4]

Question 32

Write laws of refraction. Explain the same with the help of ray diagram , when a ray of light passes through a rectangular glass slab.

OR

How does the strength of the magnetic field at the centre of a circular coil of wire depend on :

(i) The radius of the coil,

(ii) the number of turns of the wire,

(iii) the strength of the current flowing in the coil?

Question 33

(a) Name the scientist who gave the iden of evolution of species by natural selection.

(b) What conclusion did Mendel draw from his experiments about traits?

(c) Arrange the following according to evolution. Cockroach, Mango tree, Gorilla, Fish

Section - D

Q.no. 34 to 36 are Long answer questions

Question 34

(i) What are hydrocarbons? Write the name and general formula of

(a) Saturated hydrocarbons and

(b) Unsaturated hydrocarbons and draw the structure of one hydrocarbon of each type. How can an unsaturated hydrocarbon be made saturated?

OR

(i) A student performed the experiment of heating ferrous sulphate crystals in a boiling tube. He smelt fumes of a pungent gas and saw colours of ferrous sulphate disappear.

(a) Write the chemical formula of the pungent gas.

(b) Why does the colour of crystal disappear?

(c) Identify the nature of this chemical reaction.

(ii) A student took a small piece of solid quick lime in a China dish and poured over it a small amount of water. List two changes he is likely to observe in the China dish immediately after pouring water.

Question 35

Woman are often blamed for besuring daughters. As a student with knowledge in science how will you explain to your fellow students that the sex of the child is not determined by mother's genetic constitution ?

OR

What is speciation? List four factors that could lead to speciation. Which of these cannot be major factors in the speciation of a self pollinating plant species? Explain.

Question 36

(i) What is an electromagnet?
(ii) List any of its two uses.
(iii) Draw a labelled diagram to show how an electromagnet is made.
(iv) What is the purpose of the soft core used in making an electromagnet?

OR

Draw the lines of force of the magnetic field through and around

(i) Single loop of wire carrying comes.
(ii) A solenoid carrying electric current.

Section - E

Q.no. 37 to 39 are case - based/data -based questions with 2 to 3 short sub - parts. Internal choice is provided in one of these sub-parts

Question 37

Sonia and Preeti went to buy cooking pan. Sonia didn't want to spend a lot of money on it so she asked the shopkeeper to give her an aluminium pan. But Preeti informed her that cooking in aluminium can cause many health hazards. She advised her to buy an anodised aluminium pan instead. Though that was costlier, Sonia went with the second option.

(a) Why does the surface of aluminium have a dull experience whereas it is a shiny element?
(b) Write a reaction of Al_2O_3 with HCl.
(c) Rass is made up of and metals.
(d) What do you mean by anodising?

OR

Jai wanted to buy a new car. Once he was decided on the SAMPLE and company, he had three options to choose from i.e. Petrol engine, diesel engine or CNG engine. Knowing that CNG wouldn't harm the environment like diesel or petrol, he bought the car which used CNG as fuel.

(a) What is CNG?

(b) What are its main constitments?

(c) Mention the formula and names of two next higher homologues of the main constituent of CNG.

(d) Why is CNG better than petrol?

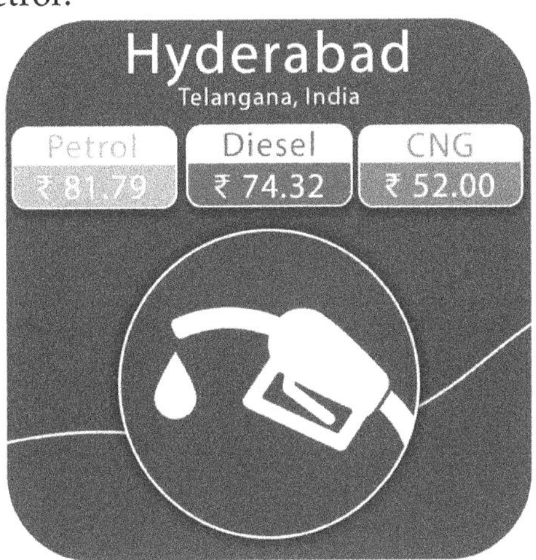

Question 38

Draw a labelled diagram of human brain. Discuss functions of cerebrum, cerebellum and medulla.

OR

(a) Draw the structure of a neuron and label the following on it:
Nucleus, Dendrite, Cell body and Axon.

(b) Name the part of neuron
(i) Where information is acquired.
(ii) Through which information travels as an electrical impulse.

Question 39

The refraction of light on going from one medium to another takes place according to two laws which are known as the laws of refraction of light. These laws are

The ratio of the sine of the angle of incidence to the sine of the angle of refraction is always constant for the pair of media in contact.

$$\frac{\sin i}{\sin r} = \mu = \text{constant}$$

This constant is called the refractive index of the second medium with respect to the first medium. The Refractive index is also defined as the ratio of the speed of light in a vacuum to the speed of light in a medium.

The incident ray refracted ray and normal all lie in the same plane.

This law is called Snell's law of refraction.

(i) When light travels from air to glass,

(a) Angle of incidence > angle of refraction
(b) Angle of incidence < angle of refraction
(c) Angle of incidence = angle of refraction
(d) Can't say
Answer(a) Angle of incidence > angle of refraction

(ii) When light travels from air to medium, the angle of incidence is 45° And the angle of refraction is 30°. The refractive index of the second medium with respect to the first medium is
(a) 1.41
(b) 1.50
(c) 1.23
(d) 1
Answer(a) 1.41

(iii) In which medium, the speed of light is minimum?
(a) Air
(b) Glass
(c) Water
(d) Diamond
Answer(d) Diamond

(iv) If the refractive index of glass is 1.5 and the speed of light in air is $3 \times 10^8\ m/s$. The speed of light in glass is
(a) $2 \times 10^8 \text{m/s}$
(b) 2.9×10^8 m/s
(c) 4.5×10^8 m/s
(d) 3×10^8 m/s
Answer(a) $2 \times 10^8 \text{m/s}$

OR

The electrical energy consumed by an electrical appliance is given by the product of its power rating and the time for which it is used. The SI unit of electrical energy is Joule. Joule represents a very small quantity of energy and therefore it is inconvenient to use where a large quantity of energy is involved. So, for commercial purposes, we use a bigger unit of electrical energy which is called a kilowatt hour. 1 kilowatt-hour is equal to 3.6×10^6 joules of electrical energy.

(i) The energy dissipated by the heater is E. When the time of operating the heater is doubled, the energy dissipated is
(a) Doubled
(b) Half
(c) Remains same
(d) Four times
Answer(a) Doubled

(ii) The power of a lamp is 60 W. The energy consumed in 1 minute is

(a) 360 J

(b) 36 J

(c) 3600 J

(d) 3.6 J

Answer(c) 3600 J

(iii) The electrical refrigerator rated 400 W operates 8 hours a day. The cost of electrical energy is ₹5 per kWh. Find the cost of running the refrigerator for one day.

(a) ₹32

(b) ₹16

(c) ₹8

(d) ₹4

Answer(b) ₹16

(iv) Calculate the energy transformed by a 5 A current flowing through a resistor of 2Ω for 30 minutes.

(a) 90 kJ

(b) 80 kJ

(c) 60 kJ

(d) 40 kJ

Answer(a) 90 kJ

Class- X Session- 2022-23
Science
SAMPLE TEST PAPER-4

Time Allowed: 3 Hrs. **Maximum Marks: 80**

General Instructions:

1. This Question Paper has 5 Sections A-E.
2. Section **A** has 20 MCQs carrying 1 mark each
3. Section **B** has 5 questions carrying 02 marks each.
4. Section **C** has 6 questions carrying 03 marks each.
5. Section **D** has 4 questions carrying 05 marks each.
6. Section **E** has 3 case-based integrated units of assessment (04 marks each) with subparts of the values of 1, 1, and 2 marks each respectively.
7. All Questions are compulsory. However, an internal choice in 2 Qs of 5 marks, 2 Qs of 3 marks, and 2 Questions of 2 marks has been provided. An internal choice has been provided in the 2marks questions of Section E
8. Draw neat figures wherever required. Take π =22/7 wherever required if not stated

Section A

Section A consists of 20 questions of 1 mark each

Question 1

Iron sulphate crystals on heating show the evolution of gas which:

(a) Turns lime water milky
(b) Makes a burning matchstick burn more brightly
(c) Burns with a pop sound
(d) Causes choking and suffocation.

Answer. (d)

Question 2

Solid calcium oxide reacts vigorously with water to form calcium hydroxide accompanied by the liberation of heat. This process is called slaking of lime. Calcium hydroxide dissolves in water to form its solution called lime water. Which among the following is (are) true about slaking of lime and the solution formed?

(a) The pH of the resulting solution will be more than seven
(b) It is an endothermic reaction
(c) It is an exothermic reaction
(d) The pH of the resulting solution will be less than seven

(a) (i) and (ii)
(b) (ii) and (iii)
(c) (i) and (iv)
(d) (iii) and (iv)

Answer. (b)

Question 3

Sodium carbonate is a basic salt because it is a salt of:

(a) Strong acid and strong base.

(b) Weak acid and weak base.

(c) Strong acid and weak base.

(d) Weak acid and strong base.

Answer. (B)

Question 4

A student was provided with four samples of solutions as shown in figures (i), (ii), (iii), and (iv). He determined the pH value of each solution by using ph paper. The correct sequence of the colour change of ph paper observed by the student will be:

(a) Indigo light red, green red

(b) Red indigo green light red

(c) Indigo, red, green yellow

(d) Green, red, yellow indigo

Answer. A

Question 5

Four test tubes marked i, ii, iii and iv was taken. 20ml of $Al_2(So_4)_3$ a solution of water was poured into each of the test tubes. A piece of zinc metal was placed in test tube i, an iron nail was put in test tube ii, copper turnings were put in test tube iii and a clean aluminium strip was placed in test tube iv. No change was observed in any of the test tubes. The correct inference drawn is:

(a) Copper is more reactive than aluminium

(b) Zinc is more reactive than aluminium

(c) Zinc is more reactive than copper

(d) Zinc, iron, and copper are less reactive than aluminium.

Answer. (d)

Question 6

Two beakers a and b contain iron (ii) sulphate solution. In breaker a, a small piece of copper and in beaker b a small piece of zinc is placed it is found that after some time a grey deposit forms on zinc but not on copper. From these observations, it can be concluded that:

(a) Zinc is the most active metal followed by iron and then copper.

(b) Zinc is the most active metal followed by copped and then iron.

(c) Iron is the most active metal followed by in and then copper.

(d) Iron is the most active metal followed by copper and then zinc.

Answer. (a)

Question 7

A student takes about 4 ml of distilled water in four test tubes marked p, q, r and s. He then dissolves in each test tube an equal amount of one salt in one test tube, namely sodium sulphte in p, potassium sulphate in q, calcium sulphate in r and magnesium sulphate in s. After that he adds an equal amount of soap solution in cach test tube. On shaking each of these test tubes well, he observes a good amount of lather (foam) in the test tubes marked:

(a) P and q

(b) Q and r

(c) P. Q and S

(d) P, r and s

Answer. (a)

Question 8

Alveoli are located at the end of

(a) Bronchi

(b) Heart

(c) Lungs

(d) Bronchioles

Answer. (a)

Question 9

The xylem in plants is responsible for

(a) Transport of water

(b) Transport of food

(c) Transport of amino acids

(d) Transport of oxygen

Answer. (a)

Question 10

The main function of the ureters is to

(a) Control the pressure of urine in urinary bladder

(b) Take urine from kidneys to urinary bladder

(c) Filter blood and remove it to urine

(d) Connect the parts of excretory system

Answer. (b)

Question 11

The kidneys in human beings are a part of the system for

(a) Nutrition

(b) Respiration

(c) Excretion

(d) Transportation

Answer. (c)

Question 12

The blood cells responsible for clotting of blood are

(a) Erythrocytes

(b) Blood platelets

(c) White blood corpuscles

(d) Red blood cell

Answer. ( )

Question 13

When white light passes through a prism, the colour that undergoes maximum deviation is

(a) Red

(b) Yellow

(c) Violet

(d) Green

Answer(c) Violet

Question 14

Frequency (v) and wavelength (λ) of light are related as

(a) $c = v\lambda$

(b) $\lambda = cv$

(c) $v = c\lambda$

(d) $\lambda = \frac{v}{c}$

where c is the velocity of light.

Answer(a) $c = v\lambda$

Question 15

In the fig., Fleming's right-hand rule is applied. The centre finger points along

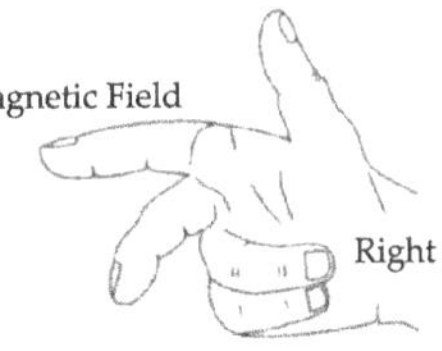

(a) Induced current

(b) Electric field

(c) Gravitational field

(d) None of these

Answer(a) Induced current

Question 16

Which of the following combinations of resistances is different from others?

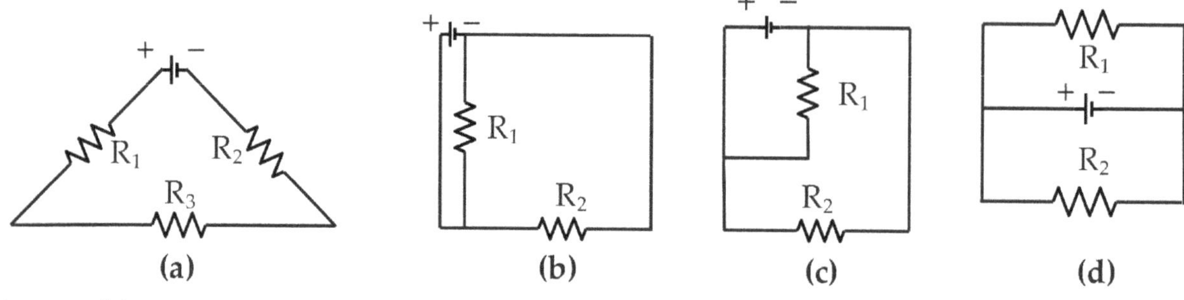

Answer(a)

Q. no 17 to 20 are Assertion - Reasoning based questions. These consist of two statements – Assertion (A) and Reason (R). Answer these questions selecting the appropriate option given below:

(a) Both A and R are true and R is the correct explanation of A

(b) Both A and R are true and R is not the correct explanation of A

(c) A is true but R is false

(d) A is False but R is true

Question 17

Assertion(A) : Assertion : Rancidity is the change in taste and odour of food materials when fats and oils present in it get oxidised by oxygen present in air.

Reason : Rancidity can be presented by refrigeration, use of antioxidants.

Answer. (b)

Question 18

Assertion(A) : Photosynthesis is considered as an endothermic reaction.

Reason (R) : Energy gets released in the process of photosynthesis.

Answer. (c)

Question 19

Assertion(A): The concentration of harmful substances is more in human being.

Reason (R) : Humans are at the apex of the food chain.

Answer. (a)

Question 20

Assertion: A convex lens is made of two different materials. A point object is placed on the principal axis. The number of images formed by the lens will be two.

Reason: The image formed by a convex lens is always virtual.

Answer(c)

Section B

Section B has 5 questions carrying 02 marks each

Q. no. 21 to 26 are very short answer questions

Question 21 **[2]**

What would be the electron dot structure of a molecule of sulphur which is made of eight atoms of sulphur?

OR

(a) What type of reaction is this?

$Cuso_4(aq) + H_2\ S(g) \rightarrow CuS(s) + H_2SO_4(aq)$

(b) What can be seen when strip of copper metal is placed in a solution of silver nitrate.

Question 22 **[2]**

What is Lymph? How is it different from blood?

Question 23 **[2]**

Differentiate between plumule and radicle.

Question 24 **[2]**

Write two differences between binary fission and multiple fission in a tabular form as observed in the cells of the organisms.

Question 25

The V-I graph for a series combination and for a parallel combination of two resistors is as shown in the figure:

Which of the two, A or B, represents the parallel combination? Give a reason for your answer.

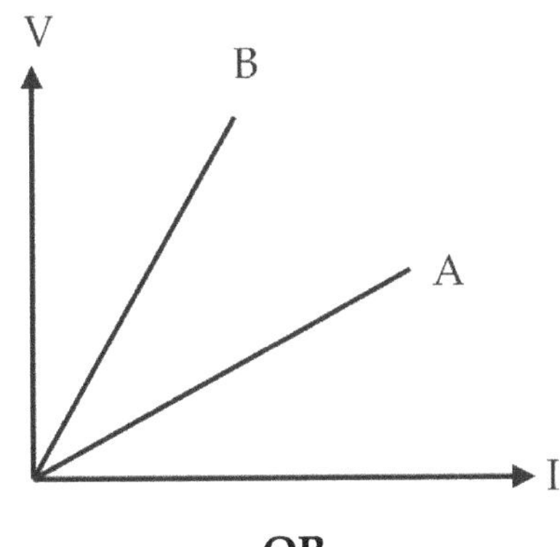

OR

How can you distinguish between a convex lens, a concave lens, and a simple plane glass plate?

Question 26

Why is it advisable to breathe through nose?

Section - C
Q.no. 27 to 33 are short answer questions

Question 27

Samples of four metals A, B, C and D were taken and added to the following solution one by one. The results obtained have been tabulated as follows:

Metal	Iron (II) sulphate	Copper (II) sulphate	Zinc sulphate	Silver nitrate
A	No reaction	Displacement		
B	Displacement		No reaction	
C	No reaction	No reaction	No reaction	Displacement
D	No reaction	No reaction	No reaction	No reaction

Use the table above to answer the following questions about metals A, B, C and D ?

(a) Which is the most reactive metal?

(b) What would you observe when B is added to a solution of copper (II) sulphate?

(c) Arrange the metals A, B, C and D in the order of decreasing reactivity.

Question 28

Write the name given to bases that are highly soluble in water? Give an example.

(a) How is tooth decay related to pH ? How can it be prevented?

(b) Why does bee sting cause pain and irritation? Rubbing of baking soda on the sting area gives relief. How?

Question 29

How are water and minerals absorbed and transported in the plants?

OR

Draw a labelled diagram of human brain. Discuss functions of cerebrum, cerebellum and medulla.

Question 30

Draw a ray diagram to illustrate how a ray of light incident obliquely on one face of a rectangular glass slab of uniform thickness emerges parallel to its original direction. Mention which pairs of angles are equal.

Question 31

Calculate the electrical energy in SI units consumed by a 100 W bulb and a 60 W fan connected in parallel in 5 minutes.

(**Answer**48,000 J)

Question 32

Draw the pattern of field lined due to a solenoid carrying electric current. Mark the North and the South poles in the diagram.

OR

What are the factors on which the strength of magnetic field produced by current-carrying solenoid depends?

Question 33

Name the hormones secreted by the following endocrine glands and specify one function of each:

(a) Thyroid

(b) Pituitary

(c) Pancreas

Section - D

Q.no. 34 to 36 are long answer questions

Question 34

Why are certain compounds called hydrocarbons? Write the general formula for homologous series of alkanes, alkenes and alkynes and draw the structure of the first member of each series. Write the name of the reaction that converts alkenes into alkanes and write the chemical equation to show the necessary conditions for the reaction to occur?

OR

Four metals a, b, c, d are in term and the following solutions. One by one observations made are tabulated below.

Metal	Iron (II) sulphate	Copper (II) sulphate	Zinc sulphate	Silver nitrate
A	No reaction	Displacement		
B	Displacement		No reaction	
C	No reaction	No reaction	No reaction	Displacement
D	No reaction	No reaction	No reaction	No reaction

(a) Which is the most active metal and why?

(b) What would be observed if B is added to solution of copper sulphate and why?

(c) Arrange A, B, C and D on increasing order of activity.

(d) Container of which metal can be used to store both zinc sulphate and silver nitrate solution.

(e) Which of the above solutions can be easily stored in a container made up of any of these metals?

Question 35

(i) Draw the structure of a neuron and label the following on it:
Nucleus, Dendrite, Cell body and Axon

(ii) Name the part of neuron

(a) Through which information is acquired

(b) Through which information travels as an electrical impulse.

OR

(i) What is phototropism and geotropism? With labelled diagrams an activity to show that light and gravity change the direction that planet part grows in.

(ii) Mention the role of each of the following plant hormones:

(a) Auxin

(b) Abscisic acid

Question 36

A small candle, 1.5cm in size is placed at 15cm in front of a concave mirror of radius of curvature 20cm. At what distance from the mirror should a screen be placed in order to obtain a sharp image? Describe the nature and size of the image. **[Answer** $v = -30\text{cm}, h_i = -3\text{cm}$**]**

OR

Sketch magnetic field lines around a current- carrying straight conductor and write any three properties.

Section - E

Q.no. 37 to 39 are case - based/data -based questions with 2 to 3 short sub - parts. Internal choice is provided in one of these sub-parts

Question 37

Manya visited her grandmother after a long while. At lunch, her grandmother surprised her with various dishes, all her favourites. However, she enjoyed the homemade pickles the most. Curious, she asked her grandmother about how it didn't get spoiled over a period?

(i) What do you think was her grandmother's reply?
(ii) Name the preceding and following homologues of this acid use.
(iii) What is antioxidant?
(iv) Name one antioxidant.

OR

In the following schematic diagram for the preparation of hydrogen gas as shown in Figure, what would happen if following changes are made?

(i) In place of zinc granules, same amount of zinc dust is taken in the test tube.
(ii) Instead of dilute sulphuric acid, dilute hydrochloric acid is taken.
(iii) In place of zinc, copper turnings are taken.
(iv) Sodium hydroxide is taken in place of dilute sulphuric acid and the tube is heated.

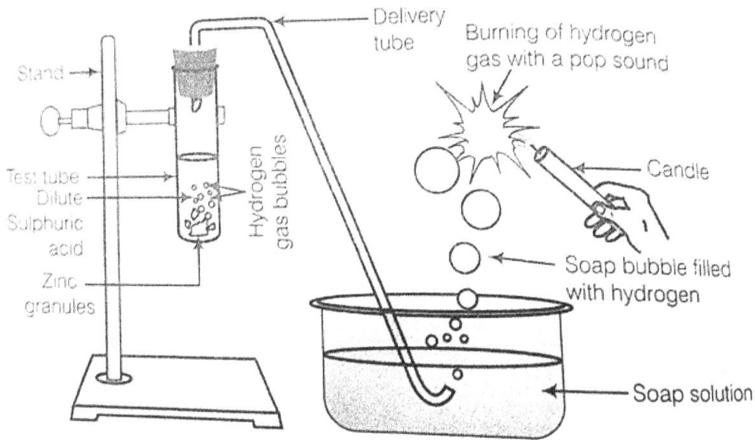

Question 38

(i) Name the part of brain which controls

(a) Voluntary action,

(b) Involuntary action.

(ii) What is the significance of the peripheral nervous system? Name the components of this nervous system and distinguish between the origin of the two.

OR

(i) What is reflex arc?

(ii) What are the components of reflex arc?

(iii) How do muscle cells move?

(iv) What is synapse?

Question 39

The relationship between potential difference and the current was first established by George Simon Ohm called Ohm's law. According to this law, the current through a metallic conductor is proportional to the potential difference applied between its ends, provided the temperature remains constant i.e., $I \propto V$ or $V = IR$; where R is constant for the conductor and it is called resistance of the conductor. Although Ohm's law has been found valid over a large class of materials, there do exist materials and devices used in electric circuits where the proportionality of V and I does not hold.

(i) If both the potential difference and the resistance in a circuit are doubled, then

(a) Current remains same

(b) Current is doubled

(c) Current is halved

(d) Current is quadrupled

Answer(a) Current remains same

(ii) For a conductor, the graph between V and l is there. Which one is correct?

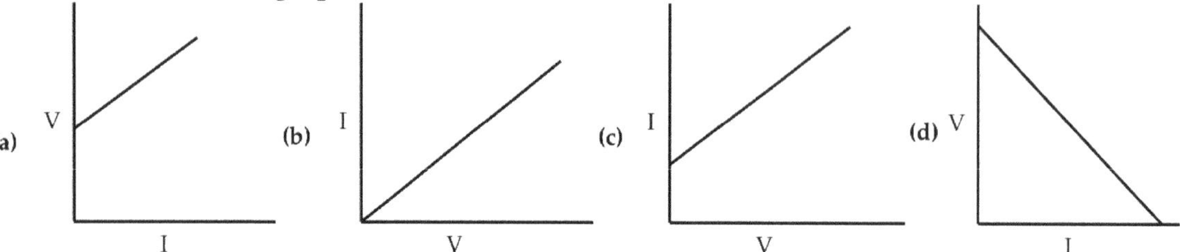

Answer(b)

(iii) The slope of V – I graph (V on x-axis and I on y-axis) gives
(a) Resistance
(b) Reciprocal of resistance
(c) Charge
(d) Reciprocal of charge.
Answer(b) Reciprocal of resistance

(iv) When a battery of 9 V is connected across a conductor and the current flows are 0.1 A, the resistance is
(a) 9Ω
(b) 0.9Ω
(c) 90Ω
(d) 900Ω
Answer(c) 90Ω

(v) By increasing the voltage across a conductor, the
(a) Current will decrease
(b) Resistance will increase
(c) Current will increase
(d) Resistance will decrease.
Answer(c) Current will increase

OR

An electric motor is a rotating device that converts electrical energy into mechanical energy. Electric motor is used as an important component in electric fans, refrigerators, mixers, washing machines, computers, MP3 players, etc.

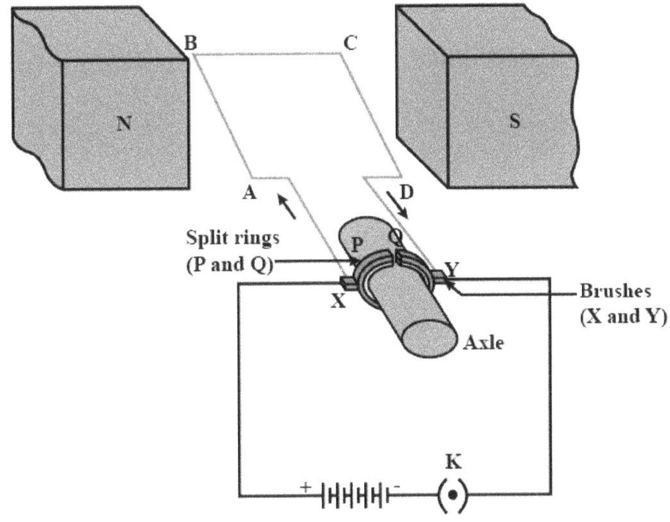

A simple electric motor

An electric motor consists of a rectangular coil ABCD of insulated copper wire. The coil is placed between the two poles of a magnetic field such that the arm *AB* and *CD* are perpendicular to the direction of the magnetic field. The ends of the coil are connected to the two halves *P* and *Q* of a split ring. The inner sides of these halves are insulated and attached to an axle. The external conducting edges of *P* and *Q* touch two conducting stationary brushes *X* and *Y*, respectively, as shown in the figure.

Commercial motors use an electromagnet in place of a permanent magnet, a large number of turns of conducting wire in the current carrying coil and a soft iron core on which the coil is wound.

(i) Choose incorrect statement from the following regarding split rings.

(a) Split rings are used to reverse the direction of current in coil.

(b) Split rings are also known as commutator.

(c) Split ring is a discontinuous or a broken ring.

(d) Both (a) and (b)

Answer(d) Both (a) and (b)

(ii) Which of the following has no effect on the size of the turning effect on the coil of an electric motor?

(a) The amount of the current in the coil.

(b) The direction of the current in the coil.

(c) The number of turns in the coil.

(d) The strength of the magnetic field.

Answer(b) The direction of the current in the coil.

(iii) When current is switched ON, an electric fan converts

(a) Mechanical energy to chemical energy

(b) Electrical energy to mechanical energy

(c) Chemical energy to mechanical energy

(d) Mechanical energy to electrical energy.

Answer(b) Electrical energy to mechanical energy

(iv) In an electric motor, device that makes contact with the rotating rings and through them to supply current to coil is

(a) Axle

(b) Brushes

(c) Coil

(d) Split rings.

Answer(d) Split rings.

(v) In an electric motor, the direction of current in the coil changes once in each

(a) Two rotations

(b) One rotation

(c) Half rotation

(d) One-fourth rotation.

Answer(c) Half rotation

Class- X Session- 2022-23

Science

SAMPLE TEST PAPER-5

Time Allowed: 3 Hrs. **Maximum Marks: 80**

General Instructions:

1. This Question Paper has 5 Sections A-E.
2. Section **A** has 20 MCQs carrying 1 mark each
3. Section **B** has 5 questions carrying 02 marks each.
4. Section **C** has 6 questions carrying 03 marks each.
5. Section **D** has 4 questions carrying 05 marks each.
6. Section **E** has 3 case-based integrated units of assessment (04 marks each) with subparts of the values of 1, 1, and 2 marks each respectively.
7. All Questions are compulsory. However, an internal choice in 2 Qs of 5 marks, 2 Qs of 3 marks, and 2 Questions of 2 marks has been provided. An internal choice has been provided in the 2marks questions of Section E
8. Draw neat figures wherever required. Take π =22/7 wherever required if not stated

Section A

Section A consists of 20 questions of 1 mark each

Question 1

Which of the following is not a physical change

(a) Boiling of water to give water vapor

(b) Melting of ice to give water

(c) Dissolution of salt in water

(d) Combustion of Liquefied Petroleum Gas (LPG).

Answer. (d)

Question 2

Solid calcium oxide reacts vigorously with water to form calcium hydroxide accompanied by the liberation of heat. This process is called slaking of lime. Calcium hydroxide dissolves in water to form its solution called lime water. Which among the following is (are) true about slaking of lime and the solution formed?

(a) It is an endothermic reaction

(b) It is an exothermic reaction

(c) The pH of the resulting solution will be more than seven

(d) The pH of the resulting solution will be less than seven

(a) i. and ii.

(b) ii. and iii.

(c) i. and iv.

(d) iii. and iv.

Answer. (b)

Question 3

Two test tubes containing 2 mL. of dilute HCl are taken. Zinc granules are added to test tube (A) and solid sodium carbonate is added to test tube (B) as shown.

The correct observation would be:

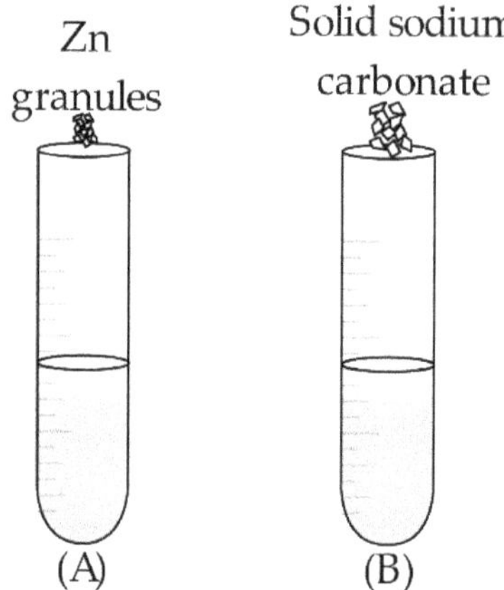

(a) Show reaction in (A) and rapid reaction in (B).

(b) Rapid reaction in (A) but a slow reaction in (B).

(c) Rapid reaction in both test tubes.

(d) No reaction in any of the tubes.

Answer. (c)

Question 4

The reaction between X and Y forms compound Z. X loses electron and Y gains electron. Which of the following properties is not shown by Z?

(a) Has a high melting point.

(b) Has a low melting point.

(c) Conducts electricity in a molten state.

(d) Occurs as a solid.

Answer. (b)

Question 5

Generally, Non-metals are not lustrous. The nonmetal having lustre is :

(a) Iodine

(b) Bromine

(c) Chlorine

(d) Graphite

Answer(a) Iodine

Question 6

On adding acetic acid to sodium hydrogen carbonate in a test tube, a student observes

(a) No reaction

(b) A colourless gas with a pungent smell.

(c) Bubbles of a colourless and odourless

(d) A strong smell of vinegar

Answer. (c)

Question 7

The correct structural formula of butanoic acid is

```
        H   H   H   O
        |   |   |   ||
(a) H — C — C = C — C — OH
        |
        H
```

```
        H   H   H   H   O
        |   |   |   |   ||
(b) H — C — C — C — C — C — OH
        |   |   |   |   |
        H   H   H   H   H
```

```
        H   H   H   H
        |   |   |   |
(c) H — C — C — C — C — OH
        |   |   |   |
        H   H   H   H
```

```
        H   H   H   O
        |   |   |   ||
(d) H — C — C — C — C — OH
        |   |   |
        H   H   H
```

Answer. (b)

Question 8

Pseudopodia are

(a) Small hair-like structures present in unicellular organisms.

(b) False feet developed in some unicellular organisms.

(c) Long, tube-like structures coming out of the mouth.

(d) Suckers which are attached to the walls of the intestines

Answer. (b)

Question 9

Which of the following statements about autotrophs is incorrect?

(a) They synthesize carbohydrates from carbon dioxide and water in the presence of sunlight and chlorophyll

(b) They store carbohydrates in the form of starch

(c) They convert carbon dioxide and water into carbohydrates in the absence of sunlight

(d) They constitute the first trophic level in food chains

Answer. (c)

Question 10

In which of the following groups of organisms, food material is broken down outside the body and absorbed?

(a) Mushrooms, green plants, Amoeba

(b) Yeast, mushroom, bread mould

(c) Mazaedium, Amoeba, Cusseta

(d) Cusseta, lice, tapeworm

Answer. (b)

Question 11

Select the correct statement

(a) Heterotrophs do not synthesize their own food

(b) Heterotrophs utilize solar energy for photosynthesis

(c) Heterotrophs synthesize their food

(d) Heterotrophs are capable of converting carbon dioxide and water into carbohydrates

Answer. (a)

Question 12

Which part of the alimentary canal receives bile from the liver?

(a) Stomach

(b) Small intestine

(c) Large intestine

(d) Oesophagus

Answer. (b)

Question 13

When a current I ampere flows through a conductor of resistance R for time t seconds, the electrical energy spent is:

(a) IR^2t

(b) IRt

(c) I^2Rt

(d) $\frac{I^2R^2}{t}$

Answer(c) I^2Rt

Question 14

Magnetic lines of force

(a) Cannot intersect at all.

(b) Intersect within the magnet.

(c) Intersect only at south and north poles.

(d) Intersect at neutral points only.

Answer(a) Cannot intersect at all.

Question 15

The image formed by a concave mirror is real, inverted and of the same size as that of the object. The position of the object is

(a) At C

(b) At F

(c) Between C and F

(d) Beyond C

Answer(a)

Question 16

The process of splitting white light into its seven constituent colours is called

(a) Reflection

(b) Refraction

(c) Scattering

(d) Dispersion

Answer(d) Dispersion

Q. no 17 to 20 are Assertion - Reasoning based questions. These consist of two statements – Assertion (A) and Reason (R). Answer these questions by selecting the appropriate option given below:

(a) Both A and R are true, and R is the correct explanation of A

(b) Both A and R are true, and R is not the correct explanation of A

(c) A is true but R is false

(d) A is False but R is true

Question 17

Assertion(A): Concentration of ore means reduction of oxide ore to metal.

Reason (R): Metals of low reactivity can be reduced by heating above.

Answer. (d)

Question 18

Assertion(A): The concentration of harmful substances is more in human beings.

Reason (R): Humans are at the apex of the food chain

Answer. (a)

Question 19

Assertion(A): Green plants of the ecosystem are the transducers.

Reason (R): Producers trap the radiant energy of the sun and change it into chemical energy

Answer. (a)

Question 20

Assertion: In diffused reflection, a parallel beam of incident light is reflected in a different direction.

Reason: The diffused reflection of light is due to the failure of the laws of reflection.
Answer (c)

Section B

Section B has 5 questions carrying 02 marks each

Q. no. 21 to 26 are very short answer questions

Question 21

An aldehyde as well as a ketone can be represented by the same molecular formula say C_3H_6O. Write their structures and name them. State the relation between the two in the languages of science.

OR

What are natural indicators? Give two examples.

Question 22

(i) Which is the universal source of energy in all cells?
(ii) What would be the consequences of a deficiency of haemoglobin in our bodies?

Question 23

How are fats digested in our bodies? Where does this process take place?

Question 24

List two factors that decide the direction of diffusion of oxygen and carbon dioxide.

Question 25

(i) State Ohm's Law.
(ii) Diagrammatically illustrate how you would connect a key, a battery, a voltmeter, an ammeter, an unknown resistance R, and a rheostat so that it can be used to verify the above law.

OR

An object is placed in front of a lens between its optical Centre and the focus and forms a virtual, erect and diminished image.
(i) Name the lens which formed this image.
(ii) Draw a ray diagram to show the formation of the image with the above stated characteristics.

Question 26

Define transpiration. How does transpiration help in the upward movement of water from roots to leaves?

Section - C

Q.no. 27 to 33 are short answer questions

Question 27

During the extraction of metals, electrolytic refining is used to obtain pure metals. (a) Which material will be used as an anode and cathode for refining silver metal by this process? (b) Suggest a suitable electrolyte also. (c) In this electrolytic cell, where do we get pure silver after passing an electric current?

Question 28

A silver article generally turns black when kept in the open for a few days. The article when rubbed with toothpaste again starts shining.

(i) Why do silver articles turn black when kept in the open for a few days? Name the phenomenon involved.

(ii) Name the black substance formed and give its chemical formula.

Question 29

What is excretion? Name some parts of our body involved in this life process.

OR

What are the important features of all respiratory structures in animals?

Question 30

Calculate the speed and wavelength of light

(i) In glass

(ii) In air,

When light waves of frequency 6×10^{14} Hz travel from air to glass of n = 1.5.

Answer((i) 2×10^8 ms^{-1}, 3.3×10^{-7} m (ii) 3×10^8 ms^{-1}, 5×10^{-7} m **)**

Question 31

Calculate the quantity of heat that will be produced in a coil of resistance 75Ω if a current of 2A is passed through it for 2 minutes. (**Answer**8571.9 J)

Question 32

(i) A straight wire conductor passes vertically through a piece of cardboard sprinkled with iron filings. Copy the diagram and show the setting of iron filings when a current is passed through the wire in the upward direction and the cardboard is tapped gently. Draw arrows to represent the direction of the magnetic field lines.

(ii) Name the law which helped you to find the direction of the magnetic field lines.

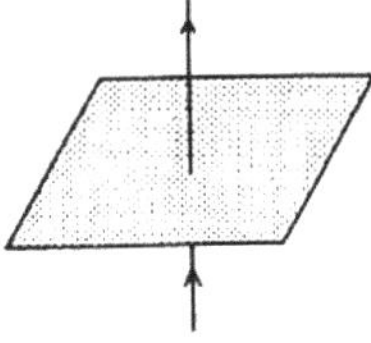

OR

On what factors the magnitude of the force on a current-carrying conductor placed in a magnetic field depends?

Answer ((i) on B, ($F \propto B$); (ii) on I($F \propto I$); (iii)l($F \propto l$))

Question 33

Give a schematic representation of different pathways of the breakdown of a glucose molecule.

Section - D

Q.no. 34 to 36 are long answer questions

Question 34

(i) Define corrosion.

(ii) What is corrosion of iron called?

(iii) How will you recognize the corrosion of silver?

(iv) Why corrosion of iron is a serious problem?

(v) How can we prevent corrosion?

OR

(i) Complete the following equations:

(a) $CH_4 \underset{O_2}{\rightarrow}$

(b) $CH_3COOH + C_2H_5OH \xrightarrow{acid}$

(c) $CH_3CH_2OH \xrightarrow[443\text{ K}]{\text{conc. } H_2SO_4}$

(ii) Write the IUPAC name of the next homologous of CH_3OH and $CH_2 = CH_2$.

Question 35

Name the chemical in a small tube hanging in a conical flask. Why is it being used?

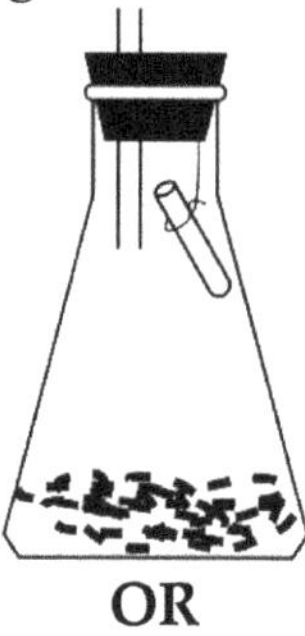

OR

(i) **(a)** Write the full form of D.N.A.

(b) State the role of D.N.A. in the cell nucleus.

(c) What will be the after-effect if the information of D.N.A. is charged?

(ii) Explain the importance of D.N.A. copying in reproduction.

Question 36

Draw the lines of force of the magnetic field through and around

(a) Single loop of wire carrying comes.

(b) A solenoid

OR

Draw the pattern of magnetic field lines of a current- carrying solenoid. When does the pattern of field lies inside the solenoid indicate? Write any three properties of magnetic field of current-carrying solenoid.

Section - E

Q.no. 37 to 39 are case-based/data-based questions with 2 to 3 short sub-parts. Internal choice is provided in one of these sub-parts

Question 37

On heating, a blue-coloured powder of copper (II) nitrate in a boiling tube, copper oxide (black), oxygen gas, and a brown gas X is formed.

(i) Write a balanced chemical equation of the reaction.

(ii) Identify the brown gas X evolved.

(iii) Identify the type of reaction.

(iv) What could be the pH range of the aqueous solution of the gas X ?

OR

(i) Give an example of a metal that:

(a) Is a liquid at room temperature.

(b) Is kept immersed in kerosene for storage.

(c) Is both malleable and ductile.

(d) Is the best conductor of heat.

(ii) Name the process of obtaining a pure metal from an impure metal through electrolysis. Suppose you have to refine copper using this process, then explain with the help of a labeled diagram the process of purification, mentioning, in brief, the materials used as (i) anode, (ii) cathode, and (iii) electrolyte.

Question 38

(i) Give two examples of each of the following:

(a) Plants having unisexual flowers

(b) Agents of pollination

(c) Physical changes during puberty are common in both boys and girls.

(ii) Why is the temperature of the scrotal sac has2°c less than the body temperature?

OR

(i) State the changes that take place in the uterus when

(a) The implantation of the embryo has occurred

(b) The female gamete/egg is not fertilized

(ii) Give reasons as to why the following processes are different from each other:

(a) Fission in Amoeba and Plasmodium

(b) Binary fission and Fragmentation

Question 39

The lenses form different types of images when objects are placed at different locations. When a ray is incident parallel to the principal axis, then after refraction, it passes through the focus or appears to come from the focus. When a ray goes through the optical center of the lens, it passes without any deviation.

If the object is placed between the focus and optical center of the convex lens, an erect and magnified image is formed. As the object is brought closer to the convex lens from infinity to focus, the image moves away from the convex lens from focus to infinity. Also, the size of the image goes on increasing and the image is always real and inverted.

A concave lens always gives a virtual, erect, and diminished image irrespective of the position of the object.

(i) The location of an image formed by a convex lens when the object is placed at infinity is

(a) At focus

(b) At 2F

(c) At optical center

(d) Between F and 2F

Answer(a) At focus

(ii) When the object is placed at the focus of a concave lens, the image formed is

(a) Real and smaller

(b) Virtual and inverted

(c) Virtual and smaller

(d) Real and erect

Answer(c) Virtual and smaller

(iii) The size of the image formed by a convex lens when the object is placed at the focus of the convex lens is

(a) Small

(b) Point in size

(c) Highly magnified

(d) Same as that of object

Answer(c) Highly magnified

(iv) When the object is placed at 2F in front of a convex lens, the location of the image is

(a) At F

(b) At 2 F on the other side

(c) At infinity

(d) Between F and the optical center

Answer(b) At 2 F on the other side

(v) At which location of an object in front of a concave lens, the image between focus and optical center is formed

(a) Anywhere between center and infinity

(b) At F

(c) At 2F

(d) Infinity

Answer(a) Anywhere between center and infinity

OR

Two or more resistances are connected in series or parallel or both, depending upon whether we want to increase or decrease the circuit resistance.

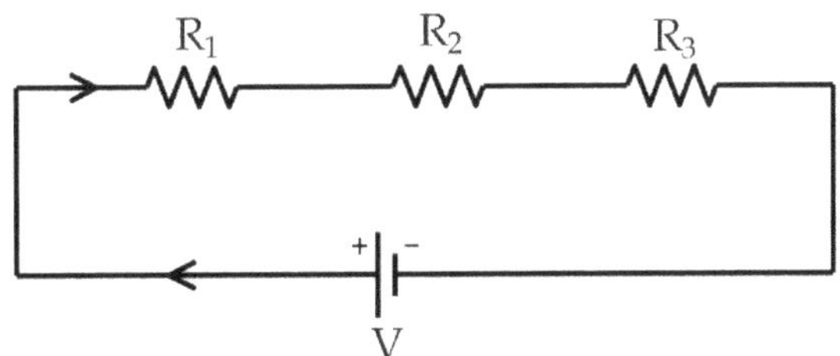

The two or more resistances are said to be connected in series if the current flowing through each resistor is the same. The equivalent resistance in the series combination is given by

$$R_S = R_1 + R_2 + R_3$$

(i) When three resistors are connected in series with a battery of voltage V and the voltage drop across resistors is V_1, V_2 and V_3, which of the relation is correct?

(a) $V = V_1 = V_2 = V_3$

(b) $V = V_1 + V_2 + V_3$

(c) $V_1 + V_2 + V_3 = 3\ V$

(d) $V > V_1 + V_2 + V_3$

Answer(b) $V = V_1 + V_2 + V_3$

(ii) When the three resistors each of resistance Rohm, are connected in series, the equivalent resistance is

(a) $\frac{R}{2}$

(b) $> R$

(c) $< R/2$

(d) $< R$

Answer(b) $> R$

(iii) There is a wire of length 20 cm and having resistance 20Ω cut into 4 equal pieces and then joined in series. The equivalent resistance is

(a) 20Ω

(b) 4Ω

(c) 5Ω

(d) 10Ω

Answer(a) 20Ω

(iv) In the following circuit, find the equivalent resistance between A and B is (R = 2Ω)

(a) 10Ω

(b) 5Ω

(c) 2Ω
(d) 4Ω

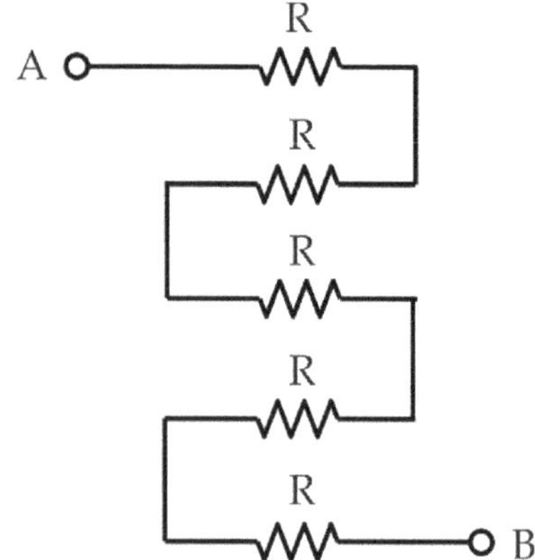

Answer(a) 10Ω

(v) In the given circuit. the current in each resistor is

(a) 3 A
(b) 6 A
(c) 9 A
(d) 18 A

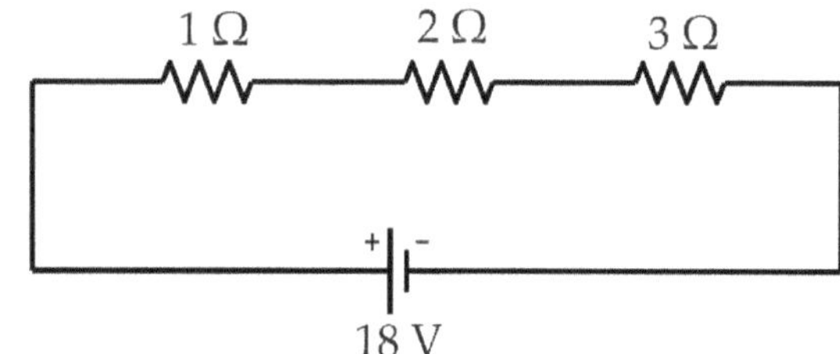

Answer(a) 3A

PREVIOUS YEAR PAPER

Class- X Session- 2022-23

Science

PREVIOUS YEAR PAPER- 2019

Time Allowed: 3 Hrs. **Maximum Marks: 80**

General Instructions:

1. This Question Paper has 5 Sections A-E.
2. Section **A** has 20 MCQs carrying 1 mark each
3. Section **B** has 5 questions carrying 02 marks each.
4. Section **C** has 6 questions carrying 03 marks each.
5. Section **D** has 4 questions carrying 05 marks each.
6. Section **E** has 3 case-based integrated units of assessment (04 marks each) with subparts of the values of 1, 1, and 2 marks each respectively.
7. All Questions are compulsory. However, an internal choice in 2 Qs of 5 marks, 2 Qs of 3 marks, and 2 Questions of 2 marks has been provided. An internal choice has been provided in the 2marks questions of Section E
8. Draw neat figures wherever required. Take π =22/7 wherever required if not stated

Section A

Section A consists of 20 questions of 1 mark each

Question 1.

State Ohm's law.

Answer

According to Ohm's law, the electric current flowing through a metallic wire is directly proportional to the potential difference V, across its ends provided its temperature remains the same.

In other words, $V \propto I$

Or $V = RI$

Where, R is a constant of proportionality called resistance of the resistor, it tends to resist the flow of charge through a conducting wire. Its SI unit is Ohm (Ω).

Question 2.

Name any two nutrients that the spent slurry has in the biogas plant.

Answer

Two nutrients that the spent slurry has in the biogas plants are nitrogen and phosphorous.

Question 3.

Draw a labelled ray diagram to show the path of the reflected ray corresponding to an incident ray of light parallel to the principal axis of a convex mirror. Mark the angle of incidence and angle of reflection on it.

Answer

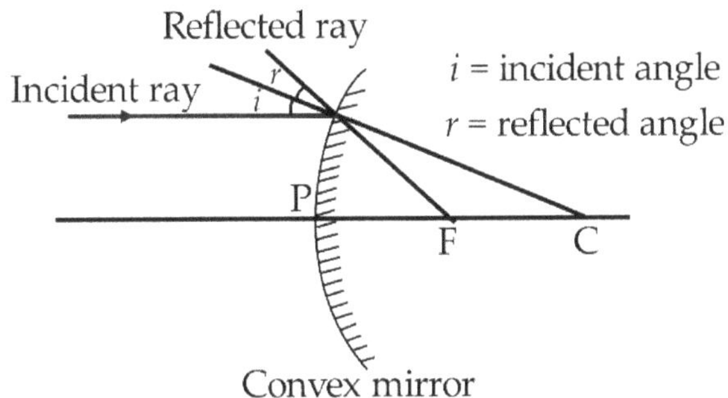

Question 4.

A compass needle is placed near a current carrying straight conductor. State your observation for the following cases and give reasons for the same in each case:

(a) Magnitude of electric current is increased.

(b) The compass needle is displaced away from the conductor.

Answer

(a) Deflection of compass needle increases- Magnetic field strength is directly proportional to the amount of current.

(b) Deflection of compass needle decreases-Magnetic field strength is inversely proportional to the distance from the wire.

Question 5.

Out of HCl and CH_3COOH, which one is a weak acid and why? Explain with the help of an example.

OR

"Sodium hydrogen carbonate is a basic salt." Justify this statement. How is it converted into washing soda?

Answer

HCl (hydrochloric acid) when comes in contact with water, liberates more H^+ ions into the solution when compared to the number of hydrogen ions liberated by the same amount of CH_3COOH (acetic acid) into the solution. Thus acetic acid (CH_3COOH) is a weaker acid.

Example: When we make two separate electrolytic cells, one with HCl (aq) as an electrolyte and the other cell with CH_3COOH (aq) as an electrolyte, in both the cells when we connect a bulb to check the voltage produced in the respective cells, we find that the bulb connected to the cell with HCl glows brighter compared to the other cell. From this, it is proved that HCl is a stronger acid because when there are more ions in the solution there will be more conduction of electricity and thus the bulb would glow brighter.

OR

When a strong base reacts with a weak acid it results in a basic salt and water.

$$NaOH + H_2CO_3 \rightarrow \underset{\text{basic salt}}{NaHCO_3} + H_2O$$

Thus we can justify that sodium hydrogen carbonate ($NaHCO_3$) is a basic salt.

Washing soda can be formed by heating of sodium hydrogen carbonate followed by recrystallisation.

$2NaHCO_3 \xrightarrow{\Delta} Na_2CO_3 + H_2O + CO_2$

Recrystallisation

$Na_2CO_3 + 10H_2O \rightarrow Na_2CO_3.10H_2O$

Question 6.

Define genetics. Why is decrease in the number of surviving tigers cause of concern from the point of view of genetics? Explain briefly.

Answer

Genetics is a branch of biology which deals with the study of genes, genetic variation and heredity in organisms.

From the point of genetics, a small population of an organism means, limited scope of variation which in turn would result in reduced traits and diversity. A decrease in the number of surviving tigers is a cause of concern because it can lead to the loss of genetic variability which can negatively impact the fitness of tiger populations. If the entire population of tigers get extinct due to any reason, it would result in the loss of their genes. This would have a direct effect on the ecological balance and effect the ecosystem adversely.

Question 7.

A concave mirror has a focal length of 20 cm. At what distance from the mirror should a 4 cm tall object be placed so that it forms an image at distance of 30 cm from the mirror ? Also calculate the size of the image formed.

OR

A real image 2/3rd of the size of an object is formed by a convex lens when the object is at a distance of 12 cm from it. Find the focal length of the lens

Answer

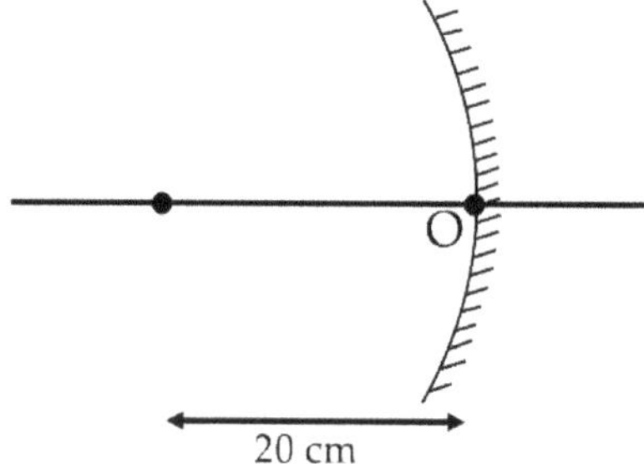

As per sign convention f = −20 cm v = −30 cm

Now mirror formula

$$\frac{1}{v} + \frac{1}{u} = \frac{1}{f}$$

$$\frac{1}{(-30)} + \frac{1}{u} = \frac{1}{(-20)} \Rightarrow \frac{1}{u} = \frac{1}{30} - \frac{1}{20} = \frac{2-3}{60} = \frac{-1}{60}$$

$$u = -60 \text{ cm}$$

So object distance = −60 cm i.e. 60 cm in front of mirror.

Now magnification = m = $\frac{-v}{u}$

$$\text{so } m = \frac{-v}{u} = \frac{h_i}{h_0}$$

$$m = \frac{-(-30)}{(-60)} \Rightarrow -\frac{1}{2} = \frac{h_i}{h_0}$$

$$h_i = -\frac{h_0}{2} = \frac{-4}{2} = -2 \text{ cm}$$

So, height of image = 2 cm and image is real & inverted

OR

Magnification = $-\frac{2}{3}$ (Negative since image is real and inverted)

$$m = -\frac{2}{3} = \frac{h_i}{h_0}$$

$$u = -12 \text{ cm}$$

$$\text{now } m = \frac{v}{u} \Rightarrow -\frac{2}{3} = \frac{v}{(-12)}$$

$$v = -\frac{2}{3} \times (-12) = 8 \text{ cm}$$

So, Real image is formed 8 cm behind the mirror.

Now lens formula

$$\frac{1}{v} - \frac{1}{u} = \frac{1}{f}$$

$$\frac{1}{8} - \frac{1}{(-12)} = \frac{1}{f}$$

$$f = \frac{24}{5} = 4.8 \text{ cm}$$

Hence, focal length is 4.8 cm

Question 8.

2 g of ferrous sulphate crystals are heated in a dry boiling tube.

(i) List any two observations.

(ii) Name the type of chemical reaction taking place.

(iii) Write balanced chemical equation for the reaction and name the products formed.

OR

You might have noted that when copper powder is heated in a china dish, the reddish brown surface of copper powder becomes coated with a black substance.

(i) Why has this black substance formed ?

(ii) What is this black substance ?

(iii) Write the chemical equation of the reaction that takes place.

(iv) How can the black coating on the surface be turned reddish brown?

Answer

(i) On heating 2 g ferrous sulphate following observations are obtained:

(a) On heating, the colour changes from light green to white.

(b) On further heating, the white substance changes to dark brown solid.

(c) The gas emitted has the characteristic odour of burning sulphur.

(ii) Decomposition reaction is taking place on heating ferrous sulphate.

(iii) $2FeSO_4 \cdot 7H_2O(s) \xrightarrow{\text{Heating}} Fe_2O_3(s) + SO_2(g) + SO_3(g) + 14H_2O(g)$

(a) The black colour is due to the oxidation of Cu.

(b) When the copper powder is heated, it combines with oxygen in the air to form copper oxide which is black in colour.

(c) $2\,Cu + O2 \rightarrow 2CuO$

(iv) We can use the wire strippers to remove this black coating of copper oxide.

Question 9.

What is a food chain? Why is the flow of energy in an ecosystem unidirectional? Explain briefly.

OR

(a) Why should National Parks be allowed to remain in their pristine form?

(b) Why is reuse of materials better than recycling?

Answer

A food chain is a series of organisms where one is eaten by the next member in the series. Organisms are grouped according to their feeding habit into trophic levels. Grass (a producer) gets eaten by insects (primary consumers), which in turn get eaten by rats (secondary consumer) and finally is itself eaten by snakes (tertiary consumer). In this food chain, the organisms placed in the higher level get energy by consuming the ones at the lower level. Consumers, like insects, eat grass and thus the energy flows from grass to insects; the opposite is not possible. Hence, the flow of energy in an ecosystem in unidirectional

OR

(a) A National park is an area designated as protected by the government and is aimed at protecting the natural environment therein. It might comprise well-developed ecosystems where interactions between the components are well established. Any perturbations in such ecosystems will cause a cascade of effects given to the relationships between the biotic and abiotic components in the ecosystems. Hence, we should abstain from producing any changes in such parks.

(b) Recycling involves processes that use waste material to produce a commodity. Several things like some plastics, papers are recyclable. However, all such processes require some inputs as well as processing. Reusing increases the time for which the commodity is in usage and thus prevents the processing and inputs required for recycling. Thus, reusing can decrease the pressure on digging up for more resources for manufacturing or recycling and hence is a better approach.

Question 10.

A white powder is added while baking cakes to make it soft and spongy. Name its main ingredients. Explain the function of each ingredient. Write the chemical reaction taking place when the powder is heated during baking.

Answer

The white powder which is added while baking cakes to make it soft and spongy is called Baking soda. Its chemical formula is $NaHCO_3$. Its main ingredients are Sodium hydrogen carbonate, tartarate salt and starch.

The function of each ingredient: The following reaction takes place when heated during cooking,

$$\underset{\text{Sodium hydrogen carbonate}}{2NaHCO_3} \xrightarrow{\text{Heating}} \underset{\text{Sodium carbonate}}{Na_2CO_3} + \underset{\text{Carbon dioxide}}{CO_2} + \underset{water}{H_2O}$$

Carbon dioxide produced during the reaction causes bread or cake to rise making them soft and spongy.

The function of the tartarate salt → When the baking powder comes in contact with water the tartaric acid gets active and reacts with the sodium bicarbonate and carbon dioxide gas is evolved in this reaction which is the reason of puffiness of the cake and bread.

The function of corn starch in the baking soda is to act a filler, it absorbs any extra moisture and prevents the baking soda from acting too quickly.

Question 11.

Two circular coils P and Q are kept close to each other, of which coil P carries a current. What will you observe in the galvanometer connected across the coil Q

(a) If current in the coil P is changed?

(b) If both the coils are moved in the same direction with the same speed?

Give reasons to justify your answer in each case.

Answer

(a) When the current in coil P is changed, a current is induced in coil Q, hence the galvanometer connected across the ends of coil Q will show the deflection.

(b) If both the coils are moved in the same direction with the same speed, their relative motion is zero. It is equivalent to not moving them at all. So because of this motion, there will not be any current induced in the coil Q, hence, the galvanometer will not show any deflection.

Question 12.

(a) Write two water conducting tissues present in plants. How does water enter continuously into the root xylem?

(b) Explain why plants have low energy needs as compared to animals

Answer

(a) Xylem vessels and tracheids are the water-conducting tissues in vascular plants. Roots of most of the vascular plants first actively absorb minerals and salts from the soil, leading to endosmosis of water into the root tissue. This creates a positive and upward hydrostatic pressure into the xylem tissue of the plant. Thereafter transpirational pull creates a suction force to pull up the water column upwards to the higher regions of the plant body. Forces of cohesion between the water molecules and adhesion between the water molecules and xylem vessel walls lead to the creation of unbroken upward column of water being pulled up.

(b) Plants are primarily stationary and do not show or use muscular energy for movement and locomotion. Thus a lot of energy is saved as they cannot use muscular energy and thus have comparatively very less energy requirement compared to the animals.

Question 13.

Why does the flow of signals in a synapse from axonal end of one neuron to dendritic end of another neuron take place but not in the reverse direction? Explain.

Answer

The dendrites contain the receptors for the neurotransmitters while the axon terminals have synaptic vesicles that are filled with the neurotransmitters. So, when the impulse is generated, the synaptic vesicles fuse with the membranes of the synaptic knobs of axon terminal and the neurotransmitters are released in the synaptic cleft. These are then sensed by the receptors present on the dendrites of the post-synaptic neuron. As dendrites do not release the neurotransmitters, the impulse cannot travel from the dendrites of one neuron to the axonal end of the other neuron. It is always unidirectional, that is, from the axonal end of the pre-synaptic neuron to the dendrites of the post-synaptic neurons.

Question 14.

Mention the environmental consequences of the increasing demand for energy. List four steps you would suggest to reduce the consumption of energy

Answer

The increasing demand for energy is met by fossil fuels like coal and petroleum. There are several environmental consequences of the increased usage of these fossil fuels as below -

(i) Fossil fuels are non-renewable sources of energy and can be exhausted faster upon being increasingly used.

(ii) The burning of fossil fuels produces smoke and that causes severe environmental pollution.

(iii) The gases produced upon combustion of fossil fuels leads to the greenhouse effect, which is responsible for the change in environmental weather all across the world.

Steps that can be taken to reduce energy consumption are on the whole is all about using energy very judiciously.

1. Use of electricity and electrical appliances like air conditioners must be reduced and should be used only when necessary.
2. Public transport means should be chosen by one and all for mass transit.
3. Prevent unnecessary waste of water.
4. Solar heaters should be used in place of electrical heaters wherever possible.

Question 15.

An ore on treatment with dilute hydrochloric acid produces brisk effervescence. Name the type of ore with one example. What steps will be required to obtain metal from the enriched ore? Also write the chemical equations for the reactions involved in the process

Answer

An ore on treatment with dilute hydrochloric acid releases brisk effervescence of colourless and odourless gas. Then the ore should be carbonate ore. As only metal carbonate on treatment with dilute hydrochloric acid releases carbon dioxide gas. **Example:** Zinc Carbonate

$$ZnCO_3 + 2\,HCl \rightarrow ZnCl_2 + H_2O + CO_2$$

Steps required to obtain metal from the enriched ore:

1. Carbonate ores are converted to their metal oxides by the calcination process.
Heating of carbonate ores in the limited supply of air to convert them into oxides is known as calcination.

$$ZnCO_3 \rightarrow ZnO + CO_2$$

2. ZnO obtained is then reduced by carbon in the form of coke.

$$ZnO + C \rightarrow Zn + CO$$

Question 16.

(a) State the reason why carbon can neither form C^{4+} cations nor C^{4-} anions, but forms covalent bonds. Also state reasons to explain why covalent compounds

i. Are bad conductors of electricity.

ii. Have low melting and boiling points.

(b) Write the structural formula of benzene, C_6H_6.

OR

(a) Define the term 'isomer'.

(b) Two compounds have same molecular formula C_3H_6O. Write the name of these compounds and their structural formula.

(c) How would you bring the following conversions:

i. Ethanol to ethene

ii. Propanol to propanoic acid

Answer

(a) Carbon can neither form C^{4+} cations nor C^{4-} anions because it involves a huge amount of energy for loosing or gaining of four electrons which is not feasible. Thus it completes its octet by sharing of electrons, i.e. forming covalent bonds.

i. Covalent compounds are bad conductors of electricity because they do not contain ions.

ii. Covalent compounds are made up of electrically neutral molecules. So, the force of attraction between the molecules of a covalent compound is very weak. Only a small amount of heat energy is required to break these weak molecular forces, due to which covalent compounds have low melting points and low boiling points.

(b) The structural formula of benzene, C_6H_6 is

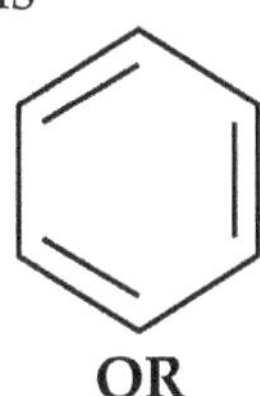

OR

(a) The organic compounds having the same molecular formula but different structures are known as isomers.

(b) Two compounds have same molecular formula C_3H_6O are

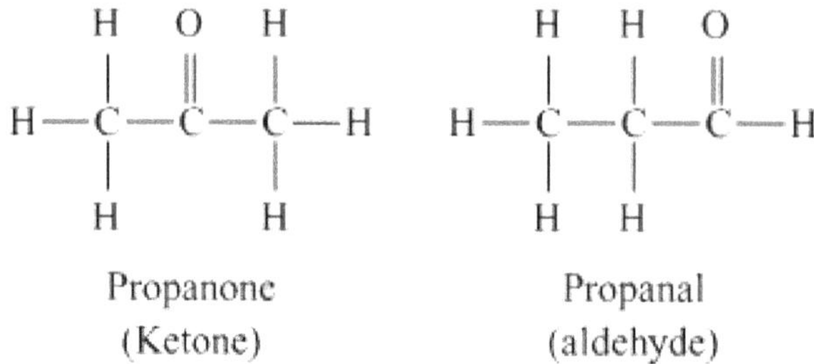

(c) i. Ethanol to ethene

$$CH_3CH_2OH \xrightarrow[\text{dehydration}]{\text{conc. } H_2SO_4;170°C} CH_2 = CH_2 + H_2O$$

ii. Propanol to propanoic acid

$$CH_3CH_2CH_2OH + 2[O] \xrightarrow{\text{alkaline } KMnO_4;\text{ heat}} CH_3CH_2COOH + H_2O$$

Question 17.

(a) A 5 cm tall object is placed perpendicular to the principal axis of a convex lens of focal length 20 cm. The distance of the object from the lens is 30 cm. Find the position, nature and size of the image formed.

(b) Draw a labelled ray diagram showing object distance, image distance and focal length in the above case.

Answer

(a) Convex lens, f = 20 cm

u = 30 cm

$$\frac{1}{v} - \frac{1}{u} = \frac{1}{f}$$

$$\frac{1}{v} = \frac{1}{f} + \frac{1}{u}$$

$$\frac{1}{v} = \frac{u+f}{uf}$$

$$v = \frac{uf}{u+f} = \frac{-30 \times 20}{-30 + 20} = 60 \text{ cm}$$

$$v = +60 \text{ cm}$$

The image will be formed at 60 cm on the other side of the lens.

Since the image distance is positive, therefore, the nature of the image is real.

Now, magnification, $m = \frac{v}{u} = \frac{60}{-30} = -2$

Since magnification is negative, therefore, the image formed will be inverted.

$$m = \frac{h_1}{h_0}$$

$$2 = \frac{h_1}{5}$$

$$h_i = 10 \text{ cm}$$

(b)

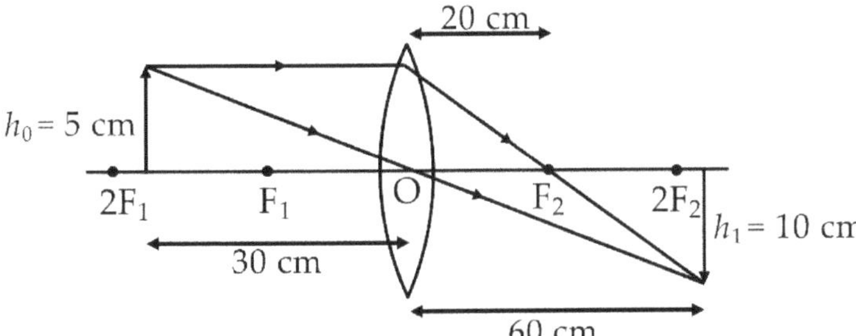

Question 18.

(i) How does metallic character of elements in Modern Periodic Table vary on moving from

(a) Left to right in a period?

(b) Top to bottom in a group?

Explain with the help of an example in each case.

(ii) If an element X is placed in group 14, what will be the nature of bond in its chloride? Write the chemical formula of the compound formed.

(iii) An element X has mass number = 35 and number of neutrons = 18. What is the atomic number of X? Write electronic configuration of X and determine its valency.

Answer

(i) **(a)** On moving from left to right in a period the metallic character of elements decreases.

This is because as we move from left to right in a period in the periodic table, the atomic size decreases as a result the electrons come closer to the nucleus and cannot be lost easily.

Example: Alkali metals and Alkaline earth metals are strong metals as they have a very high tendency to lose their valance electrons and as we move from left to right in the periodic table, the tendency to lose electrons decreases and the non-metals have a tendency to gain electrons because they have higher electronegativity than metals.

(b) On moving from top to bottom in a group the metallic character of elements increases.

This is because as we move from top to bottom in a group in the periodic table the atomic size increases as a result the electrons are far away from the nucleus and can be easily lost.

Example: Caesium has high tendency to loose electron in comparison to sodium. Thus caesium has high metallic character.

(ii) An element present in group 14 has 4 valance electrons so, to satisfy its combining capacity preferably the element will have covalent bonds in its chlorides. The chemical formula of the compound will be XCl_4.

Question 19.

Compare the power used in 2 Ω resistor in each of the following circuits:

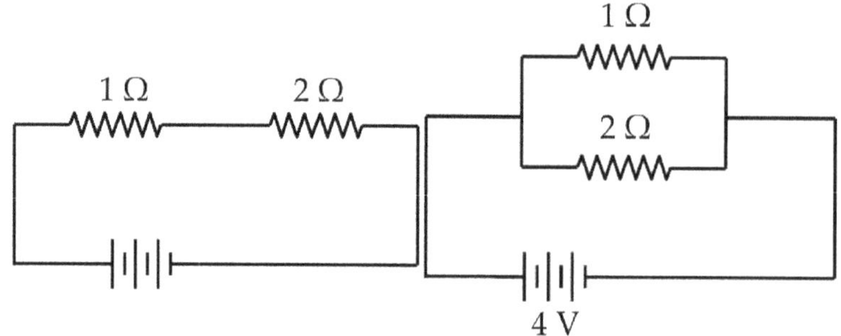

A bulb is rated 40 W; 220 V. Find the current drawn by it, when it is connected to a 220 V supply. Also find its resistance. If the given bulb is replaced by a bulb of rating 25 W; 220 V, will there be any change in the value of current and resistance? Justify your answer and determine the change.

Answer

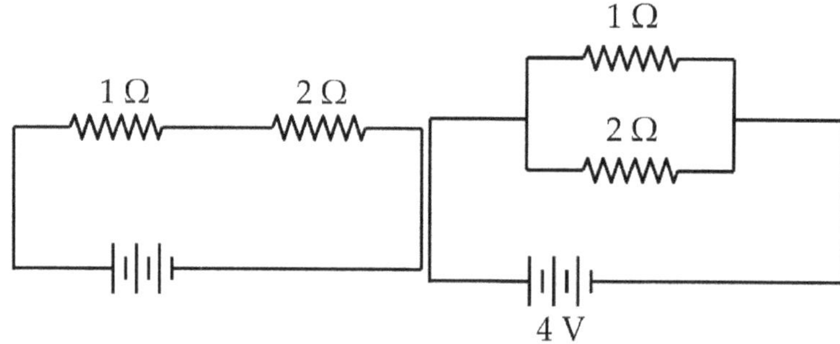

For circuit Ist.-

Total resistance $= (1 + 2) = 3\Omega$

Current $= \frac{V}{R} = \frac{6}{3} = 2\text{ A}$

Power in 2Ω Resistor $= I^2R = 4(2) = 8$Watt

For circuit IInd:-

Power in 2Ω Resistor $= \frac{V^2}{R} = \frac{16}{2} = 8$ Watt

Hence the Power consumed is the same in both cases.

OR

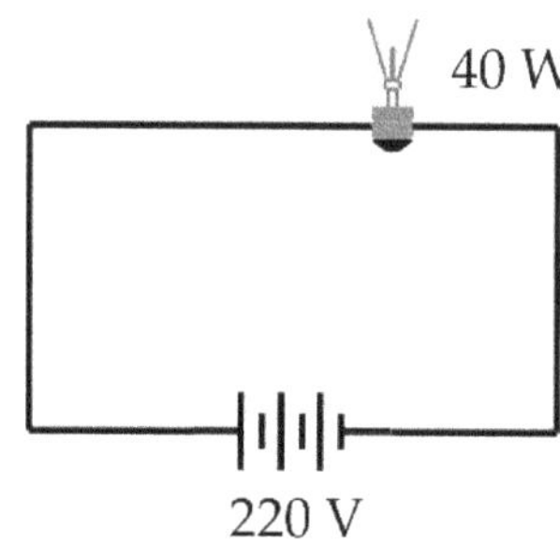

We have,

$$P = 40\text{ W} \& V = 220\text{ V}$$

$$R = \frac{V^2}{P} = \frac{(220)(220)}{40}$$

$$R = 1210\Omega$$

Current Drawn $= \frac{P}{V} = \frac{40}{220} = \frac{2}{11}\text{ A} = 0 \cdot 18\text{ A}$

Replaced Condition: -

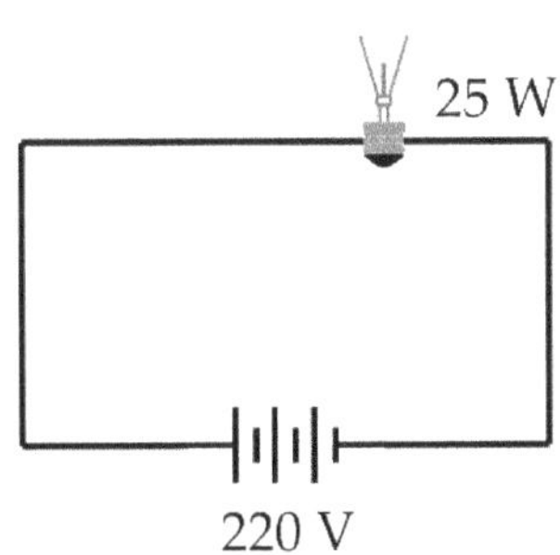

$$P = 25\text{ W} \& V = 220\text{ V}$$

$$R = \frac{V^2}{P} = \frac{220 \times 220}{25}$$

$$= 22 \times 22 \times 4$$

$$= 484 \times 4$$

$$= 1936\Omega$$

Current drawn $= \frac{P}{V} = \frac{25}{220} = 0.11\text{ A}$

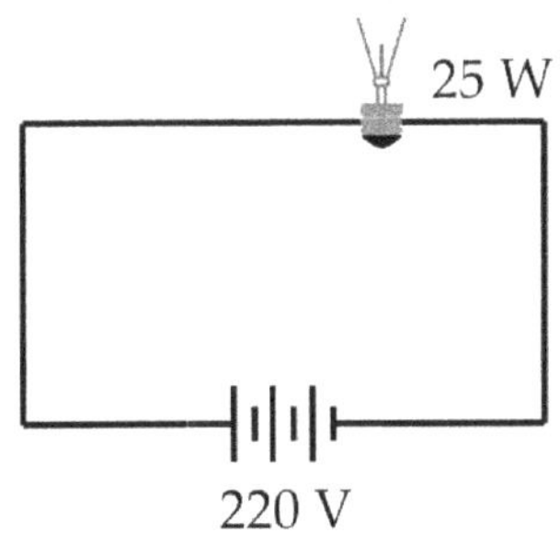

Resistance in the first case is less as compared to the IInd case, Hence current in the first case is more as compared to the IInd case.

Question 20.

(i) Distinguish between cross-pollination and self-pollination. Mention the site and product of fertilization in a flower.

(ii) Draw labelled diagram of a pistil showing the following parts: Stigma, Style, Ovary, Female germ cell

OR

(i) Draw a diagram of human female reproductive system and label the parts:

(a) which produce an egg.

(b) where fertilization takes place.

(ii) List two bacterial diseases which are transmitted sexually.

(iii) What are contraceptive devices? Give two reasons for adopting contraceptive devices in humans.

Answer

(i) Self-pollination: It is the transfer of pollen from the anther of a flower to the stigma of a flower on the same plant. There is less variation.

Cross-pollination: It is the transfer of pollen from an anther of a flower to the stigma of a flower on another plant. There is much more variation.

The site of fertilization in flowers is ovule. The products of fertilization are zygote (2n) and primary endosperm nucleus (3n).

(ii)

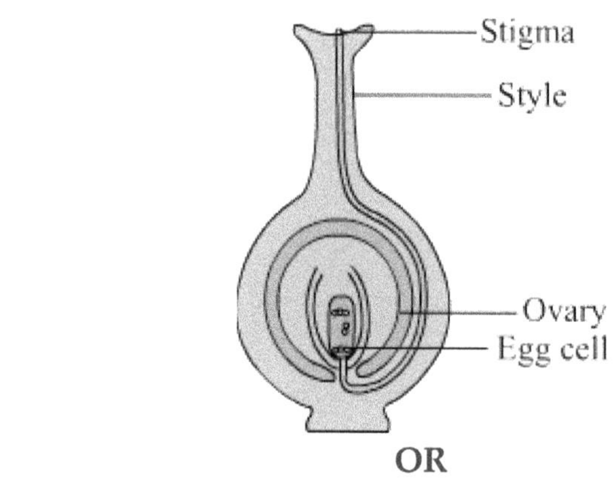

OR

(i)

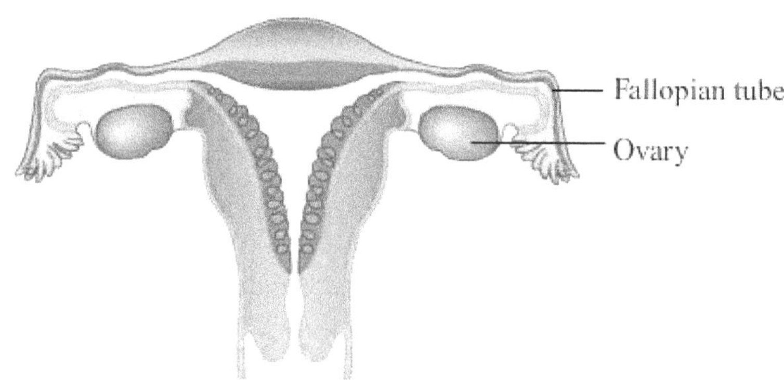

(a) Ovary produces the egg.

(b) Fertilisation takes place in the fallopian tube.

(ii) Gonorrhea and syphilis are the bacterial diseases which are transmitted sexually.

(iii) Contraceptive devices are devices which prevent fertilization and pregnancy in females. These contraceptive devices fall in the following categories :

Barrier method: In this method, the fertilization of the ovum and the sperm is prevented with the help of barriers such as a condom.

Oral contraceptive method: In this method, tablets or drugs are taken orally to prevent fertilization.

Implants and surgical methods: Contraceptive devices, such as a loop and a copperT rod, are placed in the uterus to prevent pregnancy. However, they can cause side effects on the uterus.

Reasons for adopting contraceptive devices in humans are -

- They prevent unwanted pregnancies.
- They prevent the transmission of sexually transmitted diseases.

Question 21.

(i) How do the following provide evidences in favour of evolution in organisms? Explain with an example for each.

(a) Homologous organs

(b) Analogous organs

(c) Fossils

(ii) Explain two methods to determine the age of fossils.

Answer

(i) **(a) Homologous organs:** These organs are similar in form (or are embryologically same), but perform different functions in different organisms. These organs provide strong evidence in the favour of evolution. For example, the bone structure observed in the forelimbs of birds and bats, flippers of dolphins and arms of human beings are similar and have the same pentadactyl plan, but they perform different functions.

(b) Analogous organs: These organs have different origin and different basic structure but perform same function. For example, wings of birds and wings of insects; wings of birds and wings of bats (bird wings are made of feathers while bat wings are the folds of skin) have different structure but perform same function of flying. Thus, these organs provide evidence for evolution that they are different in origin but evolve to perform same function to survive in hostile environmental conditions.

(c) Fossils: They are the impressions of dead organisms, and they can tell a great deal about the changes that various species of organisms have gone through. For example, Archaeopteryx is a connecting link between birds and reptiles and it suggests that the present animals have evolved from the existing ones through the process of continuous evolution.

(ii) **The methods to determine the age of fossils are -**

- **Radiometric dating:** In this method, the age of fossils can be determined by tracing the radioactive elements present in the rocks and by examining them chemically.
- **Relative dating:** Fossils are found in sedimentary rocks in the form of layers accumulated over a large span of time. Considering the fact that fossils found in the bottom layers are older than those found in the layers above them, geologists find the age of the fossils.

Question 22.

What would you observe on adding zinc granules to freshly prepared ferrous sulphate solution? Give reason for your answer.

Answer

Ferrous sulphate is green in colour. When zinc granules are added to ferrous sulphate, its green colour will fade away. This happens because zinc is more reactive than iron, it will displace iron and form zinc sulphate.

$Zn(s) + FeSO_4(aq) \rightarrow ZnSO_4(aq) + Fe(s)$

Question 23.

(i) How is the presence of an acid tested with a strip of red litmus paper?

OR

(ii) A student is performing an experiment to study the properties of acetic acid. Answer the following questions:

(a) Name the substance he must add to acetic acid to produce carbon dioxide.

(b) Give the relevant chemical equation for the reaction.

(c) How would he test CO2 gas in the laboratory?

Answer

(i) Red litmus changes to blue in case of base while remains the same in case of acid. So acids don't change the red litmus.

OR

(ii) **(a)** The reaction of sodium carbonate with acetic acid can be used to produce carbon dioxide gas.

(b) $CH_3COOH + Na_2CO_3 \rightarrow CO_2 + CH_3COO^-Na^+ + H_2O$

Limewater test can be used to test the presence of carbon dioxide gas. Passing the gas from limewater, it turns milky, due to the formation of insoluble suspension calcium carbonate.

$$Ca(OH)_2 + \underset{\text{(insoluble)}}{CO_2} \rightarrow CaCO_3 + H_2O$$

If more carbon dioxide is passed through the solution then the milkiness gets disappeared due to the formation of calcium bicarbonate which is soluble in water.

$$CaCO_3 + H_2O + CO_2 \rightarrow Ca(HCO_3)_2$$

Question 24.

A teacher gives a convex lens and a concave mirror of focal length of 20 cm each to his student and asks him to find their focal lengths by obtaining the image of a distant object. The student uses a distant tree as the object and obtains its sharp image, one by one, on a screen. The distances d1 and d2 between the lens/mirror and the screen in the two cases and the nature of their respective sharp images are likely to be

(a) (20 cm, 40 cm) and (erect and erect)

(b) (20 cm, 40 cm) and (inverted and inverted)

(c) (20 cm, 20 cm) and (inverted and inverted)

(d) (20 cm, 40 cm) and (erect and inverted) Give reason for your answer.

Answer

Convex lens and concave mirror both are converging in nature. The parallel rays incident on the lens or the mirror from a distant object converge on the focal plane. Thus, the distance d_1 = 20 cm and d_2 = 20 cm. As the image formed is real for lens and mirror both, so the image will be inverted. Hence, the correct answer is option C.

Question 25.

(i) The rest position of the needles in a milliammeter and voltmeter, not in use, are as shown in Figure A. When a student uses these instruments in his experiment, the readings of the needles are in the positions shown in Figure B. Determine the correct values of current and voltage the student should use in his calculations.

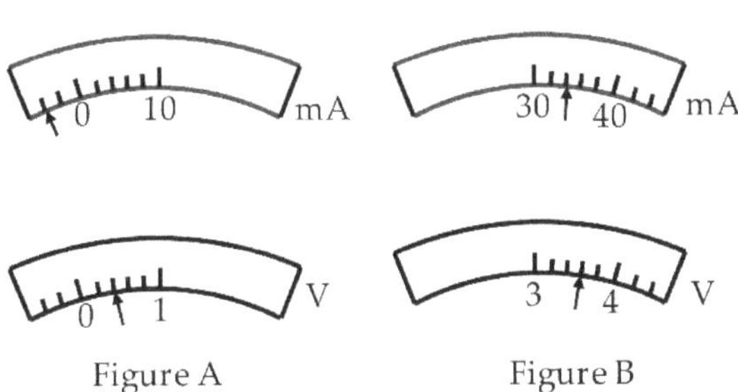

Figure A Figure B

(ii) In the experiment to study the dependence of current (I) on the potential difference (V) across a resistor, a student obtained a graph as shown.

OR

(i) What does the graph depict about the dependence of current on the potential difference?

(ii) Find the current that flows through the resistor when the potential difference across it is 2.5 V.

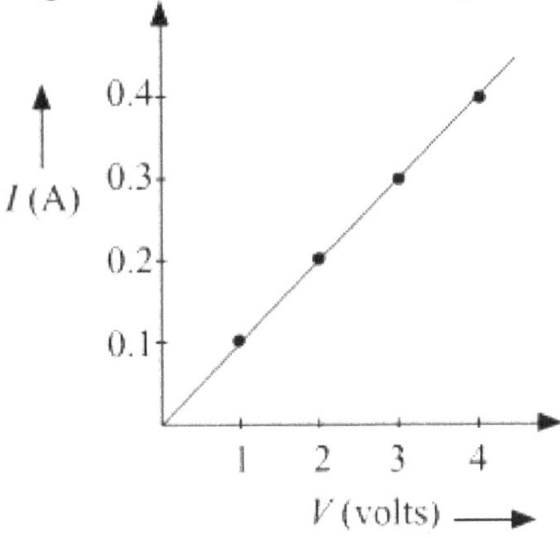

Question 26.

In the experiment "To prepare a temporary mount of a leaf peel to show stomata", glycerine and safranin are used. When and why are these two liquids used? Explain.

Answer

Glycerine is used while preparing temporary mount of leaf peel -

(a) It is a good dehydrating agent which means it avoids the drying of the specimen.

(b) It tends to reflect light due to its refractive nature, as a result of which image appears clearer under the microscope.

(c) Safranin is used to prepare temporary mount of onion peel as it binds to the component of the cells and impart them a colour which makes it easier to visualise them under the microscope.

Question 27.

Draw labelled diagram to show the following parts in an embryo of a pea seed: Cotyledon, Plumule, Radical

OR

A student observed a permanent slide showing asexual reproduction in Hydra. Draw labelled diagram in proper sequence of the observations that must have been made by the student. Name the process of reproduction also.

Answer

Embryo of a pea seed

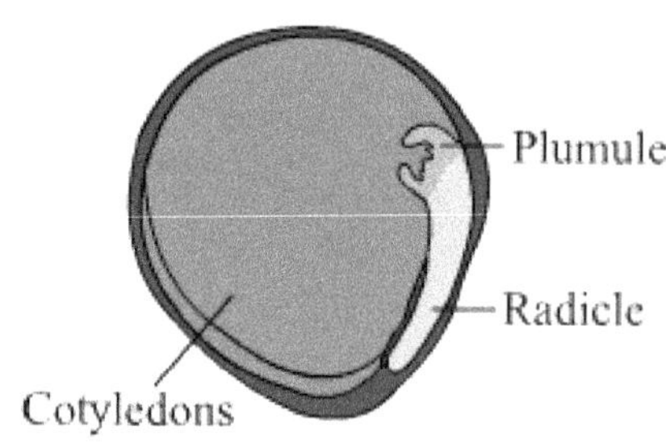

OR

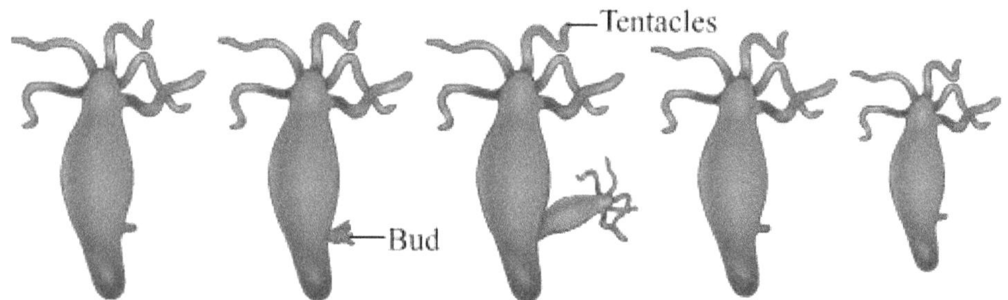

The process shown above is called budding.

Class- X Session- 2022-23

Science

PREVIOUS YEAR PAPER-2020

Time Allowed: 3 Hrs. **Maximum Marks: 80**

General Instructions:

1. This Question Paper has 5 Sections A-E.
2. Section **A** has 20 MCQs carrying 1 mark each
3. Section **B** has 5 questions carrying 02 marks each.
4. Section **C** has 6 questions carrying 03 marks each.
5. Section **D** has 4 questions carrying 05 marks each.
6. Section **E** has 3 case-based integrated units of assessment (04 marks each) with subparts of the values of 1, 1, and 2 marks each respectively.
7. All Questions are compulsory. However, an internal choice in 2 Qs of 5 marks, 2 Qs of 3 marks, and 2 Questions of 2 marks has been provided. An internal choice has been provided in the 2marks questions of Section E
8. Draw neat figures wherever required. Take π =22/7 wherever required if not stated

Section A

Section A consists of 20 questions of 1 mark each

Question 1.

Write the number of valence electrons present in a nitrogen atom **[1]**

$$\left({}^{14}_{7}\text{N}\right)$$

Answer: Five

Question 2.

Define the term induced electric current. **[1]**

Answer:

The electric current induced in a conductor due to the change in magnetic field is known as induced current.

Question 3.

Answer question number 3(a) – 3(d) on the basis of your understanding of the following paragraph and the related studied concepts.

Around the year 1800, only 30 elements were known. Dobereiner in 1817 and Newlands in 1866 tried to arrange the then known elements and framed laws which were rejected by the scientists. Even after the rejection of the proposed laws, many scientists continued to search for a pattern that correlated the properties of elements with their atomic masses.

The main credit for classifying elements goes to Mendeleev for his most important contribution to the early development of a Periodic table of element wherein the arranged the elements on the basis of their fundamental property, the atomic mass and also on the similarity of chemical properties. The formulae of their hydrides and oxides were treated as basic criteria for the classification of the elements.

However, Mendeleev's classification also had some limitations as it could not assign the position to isotopes. He also left some gaps in the periodic table.

(a) State Mendeleev's Periodic Law. **[1]**

(b) Why did Mendeleev leave some gaps in the Periodic table? **[1]**

(c) If the letter 'R' was used to represent any of the elements in the group, then the hydride and oxide of carbon would respectively be represented as

i RH_4, RO

ii RH_4, RO_2

iii RH_2, RO_2

iv RH_2, RO **[1]**

(d) Isotopes are

i Atoms of an element with similar chemical properties but different atomic masses.

ii Atoms of different elements with similar chemical properties but different atomic masses.

iii Atoms of an element with different chemical properties but same atomic masses.

iv Atoms of different elements with different chemical properties but same atomic masses.

[1]

Answer:

(a) According to the Mendeleev's periodic law, the physical and chemical properties of elements are periodic function of their atomic masses.

(b) Mendeleev predicted the existence and the properties of some elements, which were not known at that time. Therefore, he left some gaps in the Periodic table.

(c) ii

(d) i

Question 4.

Answer question numbers 4 (a) - 4 (d) on the basis of your understanding of the following paragraph and the related studies concepts-

India today is facing the problem of overuse of resources, contamination of water and soiand lack of methods of processing the waste. The time has come for the world to say goodbye to "single-use plastics". Steps must be undertaken to develop environment- friendly substitutes, effective plastic waste collection and methods of its disposal.

Indore treated 15 lakh metric tonnes of waste in just 3 years, through biomining and bioremediation techniques. Bioremediation involves introducing microbes into a landfill to naturally 'break' it down and biomining involves using trammel machines to sift through the waste to separate the 'soil' and the waste component. The city managed to chip away 15 lakh metric tonnes of waste at a cost of around Rs 10 crore. A similar experiment was successfully carried out in Ahmedabad also.

(a) State two methods of effective plastic waste collection in your school. **[1]**

(b) Name any two uses of "single use plastic" in daily life. **[1]**

(c) If we discontinue the use of plastic, how can an environment-friendly substitute be provided? **[1]**

(d) Do you think microbes will work similarly in landfill sites as they work in the laboratory? Justify your answer. **[1]**

Answer: (a) Two methods of effective plastic waste collection in the school are-

i. Curbside Recycling
ii. Drop-Off Recycling

(b) Two uses of "single use plastic" in daily life are-

i. Plastic grocery bags
ii. Plastic drinking bottles

(c) If we discontinue the use of plastic, we can use long-lasting environment-friendly substitutes like stainless steel or glass water bottles, reusable shopping bags, eco-friendly cutlery etc.

(d) Yes, microbes can work in landfill sites as they work in laboratory. The landfills can be broken down naturally by the process of bioremediation that involves the microbes.

Question 5.

Which of the following statement is correct about the human circulatory system?

(a) Blood transports only oxygen and not carbon dioxide.
(b) Human heart has five chambers.
(c) Valves ensure that the blood does not flow backwards.
(d) Both oxygen-rich and oxygen-deficient blood gets mixed in the heart. **[1]**

Answer: (C)

Explanation: Blood can flow from the atria down into the ventricles. Valves open in one direction like trapdoors to let the blood pass through. Then they close, so the blood cannot flow backwards into the atria.

Question 6.

Anaerobic process

(a) Takes place in yeast during fermentation. (b) takes place in the presence of oxygen.
(b) Produces only energy in the muscles of human beings.
(c) Produces ethanol, oxygen and energy. **[1]**

Answer: (A)

Explanation: In yeast, anaerobic fermentation takes places in the presence of sugar but absence of oxygen. Anaerobic fermentation in yeast results in the production of ethanol and carbon dioxide.

OR

Most of the digestion and absorption of the food takes place in the

(a) small intestine.
(b) liver.
(c) stomach.
(d) large intestine. **[1]**

Answer: (A)

Explanation: The small intestine is the part of digestive system where much of the digestion and absorption of food takes place. The primary function of the small intestine is to absorb nutrients and minerals present in the food.

Question 7.

Fertilization is the process of

(a) Transfer of male gamete to female gamete.

(b) Fusion of nuclei of male and female gamete.

(c) Adhesion of male and female reproductive org**Answer**

(d) The formation of gametes by a reproductive organ. **[1]**

Answer: (B)

Explanation: Fertilization is the process of fusion of haploid gametes, (male and female) to form the diploid zygote.

Question 8.

If a person has five resistors each of value $\frac{1}{5}\,\Omega$, then the maximum resistance he can obtain by connecting them is **[1]**

(a) 1 Ω

(b) 5 Ω

(c) 10 Ω

(d) 25 Ω

Answer: (A)

Series combination of resistors gives maximum resistance

$R_{equivalent} = R_1 + R_2 + R_3 + R_4 + R_5$

$R_{equivalent} = \frac{1}{5\Omega} + \frac{1}{5\Omega} + \frac{1}{5\Omega} + \frac{1}{5\Omega} + \frac{1}{5\Omega} = 1\Omega$

OR

The resistance of a resistor is reduced to half of its initial value. In doing so, if other parameters of the circuit remain unchanged, the heating effects in the resistor will become **[1]**

(a) Two times.

(b) Half.

(c) One-fourth.

(d) Four times.

Answer: (B)

Joule's law of heating is given by $H = I^2RT$

If other parameters remain constant, the amount of heat produced, H is directly proportional to R.

Question 9.

Fleming Right-hand rule gives **[1]**

(a) magnitude of the induced current.

(b) magnitude of the magnetic field.

(c) direction of the induced current.

(d) both, direction and magnitude of the induced current.

Answer: (C)

Fleming's right-hand rule states that if we stretched our right hand's thumb, index finger and middle finger in such a way so that all three are mutually perpendicular, thumb shows the direction of motion of conductor with respect to magnetic field, index finger shows the direction of magnetic field than middle finger shows the direction of induced current in the conductor.

Question 10.

Which one of the following statements is not true about nuclear energy generation in a nuclear reactor? **[1]**

(a) Energy is obtained by a process called nuclear fission.

(b) The nucleus of Uranium is bombarded with high energy neutrons.

(c) A chain reaction is set in the process.

(d) In this process a tremendous amount of energy is released at a controlled rate.

Answer: (B)

Slow moving neutrons are bombarded on the nucleus of Uranium to break the nucleus in smaller stable nuclei.

OR

The biggest source of energy on Earth's surface is **[1]**

(a) Biomass

(b) Solar radiations

(c) Tides

(d) Winds

Answer: (B)

Maximum energy present on the earth is converted form of solar energy.

Question 11.

Food web is constituted by **[1]**

(a) Relationship between the organism and the environment.

(b) Relationship between plants and animals.

(c) Various interlinked food chains in an ecosystem.

(d) Relationship between animals and environment.

Answer: (C)

In a food web, many food chains are linked together. Thus, it is a network of interlinked food chains in an ecosystem. In this network, every organism is eaten by more than one organism, who are again eaten by other different organisms. Unlike a food chain, the food web is represented by the crisscross pattern of lines.

Question 12.

Choose the incorrect statement from the following: **[1]**

(a) Ozone is a molecule formed by three atoms of oxygen.

(b) Ozone shields the surface of the Earth from ultraviolet radiations.

(c) Ozone is deadly poisonous.
(d) Ozone gets decomposed by UV radiations.
Answer: (D)
Ozone (O_3) is an inorganic molecule made up of three oxygen atoms. It is not decomposed by UV (ultraviolet) radiations, rather these radiations help in the formation of ozone. The chemical reaction involved in ozone formation is as follows:

$$O_2 \xrightarrow{UV} O + O$$

Diatomic Oxygen   Monoatomic oxygen

$$O + O_2 \rightarrow O_3$$

Triatomic oxygen (Ozone)

Question 13.

For question numbers 13 and 14, two statements are given- one labelled as Assertion (A) and the other labelled as Reason (R). Select the correct answer to these questions from the codes (a), (b), (c) and (d) as given below:

(a) Both (A) and (R) are true and (R) is the correct explanation of the assertion (A).
(b) Both (A) and (R) are true, but (R) is not the correct explanation of the assertion (A).
(c) (A) is true, but (R) is false.
(d) (A) is false, but (R) is true.

Assertion (A): Following is a balanced chemical equation for the action of steam on iron:

$3Fe + 4H_2O$ ◎◎ $Fe_3O_4 + 4H_2$

Reason (R): The law of conservation of mass holds good for a chemical equation.
Answer: (a)

Question 14.

Assertion (A): The sex of a child in human beings will be determined by the type of chromosome he/she inherits from the father.
Reason (R): A child who inherits 'X' chromosome from his father would be a girl (XX), while a childwho inherits a 'Y' chromosome from the father would be a boy (XY). **[1]**
Answer: (a) Both (A) and (R) are true and (R) is the correct explanation of the assertion (A).
All human beings have 23 pairs of chromosomes in the nuclei of their cells. Out of these two are the sex chromosomes named as X and Y.
A female has two X chromosomes while male has one X and one Y chromosome.
If the sperm containing X chromosome fertilize the egg. The zygote will contain two X sex chromosomes. This zygote will develop into a female child.
If the sperm has Y chromosome and it fertilizes the egg the zygote. The zygote will develop into the male child.
Hence, the type of sperm contributed by father determines the sex of the unborn baby.

Section B

Section B has 5 questions carrying 02 marks each.

Question 15.

Lead nitrate solution is added to a test tube containing potassium iodide solution.

(i) Write the name and colour of the compound precipitated.

(ii) Write the balanced chemical equation for the reaction involved.

(iii) Name the type of this reaction justifying your answer. **[3]**

Answer:

(i) Name of compound precipitated: Lead iodide
Colour of the compound precipitated: Yellow

(ii) $2KI(s)+Pb(NO_3) \rightarrow 2KNO_3(aq)+PbI_{2s}$

(iii) This is a double displacement reaction because in the reaction two compounds exchange their ions to form two new compounds. Here both lead nitrate and potassium iodide are exchanging their ions.

OR

What happens when food materials containing fats and oils are left for a long time/ List two observable changes and suggest three ways by which this phenomenon can be prevented. [3]

Answer: When food materials containing fats and oils are left for a long time they undergo oxidation and their taste and smell change.

This can be prevented by–

(a) Using airtight and light protecting packing

(b) Using antioxidants like vitamin A and C

(c) Filling nitrogen gas in chips container

Question 16.

List three differentiating features between the processes of galvanization and alloying. [3]

Answer:

Galvanization	**Alloying**
Galvanization is the process of depositing a thin layer of zinc metal on iron objects to protect them for rusting.	A homogeneous mixture of two or more metals or a metal and a non-metal to change the properties of pure state metals and protect them from rust.
It can be done by spraying molten zinc on the iron surface and dipping iron objects into molten zinc.	It can be done by alloying iron object with the chromium and nickel.
It does not affect the properties of iron (metal).	It changes the hardness, tensile strength and electrical resistance of a metal.

OR

Compare in tabular form the reactivities of the following metals with cold and hot water:

(i) Sodium

(ii) Calcium

(iii) Magnesium **[3]**

Answer:

Metal	**Reactivity**	**Reactions**
Sodium (Na)	It reacts vigorously	$2Na(s) + 2H_2O(l) \longrightarrow 2NaOH(aq) + H_2(g)$
	with cold water.	
Calcium (Ca)	It reacts slowly with cold water and moderately with hot water.	$Ca(s) + 2H_2O(l) \longrightarrow Ca(OH)_2 + H_2(g)$ (Hot)
Magnesium (Mg)	Magnesium does not react with cold water. It reacts slowly with hot water and vigorously with steam.	$Mg(s) + 2H_2O(I) \longrightarrow Mg(OH)_2 + H_2(g)$ (Hot) $Mg(s) + H_2O(I) \longrightarrow MgO + H_2(g)$ (Steam)

Question 17.

Carbon, a member of group14, forms a large number of carbon compounds estimated to be about three million. Why is this property not exhibited by other elements of this group? Explain. **[3]**

Answer:

(i) Tetravalency: Carbon can easily form four covalent bonds to other atoms.

(ii) Catenation: Carbon can easily form covalent bonds to other carbon atoms and the carboncarbon bonds are more stable than the other element to same element bonds formed by other member of group 14.

(iii) Formation of multiple bonds: Carbon can form not only a single bond but also it can form double or single bonds with same or different elements. Since these properties are not exhibited by other elements of this group, therefore, the number of carbon compounds is very large as compared to the other elements of group 14.

Question 18.

A cheetah, on seeing a prey, moves towards him at a very high speed. What causes the movement of his muscles? How does the chemistry of cellular components of muscles change during this event? **[3]**

Answer: A cheetah possesses an extremely flexible spine which allows for extreme flexion and extension while moving towards a prey at a very high speed.

Rapid respiration is required for a high-intensity output of the chasing activity. Thus, a cheetah consequently respires anaerobically. During anaerobic respiration, partial breakdown of glucose takes place, which leads to the accumulation of lactic acid in the muscles as the end-product.

Question 19.

Define geotropism. Draw a labelled diagram of a plant showing geotropic movement of its parts. **[3]**

Answer: Geotropism: Geotropism refers to the growth of the parts of a plant in response to gravity.

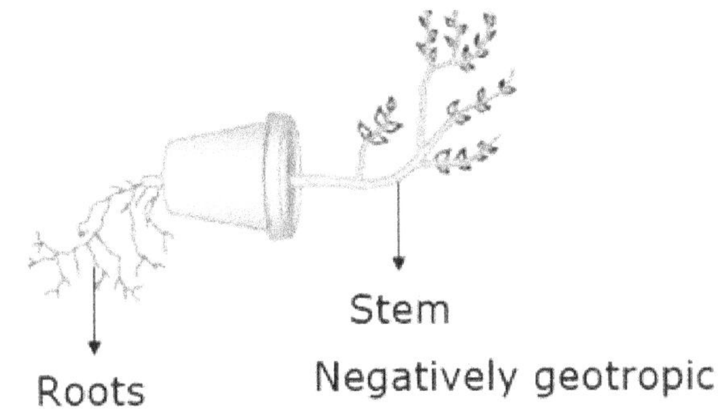

Figure: A plant showing geotropic movement

Question 20.

Define the term evolution. "Evolution cannot be equated with progress." Justify this statement.

Answer: Evolution is the gradual and continuous changes in the traits of an individual that accumulates and enables it to survive better in its surroundings.

Evolution cannot be equated with progress from lower organisms to higher organisms.

Evolution leads to the production of diversity and the shaping this diversity by environmental selection. In addition, even the simpler life forms continue to flourish as we can see in case of bacteria. These are one of the simplest life form that inhabit in extreme cold or hot conditions.

OR

"During the course of evolution, organs or features may be adapted for new functions." Explain this fact by choosing an appropriate example. **[3]**

Answer: The organs or features adapted for new functions during evolution are:

(i) Some dinosaur had feathers for insulation in cold weather but in case of birds they were used for flying.

(ii) Older life forms, such as bacteria were able to survive in most of the inhospitable habitats like, hot springs, deep-sea, thermal vents and the ice in Antarctica.

Question 21.

A concave mirror is use for image formation for different positions of an object. What inferences can be drawn about the following when an object is placed at a distance of 10 cm from the pole of a concave mirror of focal length 15 cm?

(a) Position of the image

(b) Size of the image

(c) Nature of the image

Draw a labelled ray diagram to justify your inferences. **[3]**

Answer: Given,

Position of object, u = – 10 cm

Focal length of concave mirror, f = –15 cm

(a) Using mirror formula,

$$\frac{1}{V} + \frac{1}{F} - \frac{1}{U}$$

So, the position of image is 30 cm behind the mirror.

(b) Using magnification formula, $m = \frac{h_i}{h_o} = -\frac{v}{u}$

$$\Rightarrow \frac{h_i}{h_o} = -\frac{30 \text{ cm}}{(-10 \text{ cm})} = 3 \text{ cm}$$

$$\Rightarrow h_i = 3h_o$$

So, the size of the image is three times that of the size of the object.

Here the object is placed in between focus and pole of the concave mirror, so the image formed will be virtual and magnified.

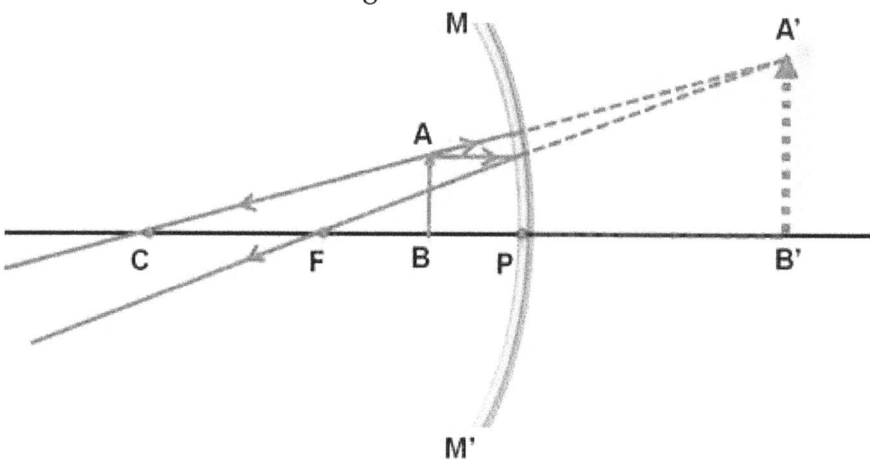

Question 22.

The refractive index of a medium 'x' with respect to a medium 'y' is 2/3 and the refractive index of medium 'y' with respect to medium 'z' is 4/3. Find the refractive index of medium 'z' with respect to medium 'x'. If the speed of light in medium 'x' is 3 × 108 ms–1, calculate the speed of light in medium 'y' [3]

Answer:

Given:

Refractive index of medium 'x"
with respect to medium 'y', $\mu_{xy} = \frac{2}{3}$

Refractive index of medium 'y"
with respect to medium 'z', $\mu_{yz} = \frac{4}{3}$

Refractive index of medium 'z"
with respect to medium 'x',

$$\mu_{zx} = \frac{1}{\mu_{xy} \times \mu_{yz}} = \frac{1}{\frac{2}{3} \times \frac{4}{3}} = \frac{9}{8}$$

Refractive index of medium 'z"
with respect to medium 'x'is $\frac{9}{8}$

Speed of light in medium 'y',

$$v = c \times \mu_{xy} = 3 \times \frac{10^8 \text{m}}{\text{s}} \times \frac{2}{3} = 2 \times \frac{10^8 \text{m}}{\text{s}}$$

Question 23.

A person may suffer from both myopia and hypermetropia defects.

(i) What is this condition called?

(ii) When does it happen?

(iii) Name the type of lens often required by the suffering from this defect. Draw labelled diagram of such lenses. [

Answer:

(i) This condition is called presbyopia.

(ii) It happens in old age.

(iii) Bifocal lens is required for clear vision by the person suffering from presbyopia.

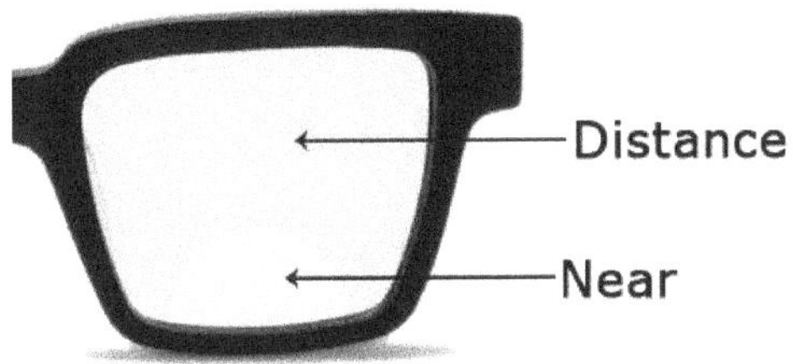

Question 24.

How will you use two identical glass prisms so that a narrow beam of white light incident on one prism emerges out of the second prism as white light? Draw and label the ray diagram. [3]

Answer: One glass prism must be placed in inverted position with respect to other, when white light passes through first prism, dispersion happens and white light splits into seven colour. When these colour light falls on the inverted prism, then light of seven colours combine to give white light.

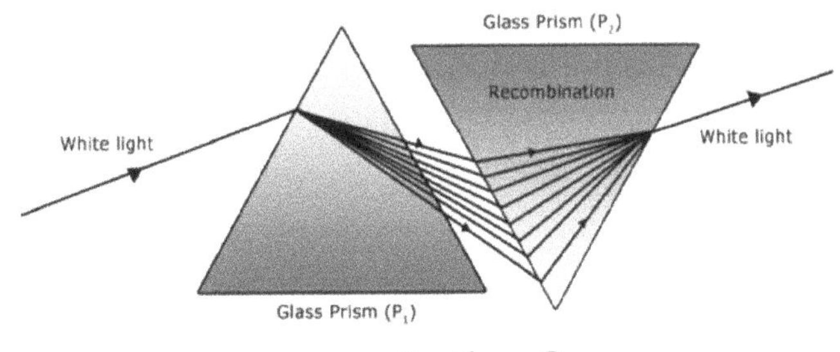

Section-C

Question 25.

A cloth strip dipped in onion juice is used for testing a liquid 'X'. The liquid 'X' changes its odour. Which type of an indicator is onion juice? 'The liquid 'X' turns blue litmus red. List the observations the liquid 'X' will show on reacting with the following:

(i) Zinc granules

(ii) Solid sodium carbonate

Write the chemical equations for the reactions involved. **[5]**

Answer: Onion juice is an olfactory indicator. Since the liquid 'X' turns blue litmus red, therefore, it is an acid.

(i) When liquid 'X' (an acid like HCl) reacts with zinc granules, bubbles of hydrogen will be formed.

$2HCl(aq)+Zn(s)\rightarrow ZnCl_2(s)+H_2\,(g)$

(ii) When liquid 'X' (an acid like HCl) reacts with sodium carbonate, carbon dioxide gas will be liberated.

$2HCl(aq)+Na_2\ CO_3(aq)\rightarrow 2NaCl(aq)+H_2O(l)+CO_2(g)$

OR

Define water of crystallization. Give the chemical formula for two compounds as examples. How can it be proved that the water of crystallization makes a difference in the state and colour of the compounds? [5]

Answer: Water of crystallisation is the number of molecules of water which are loosely bonded to one molecule of salt.

For example:

(i) $BaCl_2.2H_2O$

(ii) $CuSO_4.5H_2O$

We can prove that by heating the compound containing water of crystallisation, its colour or state change due to the removal of water of crystallisation.

For example

(a) Copper sulphate crystals containing water of crystallisation are blue but on heating they turn white.

(b) Similarly plaster of Paris is a white powder and on mixing with water it changes to gypsum which forms a hard solid mass.

Question 26.

(i) **(a)** Write two properties of gold which make it the most suitable metal for ornaments.

(b) Name two metals which are the best conductors of heat.

(c) Name two metals which **melt when you keep them on your palm.**

(ii) Explain the formation of ionic compound CaO with electron-dot structure. Atomic numbers of calcium and oxygen are 20 and 8 respectively. **[5]**

Answer:

(i) **(a)** Gold is inert metal and it has shiny surface. It is also malleable and ductile. Therefore, it is used for making ornaments.

(b) Copper and aluminium

(c) Cesium and gallium

(ii) The atomic number of calcium and oxygen is 20 and 8 respectively.

The electronic configuration of calcium will be 2, 8, 8, 2 thus, it has 2 electrons in its outermost shell. On the other hand, oxygen (2, 6) has 6 electrons in its outermost shell. By losing two electrons, calcium atom forms a calcium ion (Ca^{2+}) while by gaining 2 electrons; oxygen atom forms an oxide ion (O^{2-}). Calcium reacts with oxygen to form an ionic compound calcium oxide (CaO).

The electron dot representation for the formation of calcium oxide is given below.

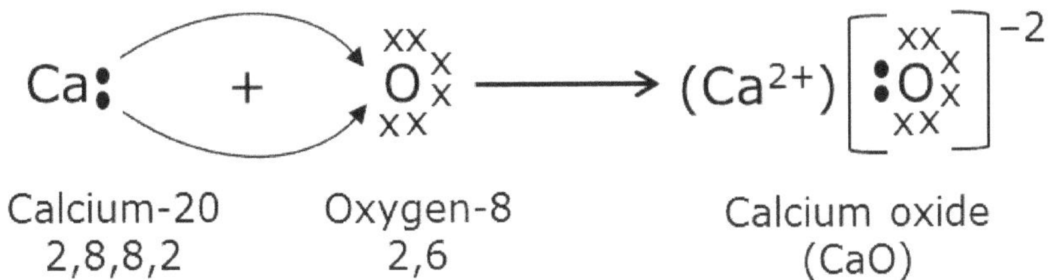

Question 27.

Why is nutrition necessary for the human body?

(a) What causes movement of food inside the alimentary canal?

(b) Why is small intestine in herbivores longer than in carnivores?

(c) What will happen if mucus is not secreted by the gastric glands? **[5]**

Answer: We obtain nutrition from the food we eat. This nutrition provides us energy for survival, growth, and reproduction.

(a) Peristalsis mainly causes the movement of food inside the alimentary canal. It is defined as a series of wave-like muscular contractions that propels the food inside an alimentary canal.

(b) The small intestine in herbivores is longer than in carnivores because herbivores are plant eating animals. Plants are made up of cellulose and fibres which are not easily digested. Therefore, for complete digestion of food, they require a longer digestive tract.
Also, many small bacteria are present in the intestine of herbivores that help in the breakdown of cellulose into glucose. This glucose is used by them as an energy source.

(c) The gastric glands present in the stomach secrete hydrochloric acid, an enzyme – pepsin, and mucus. Hydrochloric acid provides an acidic medium for the enzyme to function. Pepsin digests proteins into smaller peptides. The mucus provides protection to the inner lining of the stomach from the action of the acid.
If mucus is not secreted by the gastric glands, it may erode the inner lining of the stomach resulting in ulcer and acidity.

Question 28.

Draw a neat diagram showing fertilisation in a flower and label (a) pollen tube, (b) male germ cell, (c) female germ cell. Explain the process of fertilisation in a flower. What happens to the (i)ovary and (ii) ovule after fertilisation? **[5]**

Answer:

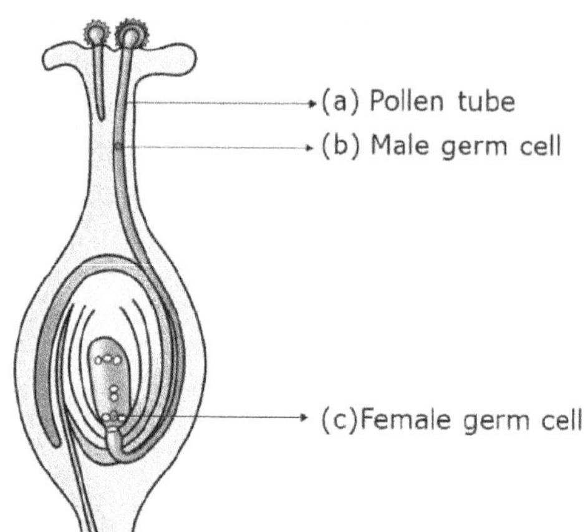

Germination of Pollen on Stigma

When a mature pollen grain reaches the stigma of a flower, it absorbs the sugary secretions of the stigma, swells up and ruptures.

It divides and releases two male gametes, which move down the style to reach the ovary via pollen tube.

On entering the ovule of the ovary through a small opening, called micropyle, one of the male gamete fuses with the female gamete to form a zygote by the process of fertilization. The other one fuses with the two polar nuclei by the process called triple fusion. Since the fertilization has occurred twice, it is said that angio spermic plants undergo double fertilization.

Post fertilization,

(a) Ovary develops into fruit

(b) Ovule develops into seed

OR

(i) What is puberty?

(ii) Describe in brief the functions of the following parts in the human male reproductive system:

(a) Testes

(b) Seminal vesicle

(c) Vas deferens

(d) Urethra

(iii) Why are testes located outside the abdominal cavity?

(iv) State how sperms move towards the female germ cell. **[5]**

Answer:

(i) The age at which sex hormones begin to produce and reproductive organs of both male and female become functional is termed as puberty. At puberty, both male and female become sexually mature.

(ii) **(a)** Testes: Testes produce male sex cells called sperms and male sex hormone called testosterone.

(b) Seminal vesicle: Seminal vesicles store sperms and add seminal fluids to the sperms that make their transport easier. The seminal fluids also provide nutrition to the sperms.

(c) Vas deferens: Vas deferens manages the transportation of the mature sperms to the urethra.

(d) Urethra: Urethra is a common passage for both urine and sperm. At a time, either of these two fluids are released from the body.

(iii) A pair of testes is located outside the abdominal cavity in a pouch-like structure called scrotum to provide accurate temperature for the process of spermatogenesis. The process of spermatogenesis requires 2-3O C less than the body temperature.

(iv) Sperms have a long tail that helps them move towards the female germ-cell.

Question 29.

Draw a schematic diagram of a circuit consisting of a battery of 3 cells of 2 V each, a combination of three resistors of 10 20 and 30 ◎◎ connected in parallel, a plug key and an ammeter, all connected in series. Use this circuit to find the value of the following :

(a) Current through each resistor

(b) Total current in the circuit

(c) Total effective resistance of the circuit [5]

Answer:

Circuit diagram :

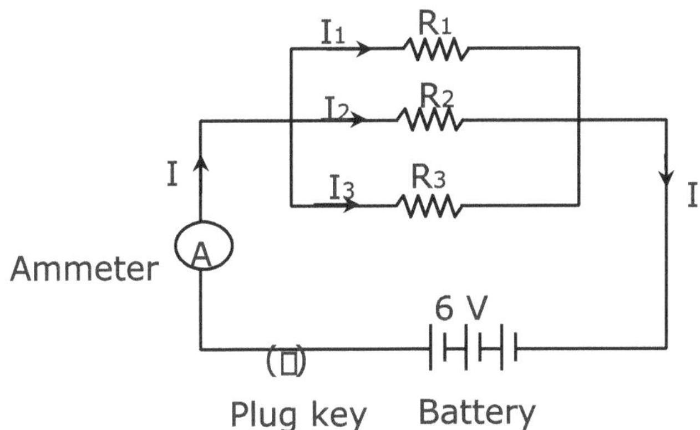

Given:

Voltage in the circuit = 2 V + 2 V +2 V = 6 V

Resistance, R_1 = 10 Ω, R_1 = 20 Ω and R_1 = 30 Ω

Let I be the total current flowing in the circuit and R be the total effective resistance of the circuit.

According to Ohm's law, V = IR

(a) Let electric current flowing through 10 Ω, 20 Ω and 30 Ω resistors be I1, I2 and I3 respectively.

According to Ohm's law, V = IR

$$I_1 = \frac{6V}{10\Omega} = 0.6A$$

$$I_2 = \frac{6V}{20\Omega} = 036A$$

$$I_3 = \frac{6V}{30\Omega} = 0.2A$$

(b) Total current flowing in the circuit,

$$I = I_1 + I_2 + I_3$$

$$I = 0.6A + 0.3A + 0.2A = 1.1A$$

(c) Total effective resistance of the circuit, $R = \frac{V}{1}$

$$\Rightarrow R = \frac{6\ V}{1.1\ A} = 5.45\Omega$$

OR

Two identical resistors, each of resistance 12 ◎, are connected in (i) series, and (ii) parallel, in turn to a battery of 6 V. Calculate the ratio of the power consumed in the combination of resistors in each case. [5]

Answer:

Given:

Voltage in the circuit = 6 V

Resistance, $R_1 = R_2 = 15\ \Omega$

(i) When the two resistances connected in series:

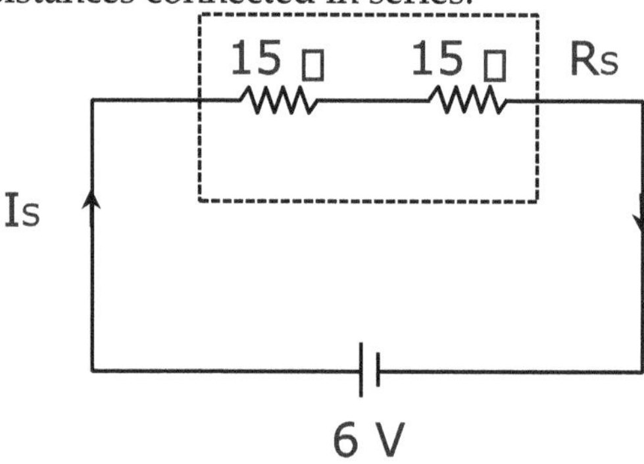

Effective resistance of the circuit, $R_S = R_1 + R_2$ $R_S = 15\ \Omega + 15\ \Omega = 30\ \Omega$

Power consumed by the circuit, $P_s = \frac{V^2}{R_s}$

$$\Rightarrow P_s = \frac{(6\ V)^2}{30\Omega} = 1.2\ W$$

(ii) When the two resistances connected in parallel:

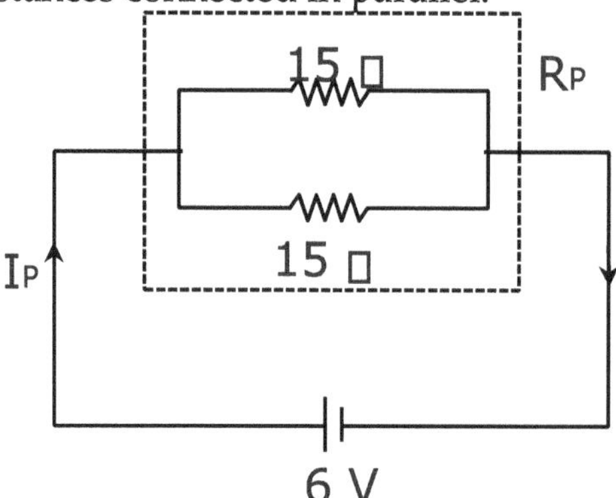

Effective resistance of the circuit, $\frac{1}{R_p} = \frac{1}{R_1} + \frac{1}{R_2} \Rightarrow \frac{1}{R_p} = \frac{1}{15\Omega} + \frac{1}{15\Omega} = \frac{1}{30\Omega}$

Power consumed by the circuit, $P_p = \frac{V^2}{R_p} \Rightarrow P_p = \frac{(6\ V)^2}{30\Omega} = 1.2\ W$

$\therefore$ Ratio $= P_S : P_P = 1.2\ W : 1.2\ W = 1:1$

So, the ratio of power consumption is $1:1$.

Question 30.

(i) State Fleming's Left-hand rule.

(ii) List three characteristic features of the electric current used in our homes.

(iii) What is a fuse ? Why is it called a safety device ?

(iv) Why is it necessary to earth metallic electric appliances? [5]

Answer:

(i) Fleming's left-hand rule states that if we stretch the thumb, the forefinger and the middle finger of our left hand in mutually perpendicular directions such that the forefinger gives the direction of current, middle finger points in the direction of magnetic field, then gives the direction of the force or motion of the conductor.

(ii) The electric current supplied to our home is alternating in nature. It has following characteristics.

(a) It is time varying current.

(b) It has frequency of 50 Hz in India.

(c) It can be transferred to long distances efficiently.

(iii) Fuse is a safety device used in electrical circuit and appliances. It is called safety device because it prevents damage to the appliances and the electrical circuit due to overloading.

(iv) The metallic electric appliances are earthed using earth wire as it provides a low resistance path to electric current thus ensuring that any leakage current to the metallic body of the appliance keeps its potential to that of the earth, and the user may not get a severe electric shock.

Class- X Session- 2022-23

Science

PREVIOUS YEAR PAPER-2022

Time Allowed: 3 Hrs. **Maximum Marks: 80**

General Instructions:

1. This Question Paper has 5 Sections A-E.
2. Section **A** has 20 MCQs carrying 1 mark each
3. Section **B** has 5 questions carrying 02 marks each.
4. Section **C** has 6 questions carrying 03 marks each.
5. Section **D** has 4 questions carrying 05 marks each.
6. Section **E** has 3 case-based integrated units of assessment (04 marks each) with subparts of the values of 1, 1, and 2 marks each respectively.
7. All Questions are compulsory. However, an internal choice in 2 Qs of 5 marks, 2 Qs of 3 marks, and 2 Questions of 2 marks has been provided. An internal choice has been provided in the 2marks questions of Section E
8. Draw neat figures wherever required. Take π =22/7 wherever required if not stated

Section A

Section A consists of 20 questions of 1 mark each

Question 1.

(i) Write the molecular formula of the following carbon compounds :

(a) Methane

(b) Propane

(ii) Carbon compounds have low melting and boiling points. Why ?

Answer

(iii) **(a)** CH4

(b) C_3H_8

(iv) Intermolecular forces are weak / not strong

Question 2.

The electrons in the atoms of two elements X and Y are distributed in three shells having 1 and 7 electrons respectively in their outermost shells.

(i) Write the group numbers of these elements in the Modern Periodic Table.

(ii) Write the molecular formula of the compound formed when X and Y combine with each other.

(iii) Which of the two is electropositive ?

Answer

(i)

	X	Y
Group Number	1	17

(ii) XY

(iii) X

Question 3.

(i) Which of the following flowers will have higher possibility of self-pollination ?

Mustard, Papaya, Watermelon, Hibiscus

(ii) List the two reproductive parts of a bisexual flower.

Answer

(i) Mustard and Hibiscus

(ii) Stamens and Pistil / Carpel

Question 4.

Which one of the two multicellular organisms Spirogyra and Planaria reproduces by regeneration and why ? Give an example of any other organism which can also reproduce by the same process.

Answer

- Planaria
- Regeneration is carried out by specialised cells which are not present in spirogyra.
- Hydra

Question 5.

(i) What is variation ? List two main reasons that may lead to variation in a population.

OR

(ii) **(a)** A cross between violet flowered plants and white flowered plants, state the characteristics of the plants obtained in the F_1 progeny.

(b) If the plants of F1 progeny are self-pollinated, then what would be observed in the plants of F_2 progeny?

(c) If 100 plants are produced in F_2 progeny, then how many plants will show the recessive trait?

Answer

(i) The differences in the traits shown by the individuals of a species.

Two reasons :

- Inaccurate / Error in DNA copying
- Sexual reproduction

OR

(ii) **(a)** F_1 Progeny : Violet flowered plants

(b) F_2 Progeny : Violet as well as white flowered plants

(c) 25 plants

Question 6.

(i) **(a)** Name and state the rule to determine the direction of force experienced by a current carrying straight conductor placed in a uniform magnetic field which is perpendicular to it.

(b) An alpha particle while passing through a magnetic field gets projected towards north.In which direction will an electron project when it passes through the same magnetic field ?

OR

(ii) **(a)** What is a solenoid ?

(b) Draw the pattern of magnetic field lines of the magnetic field produced by a solenoid through which a steady current flows.

Answer

(i) **(a)** Fleming's left-hand rule

- Stretch the thumb, forefinger and middle finger of your left hand such that they are mutually perpendicular. If the first finger points in the direction of magnetic field and the second finger in the direction of current, then the thumb will point in the direction of motion or the force acting on the conductor.

(b) South

OR

(ii) **(a)** A coil of many circular turns of insulated copper wire wrapped closely in the shape of a cylinder.

(b)

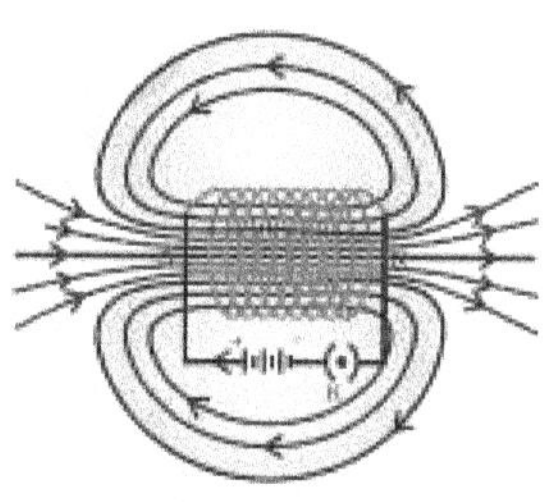

Question 7.

(i) What is ozone ? How is it formed in the upper layers of the Earth's atmosphere? How does ozone affect our ecosystem?

OR

(ii) **(a)** List two human-made ecosystems.

(b) "We do not clean a pond in the same manner as we do in an aquarium." Give reason to justify this statement.

Answer

(i)
- Ozone is a molecule formed by three atoms of oxygen.
- UV radiations split some molecular oxygen (O_2) into free oxygen atoms (O + O). These atoms then combine with molecular oxygen to form ozone.

$$O_2 \xrightarrow{uv} O + O$$
$$O + O_2 \rightarrow O_3 \text{ (Ozone)}$$

- Ozone layer shields the surface of the earth from damaging UV radiation of the sun. / Depletion of ozone layer causes harmful effects on the organism.

OR

(ii) **(a)** Aquarium, crop field, gardens, etc. (any two)

(b) A pond is a natural ecosystem. It has decomposers whereas an aquarium is an artificial ecosystem and does not contain decomposers. Therefore it needs regular cleaning for proper functioning.

Section B

Section B has 5 questions carrying 02 marks each

Question 8.

(i) List two advantages of adopting the atomic number of an element as the basis of classification of elements in the Modern Periodic Table.

(ii) Write the electronic configurations of the elements X (atomic number 13) and Y (atomic number 20).

Answer

(i)
- Atomic number is more fundamental property and it decides the properties of an element.
- Atomic number increases by one in going from one element to the next, so arrangement of elements becomes more systematic.
- Prediction of properties of elements could be made with more precision when the elements are arranged in increasing order of their atomic numbers.

OR

(ii) Electronic configuration of X - 2, 8, 3
Electronic configuration of Y - 2, 8, 8, 2

Question 9.

(i) Draw two different possible structures of a saturated hydrocarbon having four carbon atoms in its molecule. What are these two structures of the hydrocarbon having same molecular formula called ? Write the molecular formula and the common name of this compound. Also write the molecular formula of its alkyne.

OR

(ii) **(a)** Write the molecular formula of benzene and draw its structure.

(b) Write the number of single and double covalent bonds present in a molecule of benzene.

(c) Which compounds are called alkynes ?

Answer

(i)

```
    H   H   H   H
    |   |   |   |
H — C — C — C — C — H
    |   |   |   |
    H   H   H   H
```

```
    H   H   H
    |   |   |
H — C — C — C — H
    |   |   |
    H   |   H
        |
    H — C — H
        |
        H
```

- Isomers
- C_4H_{10}
- Butane
- C_4H_6

OR

(ii) **(a)** C_6H_6

```
            H
            |
    H     C      H
     \  //  \   /
      C       C
      |       ||
      C       C
     / \\   /  \
    H     C      H
          |
          H
```

(b) Single Bond 9
Double bond 3

(c) Hydrocarbons containing triple bond

Question 10.

(i) Mention one function each of the following organs in human male reproductive system :

(a) Testis

(b) Scrotum

(c) Vas deferens

(d) Prostate gland

(ii) Name the type of germ cell which (a) is motile, and (b) stores food.

Answer

(i) **(a)** Testis—To produce male gametes or sperms / To produce testosterone or male sex hormone

(b) To provide lower temperature for sperm formation

(c) Vas deferens—Transport of sperms

(d) Prostate gland— Secretion of fluid for easier transport and nutrition of sperms

(ii) **(a)** Sperm

(b) Egg / Ovum

Question 11.

(i) Three resistors R_1, R_2 and R_3 are connected in parallel and the combination is connected to a battery, an ammeter, a voltmeter and a key. Draw suitable circuit diagram to show the arrangement of these circuit components along with the direction of current flowing.

(ii) Calculate the equivalent resistance of the following network :

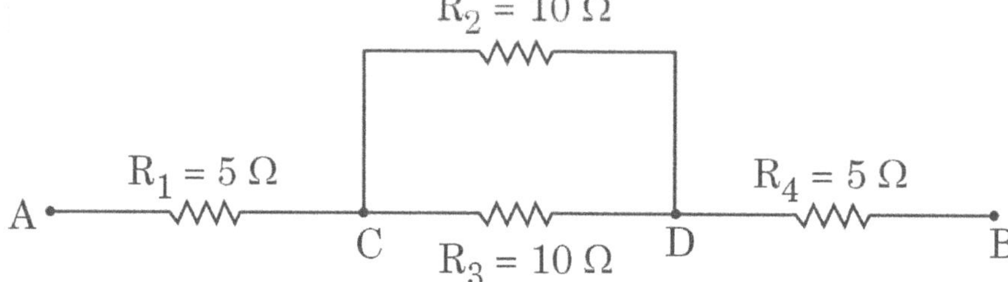

Answer

(i) Circuit diagram with given components Direction

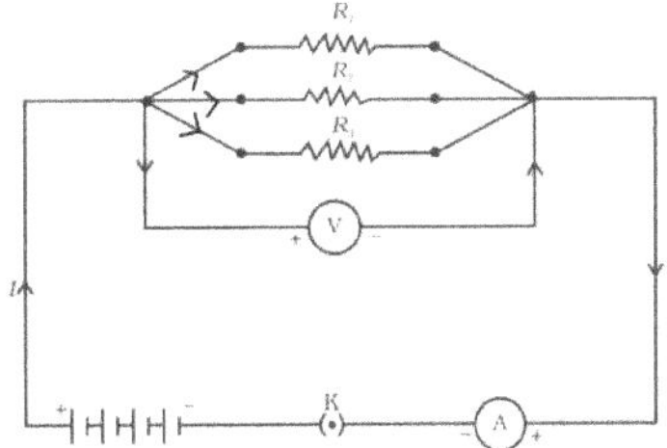

(ii) Resistance between C and D is given by

$$\frac{1}{R_{CD}} = \frac{1}{10} + \frac{1}{10} = \frac{2}{10} = \frac{1}{5}$$
$$R_{CD} = 5\,\Omega$$

D and B = $R_4 = 5\Omega$

∴ Total resistance is $R_S = R_{CD} + R_1 + R_4$

$R_{total} = 5\Omega + 5\Omega + 5\Omega$

$= 15\Omega$

Question 12.

(i) **(a)** Define Electric Power and write its SI unit. +

(b) Two bulbs rated 100 W; 220 V and 60 W; 220 V are connected in parallel to an electric mains of 220 V. Find the current drawn by the bulbs from the mains.

OR

(ii) **(a)** State joules law of heating. Express it mathematically when an appliance of resistance R is connected to a source of voltage V and the current I flows through the appliance for a time t.

(b) A 5 resistor is connected across a battery of 6 volts.
Calculate the energy that dissipates as heat in 10 s.

Answer

(i) **(a)** The rate at which electric energy is dissipated or consumed in an electric circuit.

S.I. unit-watt / V. A / joule per second

- Current drawn by first bulb

$I_1 = \frac{100\text{ W}}{220\text{ V}} = \frac{100}{220}$ ampere

- Current drawn by second bulb

$I_2 = \frac{60\text{ W}}{220\text{ V}} = \frac{60}{220}$ ampere

Both the bulbs are in parallel

Total current, $I = I_1 + I_2$

$= \left(\frac{100}{220} + \frac{60}{220}\right)$ ampere $= \frac{160}{220}$ A = 0.73 A

OR

(ii) **(a)** This law states that heat produced in a resistor is-

- directly proportional to the square of current for a given resistance / ($H \propto I^2$)
- directly proportional to the resistance for a given current / (HαR)
- directly proportional to the time for which the current flows through the resistor / (Hαt)
- H = VIt
- V = 6 V; R = 5Ω; t = 10

(b) Energy dissipated as heat in t = 10 s is

$$H = \frac{V^2}{R}t$$

$$= \frac{(6\ V)^2}{5\Omega} \times 10\ s$$

$$= 72\ J$$

Question 13.

(i) Name the group of organisms which form in the first trophic level of all food chains. Why are they called so ?

(ii) Why are the human beings most adversely affected by bio-magnification ?

(iii) State one ill-effect of the absence of decomposers from a natural ecosystem.

Answer

(i) Producers, as they can manufacture food by the process of photosynthesis.

(ii) When non-degradable harmful chemicals (pesticides / DDT, etc.) enter a food chain, they get progressively accumulated at each trophic level. Human beings occupy the top level in any food chain, therefore the maximum concentration of these chemicals get accumulated in their bodies.

(iii) Ill effects of absence of decomposers from natural ecosystem :

(a) Earth would be covered with dead bodies & foul smell

(b) Recycling of minerals will not take place

(c) Soil will not get replenished

(d) Ecosystem will get disrupted

Section C

This Section has 2 case-based questions (14 and 15). Each case is followed by 3 sub-questions (i), (ii) and (iii). Parts (i) and (ii) are compulsory. However, an internal choice has been provided in Part (iii).

Question 14.

The mechanism by which the sex of an individual is determined is called sex-determination. In human beings, sex of a newborn is genetically determined, whereas in some others it is not. There are 46 (23 pairs) chromosomes in human beings. Out of these, 44 (22 pairs) control the body characters and 2 (one pair) are known as sex chromosomes. The sex chromosomes are of two types X chromosome and Y chromosome. At the time of fertilisation, depending upon which type of male gamete fuses with the female gamete, the sex of the newborn child is decided.

(i) Why is a pair of sex chromosomes in human beings called a mismatched pair in terms of type and size ?

(ii) Out of male or female, which of them has a perfect pair of sex chromosomes ? In case of a perfect pair, will the gametes produced be of the same kind or of a different kind ?

(iii) **(a)** Name two animals whose sex is not genetically determined. Explain the process of their sex determination.

OR

(b) With the help of a flowchart only, show how sex is genetically determined in human beings.

Answer

(i) XY

Y is shorter than X

(ii) Mother/Female

Same Kind

(iii) **(a)** Reptiles & Snails

- In reptiles, the temperature at which fertilised eggs are kept determines whether the animal developing in the eggs would be a male or a female.

In snails, they can change their sex during their lifetime.

OR

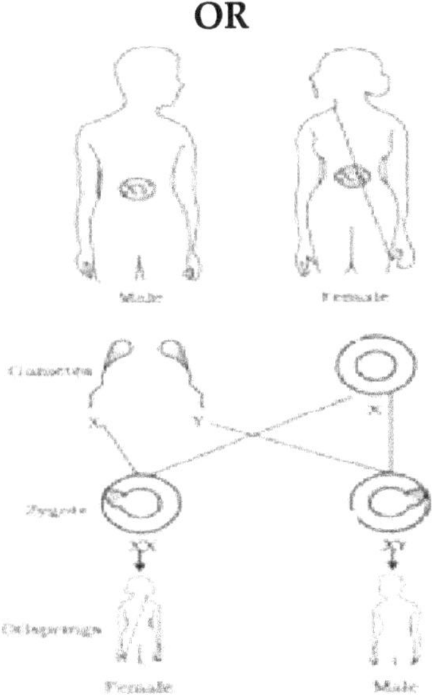

Question 15.

A student fixes a sheet of white paper on a drawing board using some adhesive materials. She places a bar magnet in the centre of it and sprinkles some iron filings uniformly around the bar magnet using a salt-sprinkler. On tapping the board gently, she observes that the iron filings have arranged themselves in a particular pattern.

(i) Draw a diagram to show this pattern of iron filings.

(ii) Draw the magnetic field lines of a bar magnet showing the poles of the bar magnet as well as the direction of the magnetic field lines.

(iii) **(a)** How is the direction of magnetic field at a point determined using the field lines ? Why do two magnetic field lines not cross each other ?

OR

(b) How are the magnetic field lines of a bar magnet drawn using a small compass needle ? Draw one magnetic field line each on both sides of the magnet.

Answer

(i)

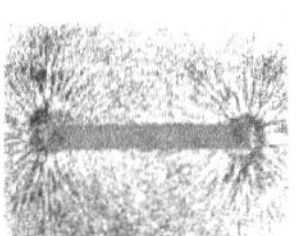

(ii)

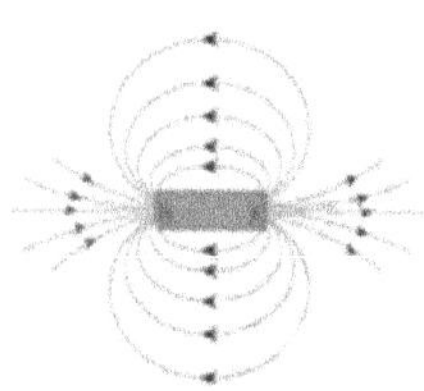

(iii) **(a)**

- By placing a compass needle on magnetic field lines, direction of north pole will give direction of magnetic field.
- If they cross or intersect , it means that at the point of interSection the compass needle would point into two directions, which is not possible.
- If they cross or intersect, it means that at the point of interSection there will be direction of two resultant fields which is not possible.

OR

(b) Take a small bar magnet, place it in the centre of the drawing on a drawing board and mark its boundary.

- Place a small compass needle near the north pole of the magnet, south pole of the compass needle points towards the north pole.
- Mark the position of two ends of the needle. Now move the needle to a new position such that the south pole of needle occupies the position previously occupied by the north pole and again mark the new position of the north pole. In this way proceed step by step till you reach the south pole of the magnet. Join the points marked to get a field line. Similarly draw one more field line on the other side of the magnet.

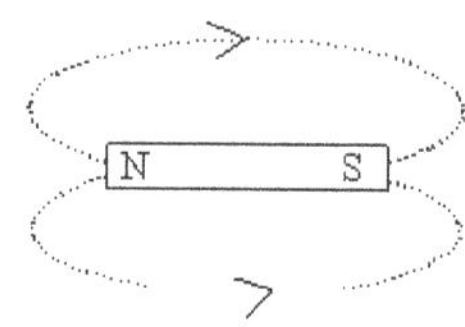

MOST EXPECTED QUESTION SAMPLE PAPER

Class- X Session- 2022-23

Science

MOST EXPECTED QUESTION SAMPLE PAPER -1

Time Allowed: 3 Hrs. **Maximum Marks: 80**

General Instructions:

1. This Question Paper has 5 Sections A-E.
2. Section **A** has 20 MCQs carrying 1 mark each
3. Section **B** has 5 questions carrying 02 marks each.
4. Section **C** has 6 questions carrying 03 marks each.
5. Section **D** has 4 questions carrying 05 marks each.
6. Section **E** has 3 case-based integrated units of assessment (04 marks each) with subparts of the values of 1, 1, and 2 marks each respectively.
7. All Questions are compulsory. However, an internal choice in 2 Qs of 5 marks, 2 Qs of 3 marks, and 2 Questions of 2 marks has been provided. An internal choice has been provided in the 2marks questions of Section E
8. Draw neat figures wherever required. Take π =22/7 wherever required if not stated

Section A

Section A consists of 20 questions of 1 mark each

Question 1

Chemical formula of rust is :

(a) $FeCO_3$

(b) Fe_2O_3

(c) $Fe_2O_3 \cdot xH_2O$

(d) $Fe_2O_3 \cdot 5H_2O$

Answer. (c)

Question 2

The following reaction is used for the preparation of oxygen gas in the laboratory

$$2KClO_3(s) \underset{\text{Catalyst}}{\overset{\text{Heat}}{\longrightarrow}} 2KCl(s) + 3O_2(g)$$

Which of the following statements(s) is(are) correct about the reaction?

(a) It is a decomposition reaction and endothermic in nature.

(b) It is a combination reaction.

(c) It is a decomposition reaction and accompanied by release of heat.

(d) It is a photochemical decomposition reaction and exothermic in nature.

Answer. (a)

Question 3

Which of the following chemical properties are shown by dilute hydrochloric acid?

i. Turns blue litmus red
ii. Turns red litmus blue
iii. Reacts with zinc and a gas is evolved
iv. Reacts with solid sodium carbonate to give brisk effervescence.

(a) i. and ii. only
(b) i. and iii. only
(c) i. iii. and iv. only
(d) ii. iii. and iv. only
Answer. (c)

Question 4

Zinc granules are placed in each of the four solutions A, B, C and D as shown. Colour change would be observed in

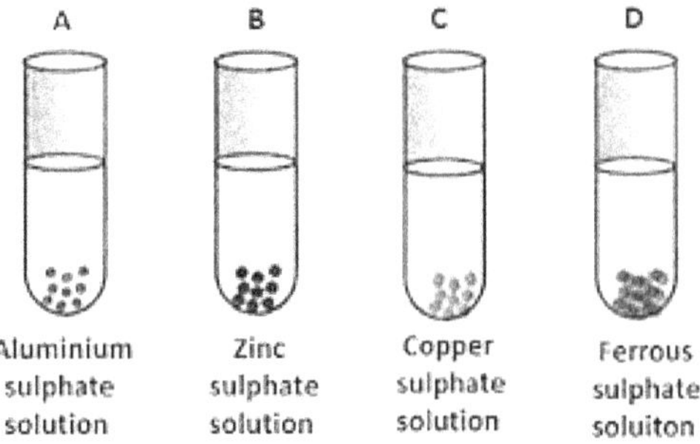

(a) A and B
(b) C and D
(c) A and C
(d) B and D
Answer. (b)

Question 5

A chemistry lab-in charge kept zinc metal in $FeS0_4$ solution and observed that after some time. green ferrous sulphate solution turns to colourless, and some brown powder is deposited on zinc. In the above reaction, zinc metal acts as:
(a) Oxidizing agent
(b) Reducing agent
(c) Dehydrating agent
(d) Catalyst
Answer. (b)

Question 6

Sodium reacts with ethanol to form:
(a) Sodium methanolate and hydrogen
(b) Sodium ethanoate and hydrogen
(c) Sodium methanolate and oxygen
(d) Sodium ethanoate and oxygen
Answer. (b)

Question 7

Which of the following is not a straight chain hydrocarbon?

(a) $H_3C - CH_2 - CH_2 - CH_2 - CH_2 - CH_3$

(b) $H_3C - CH_2 - CH_2 - CH_2 - CH_2 - CH_3$

(c) $H_3C - H_2C - H_2C - H_2C - CH_2 - CH_3$

(d)

$$\begin{matrix} CH_3 \searrow \\ CH_3 \nearrow \end{matrix} CH - CH_2 - CH_2 - CH_3$$

Question 8

In amoeba, food is digested in the:

(a) Food vacuole

(b) Mitochondria

(c) Pseudopodia

(d) Chloroplast

Answer: (a)

Question 9

In which of the following groups of organisms, food materials are broken down outside the body and absorbed?

(a) Mushroom, green plants, Amoeba

(b) Yeast, mushroom, bread mould

(c) Paramecium, Amoeba, Cuscuta

(d) Cuscuta, lice, tapeworm

Answer: (b)

Question 10

The contraction and expansion movement of the walls of the food pipe is called:

(a) Translocation

(b) Transpiration

(c) Peristaltic movement

(d) Digestion

Answer: (c)

Question 11

What are the products obtained by anaerobic respiration in plants?

(a) Lactic acid + Energy

(b) Carbon dioxide + Water + Energy

(c) Ethanol + Carbon dioxide + Energy

(d) Pyruvate

Answer: (c)

Question 12

When a few drops of iodine solution are added to rice water, the solution turns blue- black in colour. This indicates that rice water contains:

(a) Fats

(b) Complex proteins

(c) Starch

(d) Simple proteins

Answer: (c)

Question 13

Figure shows two incident rays P and Q which emerged as parallel rays R and S respectively. The device used in the box is a

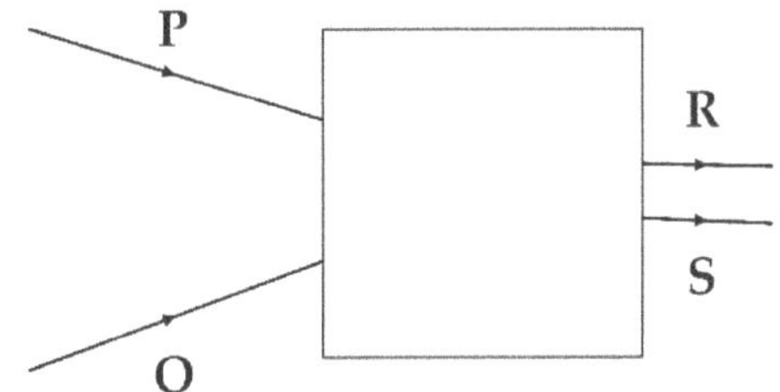

(a) Concave mirror

(b) Prism

(c) Convex lens

(d) Concave lens

Answer(d) Concave lens

Question 14

If f is focal length and R is the radius of curvature of a spherical mirror, then

(a) R = f

(b) R = 2f

(c) R = 3f

(d) R = 4f

Answer(b) R = 2f

Question 15

When the main switch of the house circuit is put off, it disconnects the:

(a) Live wire only

(b) Neutral wire only

(c) Earth wire only

(d) Both the live and neutral wires.

Answer(a) Live wire only

Question 16

What is the current in the given circuit (figure)?

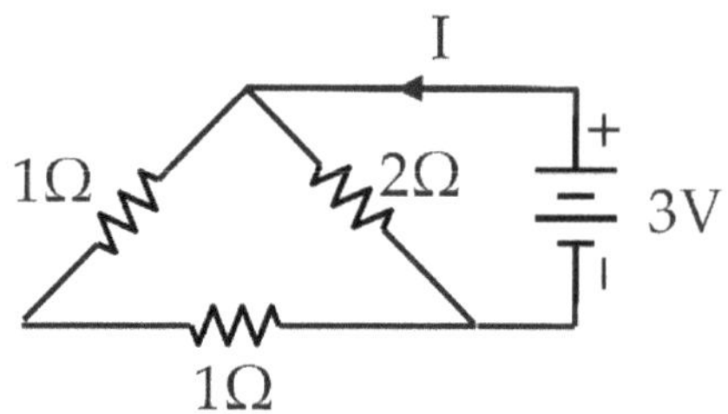

(a) 3A
(b) $\frac{1}{3}$ A
(c) $\frac{2}{3}$ A
(d) $\frac{3}{2}$ A
Answer(a) 3A

Q. no 17 to 20 are Assertion - Reasoning based questions. These consist of two statements – Assertion (A) and Reason (R). Answer these questions by selecting the appropriate option given below:

(a) Both A and R are true, and R is the correct explanation of A
(b) Both A and R are true, and R is not the correct explanation of A
(c) A is true but R is false
(d) A is False but R is true

Question 17

Assertion(A): $2NaCl \rightarrow 2Na + Cl_2$
(at cathode) (at anode)

Reason (R): The assertion is an exchange of thermal accomposition.

Answer. (c)

Question 18

Assertion(A): According to Darwin, all organisms compete with each other for existence.

Reason (R): During the struggle for existence there is survival of the fittest.

Answer. (b)

Question 19

Assertion(A): Spores are unicellular bodies.

Reason (R): The parent body simply breaks up into smaller pieces on maturation.

Answer. (c)

Question 20

Assertion: The image of a virtual object formed by a thin converging lens is always real.

Reason: In the case of a thin lens, $\frac{1}{v} - \frac{1}{u} = \frac{1}{f}$.

Answer(a)

Section B

Section B has 5 questions carrying 02 marks each

Q. no. 21 to 26 are very short answer questions

Question 21 **[2]**

When ethanol reacts with ethanoic acid in the presence of conc. H_2SO_4, a substance with fruity smell is produced. Answer the following:

(i) State the class of compound to which the fruity smelling compounds belong. Write the chemical equation for the reaction and write the chemical name of the product formed.

(ii) State the role of conc. H_2SO_4 in the reaction

OR

When soap is rubbed on a stain of curry on a white cloth, why does it become reddish brown and turns yellow again when the cloth is washed with plenty of water?

Question 22 **[2]**

What is the location of the following:

(a) DNA in a cell

(b) Gene

Question 23 **[2]**

Define the following processes of asexual reproduction:

(a) Spore formation

(b) Regeneration

(c) Multiple fission

Question 24 **[2]**

Why is vegetative propagation practised for growing some types of plant?

Question 25

Calculate the length of copper wire of resistivity $1.7 \times 10^{-8} \Omega - m$ and radius 1 mm so that its resistance is 1Ω. **[Answer** 1.84×10^2m**]**

OR

A parallel beam of light falls obliquely on a:

(i) Convex and a

(ii) Concave lens. Draw a ray diagram in each case to show the formation of the image after refraction through the lens.

Question 26

What happens to the following parts after fertilization?

Section - C

Q.no. 27 to 33 are short answer questions

Question 27

Identify the oxidizing agent (oxidant) in the following reactions:

(a) $Pb_3O_4 + 8HCl \longrightarrow 3PbCl_2 + Cl_2 + 4H_2O$

(b) $2Mg + O_2 \longrightarrow 2MgO$

(c) $CuSO_4 + Zn \longrightarrow Cu + ZnSO_4$

(d) $V_2O_5 + 5Ca \longrightarrow 2\ V + 5CaO$

(e) $3Fe + 4H_2O \longrightarrow Fe_3O + 4H_2$

(f) $CuO + H_2 \longrightarrow Cu + H_2O$

Question 28

Write the chemical formula and name of the compound which is the active ingredient of all alcoholic drinks. List its two uses. Write chemical equation and name of the product formed when this compound reacts with -

(a) Sodium metal

(b) Hot concentrated sulphury acid.

Question 29

Compare the following

(a) Unsexual and bisexual flower

(b) Self-pollination and cross pollination.

(c) Style and filament

OR

Give two examples each of the following:

(a) Plants having unisexual flowers

(b) Agents of pollination

(c) Physical changes on puberty that are common to both boys and girls.

Question 30

(a) (i) What is meant by the refraction of light?

(ii) What is the cause of the refraction of light?

(b) 'The refractive index of diamond is 2.42 '.

What is meant by this statement?

Question 31

An object 4 cm high, is placed at 25 cm in front of a concave mirror of focal length 15 cm. At what distance from the mirror should a screen be placed in order to obtain a sharp image? Find the nature and the size of the image.

Answer(.: $v = -37.5$ cm, real and imverted, size = 6 cm)

Question 32

How does AC differ from DC ? What are the advantages and disadvantages of AC over DC ?

OR

State the purpose of a fuse in an electric circuit. Name the material used for making a fuse wire.

Question 33

State the role of placenta in the development of embryo.

Section - D

Q.no. 34 to 36 are long answer questions

Question 34

State the reason why?

(vi) Carbon is not used to reduce the oxides of sodium or aluminum.

(vii) An iron strip dipped in a blue copper sulphate solution turns the blue solution pale green.

(viii) Metals replace hydrogen from acids whereas non-metals do not.

(ix) Calcium does not occur free in nature.

(x) Zinc is used in the galvanization of iron and not the copper.

OR

(iii) Write the chemical formula of hydrated copper sulphate and anhydrous copper sulphate. Give an activity to illustrate how these two are interconvertible.

(iv) Write chemical names and formula of plaster of Paris and gypsum.

Question 35

Explain the manner in which sex is determined in human beings?

OR

Women are often blamed for bearing daughters. As a student with knowledge in science how will you explain it to your fellow students that the sex of the child is not determined by mother's genetic contribution?

Question 36

Fig. shows a circuit containing a coil wound over a long and thin hollow cardboard tube. Copy the diagram

(i) Show the polarity acquired by each face of the solenoid.

(ii) Draw the magnetic field lines of force inside the coil and also show their direction.

(iii) Mention two methods to increase the strength of the magnetic field inside the coil.

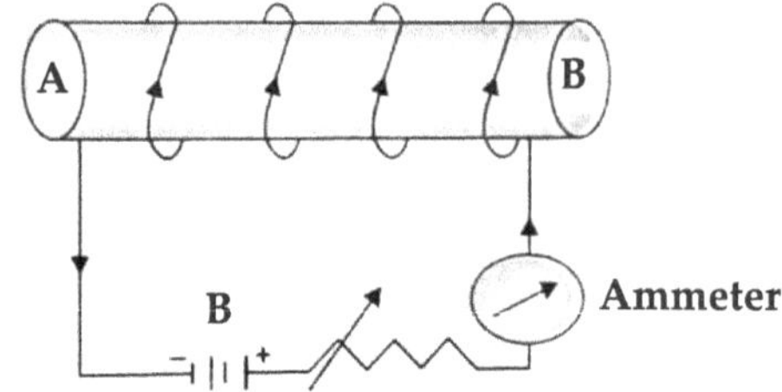

OR

(i) Draw a ray diagram to show the
(a) position and
(b) nature of the image formed when an object is placed between *F* and *P* of a concave mirror.

(ii) Find the position, nature, and size of the image of an object 3 cm high placed at a distance of 9 cm from a concave mirror of a focal length of 18 cm.

(**Ans.**: $v = 18$ cm, virtual and erect, size $= 6$ cm]

Section - E

Q.no. 37 to 39 are case-based/data-based questions with 2 to 3 short sub-parts. Internal choice is provided in one of these sub-parts

Question 37

You are provided with two containers made up of copper and aluminum. You are also provided with solutions of dilute HCl, dilute HNO_3, $ZnCl_2$ and H_2O. In which of the above containers these solutions can be kept?

OR

(i) Given below are the steps for extraction of copper from its ore.
Write the reaction involved.
(a) Roasting of copper (7I) sulphide
(b) Reduction of copper (I) oxide with copper (I) sulphide.
(c) Electrolytic refining

(ii) Draw a neat and well labelled diagram for electrolytic refining of copper.

Question 38

(i) What are monohybrid and dihybrid cross?
(ii) How Mendel proved that tallness is the dominant trait and dwarfness is recessive in a pea plant?. Explain with the help of a monohybrid cross.

OR

(i) What is a dominant trait with respect to height in pea plant. Give any two examples.
(ii) What is F_2 generation?

Question 39

The obstruction offered by a conductor in the path of the flow of current is called resistance. The SI unit of resistance is the ohm (Ω). It has been found that the resistance of a conductor depends on the temperature of the conductor. As the temperature increases, the resistance also increases. But the resistance of alloys like manner, constantan, and nichrome is almost unaffected by temperature. The resistance of a conductor also depends on the length of the conductor and the area of the cross-Section of the conductor. More be the length, more will be the resistance, more be the area of cross-Section, lesser will be the resistance.

(i) Which of the following is not will desire in the material being used for making electrical wires?

(a) High melting point
(b) High resistance
(c) High conductivity
(d) None of these
Answer(d) None of these

(ii) The $V - I$ graph for two metallic wires A and B is given. What is the correct relationship between their temperatures?

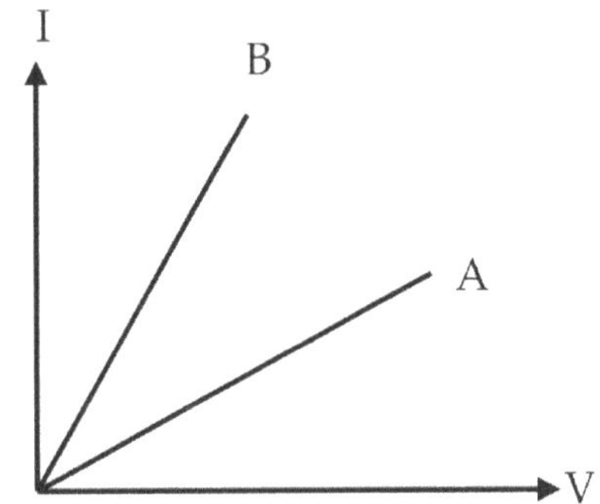

(a) $T_A < T_B$
(b) $T_A > T_B$
(c) $T_A = T_B$
(d) None of these
Answer(c) $T_A = T_B$

(iii) Two wires of the same material one of length L and area of cross-Section A, other are of length 2L and area $\frac{A}{2}$. Which of the following is correct?

(a) $R_1 = R_2$
(b) $R_1 = 4R_2$
(c) $R_2 = 4R_1$
(d) $R_1 = 2R_2$
Answer(c) $R_2 = 4R_1$

(iv) For the same conducting wire

(a) Resistance is higher in summer

(b) Resistance is higher in winter

(c) Resistance is the same in summer or winter

(d) None of these

Answer(a) Resistance is higher in summer

(v) A wire of resistance 20Ω is cut into 5 equal pieces. The resistance of each part is

(a) 4Ω

(b) 10Ω

(c) 100Ω

(d) 80Ω

Answer(a) 4Ω

OR

The relationship between the distance of an object from the lens (u), the distance of the image from the lens (v), and the focal length (f) of the lens are called the lens formula. It can be written as $\frac{1}{f} = \frac{1}{v} - \frac{1}{u}$.

The size of the image formed by a lens depends on the position of the object from the lens. A lens of short focal length has more power whereas a lens of long focal length has less power. When the lens is convex, the power is positive and for a concave lens, the power is negative.

The magnification produced by a lens is the ratio of the height of an image to the height of the object as the size of the image relative to the object is given by linear magnification (m).

When m is negative, an image formed is real and when m is positive, an image formed is virtual. If $m < 1$, the size of the image is smaller than the object. If $m > 1$, the size of the image is larger than the object.

(i) An object 4 cm in height is placed at a distance of 10 cm from a convex lens of a focal length of 20 cm. The position of the image is

(a) −20 cm

(b) 20 cm

(c) −10 cm

(d) 10 cm

Answer(a) −20 cm

(ii) In the above question, the size of the image is

(a) 16 cm

(b) 8 cm

(c) 4 cm

(d) 2 cm

Answer(b) 8 cm

(iii) An object is placed 50 cm from a concave lens and produces a virtual image at a distance of 10 cm in front of the lens. The focal length of a lens is

(a) -25 cm

(b) -12.5 cm

(c) 12.5 cm

(d) 10 cm

Answer(b) -12.5 cm

(iv) A convex lens forms an image of magnification -2 of the height of the image is 6 cm, and the height of an object is

(a) 6 cm

(b) 4 cm

(c) 3 cm

(d) 2 cm

Answer(c) 3 cm

(v) With a concave lens of a focal length of 5 cm, the power of the lens is

(a) 20D

(b) -20D

(c) 90D

(d) -5D

Answer(b) -20D

Class- X Session- 2022-23

Science

MOST EXPECTED QUESTION SAMPLE PAPER -2

Time Allowed: 3 Hrs. **Maximum Marks: 80**

General Instructions:

1. This Question Paper has 5 Sections A-E.
2. Section **A** has 20 MCQs carrying 1 mark each
3. Section **B** has 5 questions carrying 02 marks each.
4. Section **C** has 6 questions carrying 03 marks each.
5. Section **D** has 4 questions carrying 05 marks each.
6. Section **E** has 3 case-based integrated units of assessment (04 marks each) with subparts of the values of 1, 1, and 2 marks each respectively.
7. All Questions are compulsory. However, an internal choice in 2 Qs of 5 marks, 2 Qs of 3 marks, and 2 Questions of 2 marks has been provided. An internal choice has been provided in the 2marks questions of Section E
8. Draw neat figures wherever required. Take π =22/7 wherever required if not stated

Section A

Section A consists of 20 questions of 1 mark each

Question 1

Shashank was asked to carry out a displacement reaction which would show the following

i. Formation of colourless solution

ii. Black deposits

The reactants he should use are

(a) Fe (s) and $Al_2(SO_4)_3(aq)$

(b) Al (s) and $FeSO_4(aq)$

(c) Zn (s) and $CuSO_4(aq)$

(d) Fe (s) and $ZnSO_4(aq)$

Answer. (b)

Question 2

When a solution of acid is mixed with a solution of base :

(i) The temperature of solution increases

(ii) Salt formation occurs

(iii) The temperature of solution decreases

(iv) The temperature remains same

(a) (i). and (ii).

(b) (ii). and (iii)

(c) (iii) and (iv)

(d) (ii) and (iv)

Answer. (a)

Question 3

Which of the following is not a base

(a) NaOH

(b) $Ba(OH)_2$

(c) C_2H_5OH

(d) $Ca(OH)_2$

Answer. (c)

Question 4

Raman took three metals labelled P, Q and R. He carried out displacement reactions with his salt solutions and found that P is less reactive than R but more reactive than Q. The metals P, Q and R respectively could be:

(a) Zinc, Copper, Aluminium

(b) Copper, Zinc, Aluminium

(c) Aluminium, Copper, Zinc

(d) Copper, Aluminium, Zinc

Answer(A)

Question 5

In amalgam, a metal is dissolved in :

(a) Ag

(b) Hg

(c) Mg

(d) Pb

Answer. (b)

Question 6

Molecular formula of butane is C_4H_{10}, it has covalent bonds :

(a) 11

(b) 12

(c) 13

(d) 14

Answer. (c)

Question 7

When you add about 2 mL of acetic acid to a test containing an equal amount of distilled water and leave the test tube to settle after shaking its contents, then after about 5 minutes what will you observe in the test tube?

(a) A white precipitate settling at its bottom.

(b) A clear colourless solution.

(c) A layer of water over the layer of acetic acid.

(d) A layer of acetic acid over the layer of water.

Answer. (b)

Question 8

The respiratory pigment in human beings is:

(a) carotene

(b) chlorophyll

(c) haemoglobin

(d) mitochondria

Answer: (c)

Question 9

Which of the following is the important characteristic of Emphysema:

(a) Destruction of the alveolar wall and air sacs in the lungs are damaged.

(b) Increase in the growth of the lung tissue.

(c) Inflammation in the wall of bronchi.

(d) Thickening of the artery walls of the lungs.

Answer: (a)

Question 10

The opening and closing of the stomatal pore depends upon

(a) Oxygen

(b) temperature

(c) water in the guard cells

(d) concentration of CO_2

Answer: (c)

Question 11

A plant gets rid of excess water through transpiration. Which is a method used by plants to get rid of solid waste products?

(a) shortening of stem

(b) dropping down of fruits

(c) shedding of yellow leaves

(d) expansion of roots into the soil

Answer: (c)

Question 12

Digestion of food starts from which organ of the human digestive system?

(a) Mouth due to the presence of saliva

(b) Oesophagus that moves the food in gut

(c) That releases juices for fat breakdown

(d) Which helps in mixing food with digestive juices

Answer: (a)

Question 13

What is the resistance between P and Q ?

(a) $\frac{3}{4}\Omega$

(b) $\frac{4}{3}\Omega$

(c) $\frac{16}{3}\Omega$

(d) Infinity

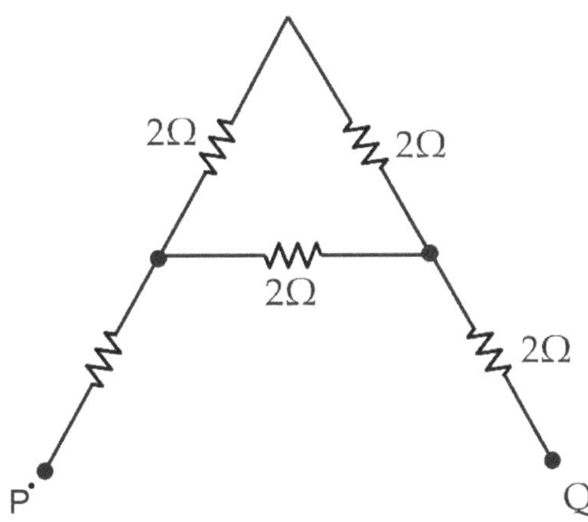

Answer(c) $\frac{16}{3}\Omega$

Question 14

According to international convention of colour coding of insulation of wires in a cable:

(a) Live is red, neutral is blue and earth is brown.

(b) Live is red, neutral is green and earth is black.

(c) Live is brown, neutral is blue and earth is black.

(d) Live is brown, neutral is blue, and earth is green.

Answer(d) Live is brown, neutral is blue, and earth is green.

Question 15

The mirror used by a dental surgeon is

(a) Plane

(b) Convex

(c) Concave

(d) Any one of the above

Answer(c) Concave

Question 16

The image formed of an object placed between the optical centre and focal of a convex lens is

(a) Virtual and diminished

(b) Virtual and enlarged

(c) Real and enlarged

(d) Real and diminished

Answer(b) Virtual and enlarged

Q. no 17 to 20 are Assertion - Reasoning based questions. These consist of two statements – Assertion (A) and Reason (R). Answer these questions by selecting the appropriate option given below:

(a) Both A and R are true, and R is the correct explanation of A

(b) Both A and R are true, and R is not the correct explanation of A

(c) A is true but R is false

(d) A is False but R is true

Question 17

Assertion(A): Ionic compound generally have high melting and boiling points

Reason (R): The interaction between ions of an ionic compounds are electrostatic in nature which is weak force.

Answer. (c)

Question 18

Assertion(A): Plants have low energy needs.

Reason (R): Plant bodies have large proportion of dead cells.

Answer. (A)

Question 19

Assertion(A): Blood pressure is arterial blood pressure.

Reason (R): It is measured by sphygmomanometer.

Answer. (b)

Question 20

Assertion: In the case of a concave mirror, the minimum distance between a real object and its real image is zero.

Reason: If a concave mirror forms a virtual image of a real object, the image is magnified.

Answer (b)

Section B

Section B has 5 questions carrying 02 marks each

Q. no. 21 to 26 are very short answer questions

Question 21 **[2]**

What is thermite reaction? Explain with example.

OR

What change in color is observed when white silver chloride is left exposed to sunlight? What type of chemical reaction is this?

Question 22 **[2]**

What is a dominant trait with respect to height in pea plant. Give any two examples.

Question 23 **[2]**

Where are the genes located? What is the chemical nature of gene?

Question 24 **[2]**

Why do human beings look different from each other? What do you mean by species?

Question 25

A wire of uniform thickness with a resistance of 27Ω is cut into three equal pieces and they are joined in parallel. Find the resistance of the parallel combination.
(**Answer**3Ω)

OR

An object is placed in front of a lens between its optical centre and focus. The image formed is virtual, erect, and diminished. Identify the lens. Draw a ray diagram to show the formation of this image.

Question 26

What is speciation? Discuss any two factors that lead to speciation.

Section - C

Q.no. 27 to 33 are short answer questions

Question 27

(a) For making cake, baking powder is taken. If at home your mother uses baking soda instead of baking powder in cake

(b) How will it affect the taste of the cake and why?

(c) How can baking soda be converted into baking powder?

(d) Write the chemical equation to describe how baking soda is produced on large scale. Also write the chemical name of the products obtained.

Question 28

(a) What is a detergent?

(b) Give structural differences between soaps and detergents.

(c) Name the hydrophilic part in soaps and detergents.

Question 29

"Natural selection and speciation lead to evolution". Justify the statement.

OR

What is DNA copying? State its importance

Question 30

(i) State the laws of refraction of light.

(ii) Write a relation between the angle of incidence (i), angle of emergence (e), angle of the prism (A), and angle of deviation (d) for a ray of light passing through an equilateral prism.

Question 31

Two heaters of 200 W each and two bulbs of 40 W each operate 4 hours daily on the supply of 200 V. If the cost of energy is ₹3 per kWh. Find the bill for the month of November.

Answer(₹172.80)

Question 32

A short sighted person can read distinctly a bool when placed at a distance of 20 cm. what is the nature and power of lens used in his spectacle to read the book at 25 cm distance?

OR

Explain the blue colour of sky?

Question 33

How is the age of fossil determined?

Section - D

Q.no. 34 to 36 are long answer questions

Question 34

(i) Write balanced chemical equation for the reaction taking place when :

(a) Zinc carbonate is calcinated.

(b) Zinc sulphide is roasted.

(c) Zinc oxide is reduced in the zinc.

(d) Cinnabar is heated in the air.

(e) Manganese dioxide is heated with aluminium powder.

OR

(i) An element ' X ' on reacting with oxygen forms an oxide X_2O. The oxide dissolves in water and turns blue litmus red. Predict the nature of the element whether metal or nonmetal?

(ii) A solution of copper sulphate was kept in an iron pot. After few days, the pot developed some holes in it. How will you account for this?

Question 35

(i) What is phototropism and geotropism? With labelled dingrams describe an activity to show that light and gravity change the direction that plant part grows in.

(ii) Mention the role of each of the following plant hormones:

(a) Auxin

(b) Abscisic acid.

OR

Draw and describe the role of various parts of human brain.

Question 36

(a) What are magnetic field lines? How is the direction field at a point determined?

(b) Draw two field lines around a bar magnet along its length on its sides and mark the field direction as there by arrow marks.

(c) List any three properties of magnetic field lines.

OR

An object $0.2m$ high is placed at a distance of $0.4m$ front a concave of radius of curvature $0.3m$ Find the position, nature, and size of the image forward.

Answer $h = -6.12$ m

Section - E

Q.no. 37 to 39 are case-based/data-based questions with 2 to 3 short sub-parts. Internal choice is provided in one of these sub-parts

Question 37

A compound C (molecular formula, $C_2H_4O_2$) racts with Na metal to form a compound R and evolves a gas which burns with a pop sound. Compound C on treatment with an alcohol A in presence of an acid forms a sweet-smelling compound S (molecular formula, $C_3H_6O_2$). On addition of NaOH to C, it also gives R and water. S on treatment with NaOH solution gives back R and A.

Identify C, R, A, S and write down the reactions involved.

OR

Rahul is a ten year old boy. He had purchased a packet of potato chips more than a moniti agc. Rahul opened the packet at that time but could eat only some of the potato chips from it. He then kept the open packet containing remaining potato chips on his book rack. He wanted to eat the remaining potato chips today. Just when Rahul was about to put these potato chips into his mouth, his elder sister Pavni, who is a student of class X, entered the room. She found that these potato chips were giving unpleasant smell. When she put one potato chip in her mouth, it had also unpleasant taste. Pavni took away the packet from Rahul and did not allow him to eat these potato chips. She threw away the potato chips into a dustbin.

(i) What name is given to the condition in which potato chips kept open for a considerable time give out unpleasant smell and taste?

(ii) Which chemical reaction is responsible for the spoilage of potato chips kept exposed by Rahul for a considerable time?

(iii) What produces the unpleasant smell as well as unpleasant taste in potato chips? Explain.

(iv) With which gas the plastic bags containing potato chips are filled and then sealed by manufacturers? How does it help?

(v) What values are displayed by Pavni in this episode?

Question 38

(i) How does chemical coordination occur in plants? Explain with the help of four examples.

(ii) Trace the sequences of events through a reflex are which occur when a bright light is focused on your eyes.

OR

What are the different components of blood? Give the function of each of them.

Question 39

The rate of flow of charge is called electric current. The SI unit of electric current is Ampere (A). The direction of the flow of current is always opposite to the direction of the flow of electrons in the current.

The electric potential is defined as the amount of work done in bringing a unit-positive test charge from infinity to a point in the electric field. The amount of work done in bringing a unit positive test charge from one point to another point in an electric field is defined as a potential difference.

$$V_{AB} = V_B - V_A = \frac{W_{BA}}{q}$$

The SI unit of potential and potential difference is volt.

(i) The 2C of charge is flowing through a conductor in 100 ms, and the current in the circuit is

(a) 20 A
(b) 2 A
(c) 0.2 A
(d) 0.02 A

(ii) Which of the following is true?

(a) Current flows from the positive terminal of the cell to the negative terminal of the cell outside the cell.
(b) The negative charge moves from lower potential to higher potential.
(c) The direction of flow of current is the same as the direction of flow of positive charge.
(d) All of these

(iii) The potential difference between the two terminals of a battery, if 100 joules of work is required to transfer 20 coulombs of charge from one terminal of the battery to other is

(a) 50 V
(b) −5 V
(c) 0.5 V
(d) 500 V

(iv) The number of electrons flowing per second in a conductor if 1 A current is passing through it

(a) 6.25×10^{20}
(b) 6.25×10^{19}
(c) 6.25×10^{18}
(d) 6.25×10^{-19}

(v) The voltage can be written as

(a) Work done × charge × time
(b) $\frac{\text{Work done}}{\text{Current} \times \text{time}}$

(c) $\frac{\text{Work done} \times \text{time}}{\text{Current}}$

(d) Work done × charge

OR

A lens is a piece of any transparent material bounded by two curved surfaces. There are two types of lenses convex lens and concave lens.

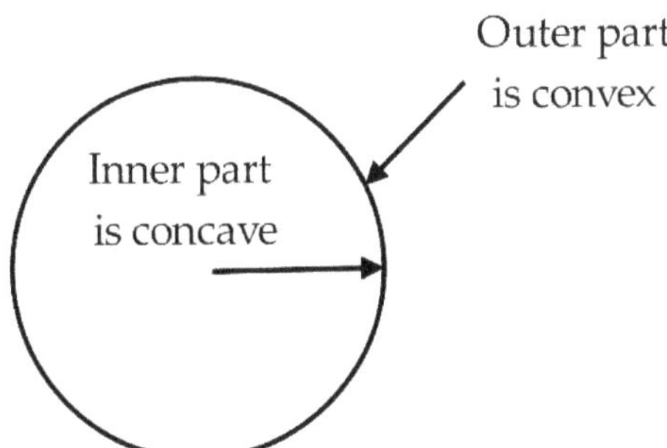

A convex lens is made up of a transparent medium bounded by two spherical surfaces that thicker in the middle and thinner at the edges. A concave lens is also made up of a transparent medium such that thicker at the edge and thinner at the middle. The midpoint of the lens is called the optical center.

A point on the principal axis, where the incident parallel rays meet or appear to come out after refraction is called the focus.

A convex lens converges a parallel beam of light to the other side whereas a concave lens spreads out.

(i) Which of the following lenses would you prefer to use while reading small letters found in a dictionary?

(a) A convex lens

(b) A concave lens

(c) Plano-convex

(d) Concavo-convex

Answer(a) A convex lens

(ii) Which type of lenses are shown in given figures (i) and (ii)?

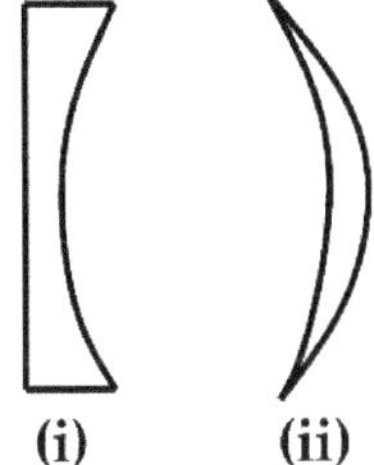

(a) Plano concave, concave-convex

(b) Plano-convex, convex-concave

(c) Double concave, concave-convex

(d) Convex-concave, double convex

Answer(a) Plano concave, concave-convex

(iii) A small bulb is placed at the focal point of a converging lens. When the bulb is switched on, the lens produces

(a) A convergent beam of light

(b) A divergent beam of light

(c) A parallel beam of light

(d) A patch of colored light.

Answer(c) A parallel beam of light

(iv) The part of the lens through which the refraction takes place is called

(a) Aperture

(b) Centre of curvature

(c) Principal axis

(d) Focus

Answer(a) Aperture

www.ingramcontent.com/pod-product-compliance
Ingram Content Group UK Ltd.
Pitfield, Milton Keynes, MK11 3LW, UK
UKHW061703190726
13853UKWH00008B/2384

9 789355 564900